STUDY GUIDE TO ACCOMPA

STATISTICS
CONCEPTS AND APPLICATIONS

David R. Anderson

Dennis J. Sweeney

Thomas A. Williams

Prepared by
Iris B. Ibrahim
Department of Mathematical Sciences
Clemson University

West Publishing Company
St. Paul New York Los Angeles San Francisco

50 West Kellogg Boulevard
P.O. Box 64526
St. Paul, MN 55164-1003

Printed in the United States of America

ISBN 0-314-96585-8

PREFACE

To learn the fundamentals of probability and statistics, the student must master certain methods and terminology. The purpose of this study guide is to help the reader organize and summarize the material presented in the textbook, STATISTICS: CONCEPTS AND APPLICATIONS by Anderson, Sweeney, and Williams; to present the student with additional examples and their detailed solutions; and to supplement this material with exercises which are designed to allow the student to evaluate his or her understanding of the basic concepts.

This guide is not intended as a replacement for the text, but rather as an individual student study aid. It contains the same chapter organization and chapter titles as the text. To help the student assimilate the basic ideas and techniques of probability and statistics, this Study Guide contains the following items for each chapter of the textbook:

1. What Am I Learning? - A chapter outline which includes a brief summary of the major concepts in the chapter. Key terms that the student should be familiar with when completing each chapter of the text have been italicized.

2. Which Formula Should I Use? - Formulas which have been organized in concise form for easy reference. When to use which formula is sometimes confusing to the student. To help eliminate this problem, the conditions for use for each formula are given. Some of the formulas have been condensed and written in a direct-substitution form. Thus, in some cases, the formula looks different, but is equivalent to, the form that is presented in the text.

3. Here's How It's Done! - A variety of examples, with their step-by-step solutions. These examples may be used to master the major concepts of problem solving while reinforcing the concepts presented in the textbook. Also included in the

detailed solutions are tips and hints as to how the student should avoid common "silly" errors.

4. Have I Learned The Material? - A self-quiz which allows the student to evaluate his or her progress in the course. In this part, two forms of exercises are presented. First, there are problems to help the student polish his or her skills through practice. Sufficient space is provided in this guide to carry out the necessary computations and give the answer for each problem. Secondly, multiple choice questions are given. These focus on the major concepts and are not meant to be comprehensive. The problems and multiple choice questions are designed to appear as a student might see the material on an actual test. Thus, they do not follow the specified order in which the material is covered in the text and examples. Answers to these self-testing problems and multiple choice questions are given at the end of each chapter of this guide.

Throughout many years of teaching probability and statistics, I have seen certain recurrent problems that students have with this material. One key hint I can give you, the student, to the successful completion of your course is "do not try to learn everything the night before the test"! Above everything else, mathematics is a subject in which "practice makes perfect". It is essential that you keep up with the material so that you can build new concepts on the fundamentals of the ones with which you are already familiar. This guide is geared to this end. I hope you find this Study Guide instructive and helpful.

Iris B. Ibrahim

CONTENTS

Chapter 1
INTRODUCTION

WHAT AM I LEARNING?

Chapter Outline and Summary

The subject of *statistics* is concerned with the procedures by which information is collected, organized, interpreted, and presented. The facts which are collected from observations are called *data.* These numerical measurements are selected from the *population* which is the complete collection of data under consideration. A subset or portion of the population is called a *sample.* The word statistics refers to a collection of numerical data as well as a method of dealing with data.

The study of statistics is divided into two main areas: descriptive statistics and statistical inference. *Descriptive statistics* is a collection of tools and techniques for characterizing and summarizing data to present the information in a convenient, usable, and understandable form. The methods of *statistical inference* deal with taking the information obtained in the sample and using it to make conclusions, decisions, or generalizations about the population from which the sample is chosen.

It is usually impractical to examine an entire population (that is, take a census) because the population may be extremely large or undergoing continuous change, the examination procedure may be too time consuming or too costly, and obtaining the required information may in some cases destroy the product. Hopefully, when chosen correctly, the sample is representative of the population and the *inference* (that is, the decision, estimate, or prediction) about the population will be valid. However, since the inference is based on the information obtained from a subset of the population, errors will occur. It is therefore necessary to have a measure of the reliability of the inference to assess its practical value. Probability concepts will be used to make statements about the precision of the inferences.

Chapter 1

Statistics is one of the most useful and important tools in the social, behavioral, physical and medical sciences. Statistical information is collected for virtually every field of human activity.

HERE'S HOW IT'S DONE!

Examples

1. The manager of a large department store wishes to determine the percentage of shoppers in his store who use a charge card for purchases. He records whether purchases are made with a charge card or cash for each of 100 customers.

(a) What is the population of interest to the manager?

Solution:
(a) The population, being the set of all data under consideration, is the set of all shoppers in the department store.

(b) What is the sample for this problem?

Solution:
(b) The sample, which is a subset of the population, is the collection of 100 shoppers the manager observes.

(c) What is the desired statistical inference?

Solution:
(c) The statistical inference is to predict the percentage of all shoppers in the store who use charge cards. To estimate this percentage for the population, the manager would take the sample percentage. The sample percentage is obtained by dividing the number of people inthe sample of 100 customers who use charge cards by 100.

2. The board of directors of a company currently employing in excess of 4000 people wants an estimate of the cost of a proposed retirement plan for those employees. Therefore, they need data on the ages of the employees of the company. They obtain the ages of 250 employees and compute the average number of years until retirement for this group.

(a) Identify the population and the sample for this problem.

Solution:
(a) The population consists of all employees of this company, with the number of years until retirement for each as the data of interest. The sample consists of the 250 employees.

(b) What inference is implied in the problem?

Solution:

(b) The inference is to predict the average number of years until retirement for all the company's employees based on the corresponding data obtained in the sample of 250 employees. Using this average, the board of directors is able to estimate the expected cost of the proposed retirement plan.

3. A survey of 50 families selected from small towns showed that the average number of times per week the families ate the evening meal outside the home was 1.20.

(a) What is the population of interest in this study?

Solution:

(a) The population is the collection of all families in small towns.

(b) In the statistical inference process, we would like to estimate the average number of times per week dinner is eaten outside the home for all the families in small towns. What would be an estimate of this value?

Solution:

(b) Provided all the procedures of the statistical experiment are performed correctly, the estimate is 1.20.

(c) Are you certain that this value is the correct number of times dinner is eaten outside the home for the population?

Solution:

(c) No, because this estimate was obtained from sample data, which varies from sample to sample, there is always the possibility of making an error.

4. Give a population from which each of the following samples may have been selected. Also, discuss the role of statistical inference in the contest of each problem.

(a) Ten registered voters are questioned in each of one-third of the precincts of a state as to their preference of senatorial candidates.

Solution:

(a) The common element for all the people in the sample is that each is a registered voter. Thus, the population is very likely all the registered voters in the state.

(b) A sample of 15 cups of coffee is taken from a coffee machine and the average content of each cup is computed.

Solution:

(b) The population consists of all the cups of coffee dispensed by the machine. The purpose of taking the sample could be to see if the machine is dispensing the drink in the manner in which it was designed. The statistical inference would then be to estimate the true average amount of coffee dispensed by the machine for all the cups of coffee it gives to see if the customer is likely to obtain that for which he/she has paid. If the sample results deviate a significant amount from the original machine specifications, adjustments should be made.

5. A standardized test consisting of 10 true-false questions is given to a group of 15 people completing a two-hour session in cooking with a microwave oven. The data of interest is the number of correct answers on the test which is defined as the person's score on the test. The results for the 15 people are as follows:

7	9	8	10	7
5	6	9	8	10
8	9	6	8	10

(a) Give a descriptive statistic that summarizes this data in a single numerical value.

Solution:

(a) By adding the 15 values for the number of correct answers on the test and dividing by the number of data values, 15, we obtain $200 / 15 = 8$. Thus, a possible descriptive statistic is: The average score on the test for the 15 people completing the course is 8.

Note: There are other single numerical value descriptive statistics that could be given, and these are discussed in Chapter 3.

(b) In order to give the instructors of the session a better idea of the effectiveness of this session, give a table which summarizes the above data.

Solution:

(b) One possible table for summarizing the 15 test scores is the following:

Score on Standardized Test	Number of Participants Receiving Score
5	1
6	2
7	2
8	4
9	3
10	3

HAVE I LEARNED THE MATERIAL?

Problems

1. A large bank wishes to estimate the average annual income of persons in a town where the bank is considering locating a branch office. Fifty people living in the town are surveyed and the annual income of each is measured.

   (a) What is the population of interest to the bank?

   (b) What is the sample for this problem?

   (c) What is the desired statistical inference?

2. Consider the following situations. Which would use descriptive statistics, and which would use statistical inference?

   (a) A manager wishes to determine the individual batting averages of his baseball team.

   (b) A legislator, arguing in favor of a bill requiring motorcyclists to wear safety helmets, gives data on the number of deaths of motorcyclists due to head injuries.

   (c) A lawyer interviews 300 doctors and finds that 39% of them stated that they had been involved in one or more malpractice suits.

   (d) A coin, suspected of being "loaded", is flipped 100 times. The results were 10 heads and 90 tails.

3. Consider the statement: "The average number of customers eating lunch at Joe's Diner on weekdays is 25".

   (a) How might this average value be used in the method of descriptive statistics?

   (b) How might this average value be used in statistical inference?

4. Consider the summary table given in Example 3:

Score on Standardized Test	Number of Participants Receiving Score
5	1
6	2
7	2
8	4
9	3
10	3

   (a) Which score occurs most frequently on this test?

   (b) What percentage of the 15 participants made a score of at least 8?

   (c) Discuss how the descriptive statistic value of 8 obtained in this example could be used in statistical inference.

5. The FDA recently reported that 1 out of every 4 Americans is overweight. To help these overweight people lose weight, a group of doctors has developed a "bubble implant" which when placed in the stomach of the overweight person makes the person feel he/she is full and consequently eat less. The FDA reported that they are "waiting for long term data" before recommending the bubble implant. Discuss the last statement made by the FDA.

6. A large management company orders 20,000 light bulbs from a manafacturer who states that the average life of the light bulbs is 1000 hours. The company tests 20 of the light bulbs in the shipment and uses the results to decide whether or not the shipment should be accepted.

   (a) What is the population for this problem?

   (b) What is the sample?

   (c) What data is obtained from the sample?

   (d) What is the desired inference?

   (e) The sample in this problem is relatively small. Why, do you suppose, were there not more light bulbs tested?

Chapter 1

Multiple Choice Questions

For each of the following multiple choice questions, circle the correct answer:

1. In statistics, a population

   (a) is the number of elements in a set of data
   (b) is a subset selected from a larger group
   (c) is the entire set of data under consideration
   (d) is a decision based on the results of sample information.

2. A statistical sample

   (a) is the complete set of data under consideration
   (b) is a set of elements selected from a population
   (c) always contains at least 100 data values
   (d) may be larger than the population.

3. Descriptive statistics is

   (a) a group of predictions about a population
   (b) the study of inferences
   (c) the study of methods for data summarization
   (d) a measure of the reliability of a statistical decision.

4. A statistical inference is

   (a) a statement made about a sample based on the information in that sample
   (b) a decision, estimate, or prediction about the sample based on information contained in the population
   (c) the process of stating, without any possibility of error, a conclusion about a population
   (d) a decision, estimate, or prediction about the population based on the information contained in a sample from that population.

5. The use of the results of an exit poll in an election is an example of

   (a) descriptive statistics
   (b) statistical inference
   (c) a sample
   (d) a population.

6. An examination of the scores on the first test in a certain freshman mathematics course is an example of

   (a) descriptive statistics
   (b) statistical inference
   (c) a sample
   (d) a population.

7. In which of the following situations would it be better to sample the population rather than obtain all the data for the population?

   (a) a TV station, covering a large broadcast area, wishes to determine the percentage of viewers watching the evening news telecast on that station
   (b) a teacher wishes to determine the average grade on the final examination in his class of 35 students
   (c) both a) and b)
   (d) neither a) nor b).

8. Student Government officers are used to represent the entire student body. Thus, these officers constitute a

   (a) census
   (b) population
   (c) sample
   (d) all of the above.

9. The "reliability" of a statistical inference refers to

   (a) how large the population is
   (b) how accurately the sample data is presented
   (c) how good, or accurate, the statistical inference is
   (d) none of the above.

10. The term "statistics" refers

    (a) to a collection of numerical data
    (b) to the method of how the numerical values are collected, analyzed, and interpreted
    (c) only to a method of weather forecasting
    (d) both a) and b).

Chapter 1

Answers to Problems

1. Population: The annual incomes of all the people in the town.
   Sample: The annual incomes of the fifty people questioned by the bank.
   Inference: To estimate the average income of all the people in the town.

2. (a) Since the manager is describing a set of data for the team, the batting average is a descriptive statistic.

   (b) Because the legislator is using the data to argue that wearing safety helmets reduces the number of deaths due to head injuries, the data is used in the area of statistical inference.

   (c) Since the figure 39% is given as a description of the data set and not used to make an estimate or decision about all doctors, it is a descriptive statistic.

   (d) Due to the fact that the results of the sample of 100 flips are probably being used to decide whether or not the coin is loaded or fair for the population of the outcomes of a very large or infinite number of flips, this is a use of statistical inference.

3. (a) If Joe has been collecting data on the number of customers eating lunch at his diner on weekdays and if he uses this value of 25 to describe that set of data, he is using descriptive statistics.

   (b) If Joe uses this average value of 25 to make a prediction or decision by describing a larger set of data, he is in the area of statistical inference. For example, the value of 25 may have been obtained from data collected over a 3 month period. Joe may use the value to decide whether or not he needs additional help at lunchtime.

4. (a) From the table, it is easily seen that the score of 8 occurs the most frequently.

   (b) A score of at least 8 means a score that is greater than or equal to 8. There are 10 such scores. Thus, the percentage is approximately 67%.

   (c) The instructors may use the results of this session to predict the average score on all sessions given. They may possibly judge the effectiveness of other sessions, given to similar groups of participants, by comparing the average score on the tests given in those sessions to this average score.

5. To recommend the procedure, the FDA is essentially predicting that it will be helpful and safe for the general public. Before doing this, they must know if it works without harmful side effects. Thus, they must have a sample that is representative of the population of human beings. They would also want the error in their prediction to be as small as possible. Thus, they would want to gather as much data as is possible before making the recommendation.

   Note: The relationship between sample size and error in prediction will be discussed further in Chapter 9.

6. (a) The population consists of the 20,000 bulbs in the shipment from the manufacturer.

   (b) The sample consists of the 20 light bulbs that are tested by the company.

   (c) The data obtained in the sample is the number of hours until burnout of each of the 20 bulbs tested.

   (d) The desired inference is to predict, for the entire shipment of 20,000 bulbs, the average number of hours of life.

   (e) In this case, testing destroys the product. The light bulbs, once tested, cannot be used again.

Chapter 1

Answers to Multiple Choice Questions

1. c
2. b
3. c
4. d
5. b
6. a
7. a
8. c
9. c
10. d

Chapter 2
DESCRIPTIVE STATISTICS I:
TABULAR AND GRAPHICAL METHODS

WHAT AM I LEARNING?

Chapter Outline and Summary

The process of assigning a label or numerical value to an observation is called *measurement.* Data obtained through measurement can be classified as nominal, ordinal, interval, or ratio.

The type of measurement is *nominal* when the measure assigned is used as a name or label for purposes of identification. The level of measurement is *ordinal* when the assigned measure indicates position in an ordered series and does not tell numerically how much of a difference exists betwen positions. The only mathematical relationships that exist between data measured on an ordinal scale are "greater than" and "less than". *Qualitative data* is data obtained from nominal or ordinal level measurement. Mathematical operations such as addition, subtraction, multiplication, and division are not used with qualitative data.

When measurement is made with scales employing numerical values, the data obtained is called *quantitative.* This type of data permits the use of standard arithmetic operations. Quantitative data may be obtained from two levels of measurement : interval and ratio. The level of measurement is *interval* when there is a fixed numerical unit of measurement and each measure assigned is expressed in terms of those units. *Ratio*-level measurements are those where there is a fixed numerical unit of measure and the zero point is inherently defined on the scale of measurement. The only difference between interval and ratio level of measurement is that there is a true or fixed zero point in the ratio-level measurement whereas the zero point in the interval-level measurement is arbitrary. Proportions and ratios are not meaningful in interval-level measurements as they are in ratio-level measurements.

Sample data, when initially obtained, should be organized in some systematic fashion in order to be analyzed. Recall that descriptive statistics is a collection of tools and techniques for characterizing and summarizing data to present the information in a convenient, usable, and understandable form. One of the most useful methods of summarizing data is a frequency distribution.

A *frequency distribution* is a table in which a mass of data has been divided into nonoverlapping groups called *classes* to bring out general characteristics. This grouping, for qualitative data, is done by recording the frequency of the data values, where the *frequency* of a class is the number of times the value or values in that class occur in the set of data. The *relative frequency* of a class is the proportion of the total number of data items that fall in that class. A *relative frequency distribution* differs from a frequency distribution only in that the relative frequencies are given in the table rather than the frequencies.

A *bar graph* is a graphical summary of qualitative data in which a bar (usually vertical) is drawn for each class in the frequency distribution. The height of each bar is the frequency of the class, all bars should be of the same width, the vertical axis should start at a frequency of zero, and the bars are separated from each other for clarity and to prevent visual distortion.

A *pie chart* is a tool of descriptive statistics for qualitative data wherein the percentage distribution of the frequencies (that is, the relative frequencies) are shown as sectors of a circle. These "pie slices" are identified by taking the relative frequency of a class multiplied by 360° to get the number of degrees in the sector corresponding to a particular class. The sector is then drawn as a portion of the circular pie chart using a protractor.

The guidelines for constructing a frequency distribution for quantitative data involve grouping the data into nonoverlapping classes of equal width with the number of classes usually between five and twenty. This grouping does involve loss of the individual data values, but the essential characteristics of the information are still present. In the frequency distribution, the stated or *apparent* class limits are not often the *real class limits* when the data has been rounded. The real class limit is equal to the apparent class limit plus or minus one-half of the *unit difference.* The unit difference is the smallest difference possible between the values that are rounded.

The relative frequency distribution for quantiative data is defined in the same way as for qualitative data.

Often it is helpful to arrange the data in a frequency or relative frequency distribution into a cumulative frequency distribution or cumulative relative frequency distribution. *Cumulative frequencies* are the sum of the frequencies from the lowest to the highest class. Thus, the cumulative frequency distribution shows the total number of data items with value less than or equal to the real upper limit for the class. Note that the cumulative relative frequency distribution may be obtained by "accumulating" the relative frequencies in the relative frequency distribution or by dividing each entry in the cumulative frequency distribution by the total number of observations.

The quantitative data may also be summarized in pictorial form with graphs called histograms, frequency polygons, and ogives. A *histogram* is a graph of a frequency distribution for quantitative data in which the real class limits are plotted on the horizontal axis and the frequency of each class is plotted on the vertical axis. Adjacent (touching) rectangles are formed with the class width being the width of each rectangle and the corresponding class frequency being the height of the rectangle.

A *frequency polygon* is a line graph formed by connecting, with straight line segments, the points obtained by taking horizontal values equal to the average of the class limits (called *class midpoints*) and corresponding vertical values as the frequencies of the classes. This line graph is "tied down" to the horizontal axis with a class of zero frequency assumed at each end of the frequency distribution. Histograms and frequency polygons may be constructed for relative frequency distributions in a similar manner using relative frequencies instead of frequencies.

An *ogive* is a graph of a cumulative frequency or cumulative relative frequency distribution. To construct such a graph, place the real upper limit for each class on the horizontal axis and cumulative frequency (or cumulative relative frequency) on the vertical axis. Connect, with straight line segments, the points formed with these horizontal and vertical coordinates for each of the classes. Again, as in the frequency polygon, "tie the graph down" to the axis (but on the <u>left</u> only) with one additional point plotted above the lower real limit for the first class at a height of zero.

Exploratory data analysis is the use of arithmetic and simple pictures to more effectively look at data. One such technique for quantative data is the *stem-and-leaf diagram* which shows the original data values in a display giving both rank order and shape. The label for each stem is usually the one- or two-digit portion of the first part of the numerical data value, and the leaf is the remaining portion of the numerical value.

Chapter 2

The measurement classifications given in Chapter 2 are summarized as follows:

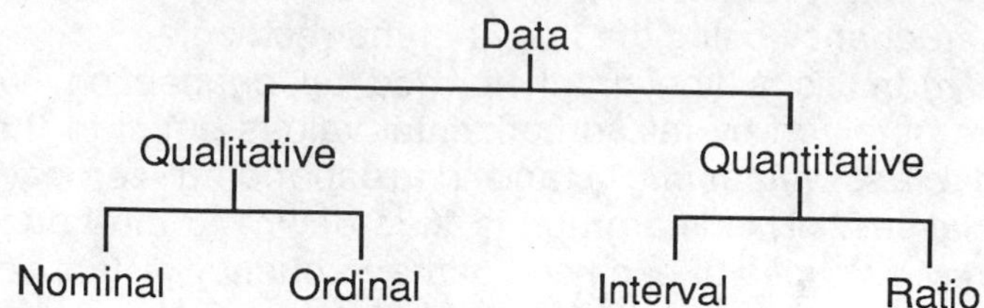

with the following descriptive statistic techniques:

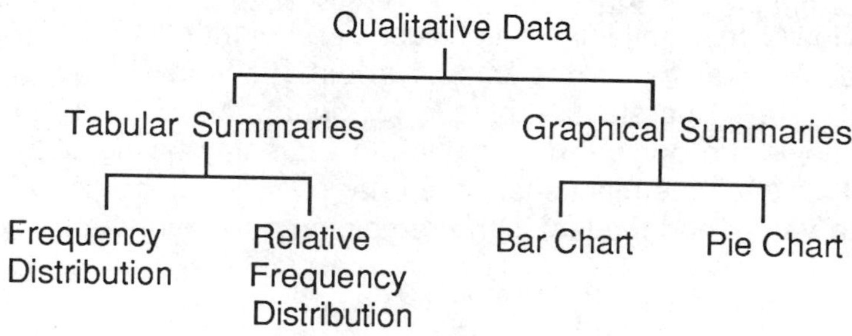

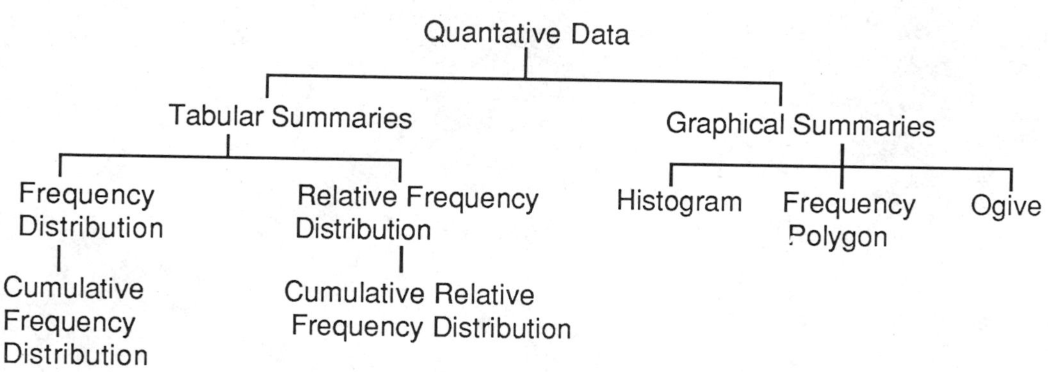

Chapter 2

WHICH FORMULA SHOULD I USE?

Formulas

When:

determining the relative frequency of a class for a data set having a total of n observations,

Use:

$$\text{Relative Frequency of a Class} = \frac{\text{Frequency of the Class}}{n} \qquad [1]$$

When:

determining the approximate number of classes for a frequency distribution with quantative data,

Use:

$$\text{Approximate number of Classes} = \frac{\text{Largest Data Value} - \text{Smallest Data Value}}{\text{Class Width}} \qquad [2]$$

When:

determining the real class limits for rounded data for use in cumulative frequency or cumulative relative frequency distributions, histograms, frequency polygons, or ogives,

Use:

$$\text{Real Lower Limit} = \text{Apparent Lower Limit} - \tfrac{1}{2}(\text{Unit Difference}) \qquad [3]$$

$$\text{Real Upper Limit} = \text{Apparent Upper Limit} + \tfrac{1}{2}(\text{Unit Difference}) \qquad [4]$$

Chapter 2

HERE'S HOW IT'S DONE!

Examples

1. Classify the data obtained from the answers to the following questions as "nominal", "ordinal", "interval", or "ratio". Also, classify each as "qualitative" or "quantative".

(a) What is your major field of study?

Solution:

(a) The data obtained would be answers such as "Business Administration", "Physical Sciences", "Social Sciences", etc. Because these names are labels for purposes of identification, the data is nominal and therefore qualitative.

(b) What is your weight?

Solution:

(b) The values given as answers would be numerical values such as 120, 142, 195, 110, etc. These values are measured on a scale with a fixed numerical unit of measure (pounds) where the zero point is fixed (the absence of weight). Thus, the data is ratio and hence quantative.

(c) What page of this book are you presently reading?

Solution:

(c) This is page 20 of the text portion of this book. The number 20 indicates that this is the twentieth page in the ordered series of page numbers. Notice that it makes no sense to "add" page 20 to page 21, but one can talk about page 20 being before (less than) page 21. Thus the level of measurement being used is ordinal and therefore qualitative.

(d) Stand on the seat of a chair. What is the distance from the top of your head to the ceiling?

Solution:

(d) This distance would probably be measured with some type of ruler. Thus, there is a fixed unit of measurement (foot, inch, etc.). However, there is no zero point inherently defined for the measurement of the required distance because the heights would not necessarily all be measured from the same chair. Thus, the measurement is interval and quantative.

2. What level of measurement did you use the last time you ordered a soft drink at a fast-food restaurant?

Solution:

Small, medium, and large are the usual measures assigned to the soft drinks. Rather than being just labels for the drinks, these measurements imply an ordering by size. A large soft drink contains more than a medium soft drink, and a medium soft drink contains more than a small soft drink in terms of the amount of beverage received. The actual amount of difference in beverage between the sizes is determined by the amount of ice in the cups and the size of the cups used by the particular fast-food restaurants.

3. Thirty residents of Ponchatoula, Louisiana were asked to name their favorite pay-TV channel. The results were as follows:

HBO	MAX	HBO	DSN	MTV
SHO	TMC	MTV	SHO	HBO
HBO	DSN	MAX	TMC	TMC
MAX	SHO	TMC	HBO	MAX
SHO	DSN	MTV	MAX	HBO
SHO	HBO	MAX	HBO	HBO

(a) Summarize this data by constructing a frequency distribution. Which pay-TV channel is preferred by the residents of Ponchatoula?

Solution:

(a) First, notice that this nominal (and therefore qualitative) data can be grouped into the classes: DSN, HBO, MAX, MTV, SHO, and TMC. Next, count the number of data items associated with each pay-TV channel. Prepare a tally sheet from the original data to obtain the frequencies of each of the (nonoverlapping) classes. Use these tallies to give the following frequency distribution:

Preferred Pay-TV Channel	Frequency
DSN	3
HBO	9
MAX	6
MTV	3
SHO	5
TMC	4

Using the frequency distribution it is easy to see that HBO is preferred.

Hint: To make certain that you have not missed counting a data item, check to see that the sum of the frequency column is the total number of data items given in the problem.

(b) Summarize the data by constructing a relative frequency distribution.

Solution:

(b) The total number of data items is 30. Thus, we use formula [1] to obtain the relative frequency of the first class, DSN, as 3/30 = .10. Obtaining the relative frequencies of the other classes in the same manner, we have the following as the relative frequency distribution for this data:

Preferred Pay-TV Channel	Relative Frequency
DSN	.10
HBO	.30
MAX	.20
MTV	.10
SHO	.17
TMC	.13

Hint: Be sure to correctly round off the relative frequencies when expressing them as decimal numerals. In some cases, however, it is still possible that the sum of the relative frequencies, which should be 1, will be 0.99 or 1.01 due to round-off error.

(c) Summarize the data by constructing a bar graph for the frequency distribution. What would be the only change in the graph if the bar graph were done for the relative frequency distribution?

Solution:

(c) Recall that the bar graph is a graphical representation of the frequency distribution. On the horizontal axis, we specify a fixed distance to represent the width of the bar. Although there are no hard-and-fast rules for specifying this distance, keep in mind that we wish the finished bar graph to be visually appealing. Thus, do not choose the bars too "fat" or too "skinny". Since we have six classes, the bar graph will have six nonoverlapping bars with the frequency of each bar represented on the vertical axis. To prevent visual distortion, the vertical axis is drawn "to scale" and begins with a frequency of zero.

When drawing the bar graph, be sure to label the axes. The graph should present the data in a form that is clear and understandable.
Without knowing what the values on the vertical axis or the bars on the horizontal axis represent, the bar graph does not give a complete

picture of the data.

If this graph were done for the relative frequency distribution, the only change would be that the relative frequencies would be given on the vertical axis. Because these frequencies and relative frequencies are ratio-level measurements, the axes are proportional and the graph of the relative frequency distribution would appear the same.

Bar Graph for Example 3:

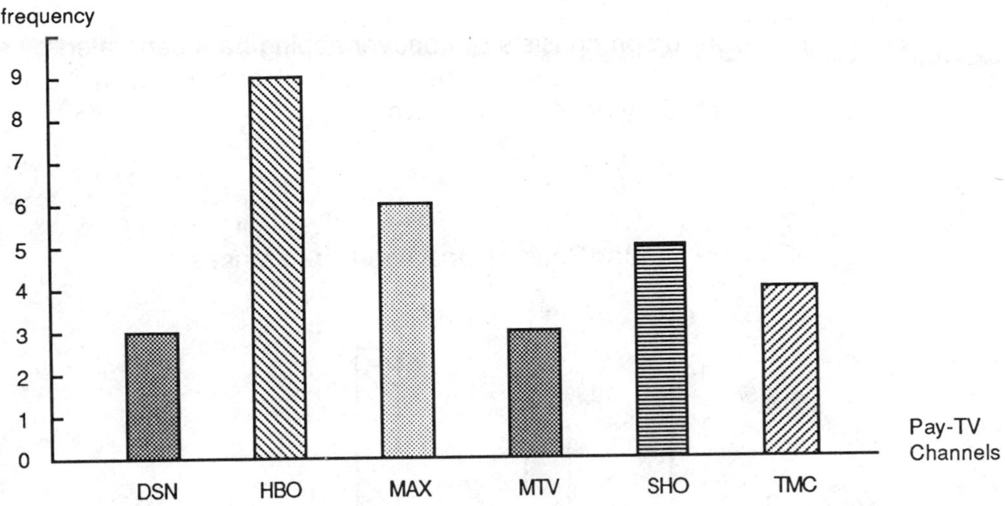

4. Forty dog owners were asked the question "Which type of dog food, canned, dry, moist, or table scraps, do you most often feed your pet?" The results are summarized in the following frequency distribution:

Type of Dog Food	Frequency
Canned	12
Dry	10
Moist	15
Table Scraps	3

a) Classify the data for this problem.

Solution:

a) The data for this problem consists of the responses of the 40 people to the question they were asked. Since they would give an answer of "canned", "dry", "moist", or "table scraps", the data is nominal and therefore qualitative.

b) Which type of dog food is most often used to feed the pets of these 40 people?

Solution:

b) From the frequency distribution, we see that the highest frequency is 15. Thus, the most often used type of dog food for these people is the moist kind. (Notice how easily you can obtain the most frequently chosen type of dog food from the following bar chart of the data.)

c) Display the frequency distribution of dog food preferences with a bar chart.

Solution:

Recall that a bar graph consists of nonoverlapping bars separated by spaces for visual clarity. The frequencies of the data are placed on the vertical axis which starts with a frequency of zero. Thus, we have:

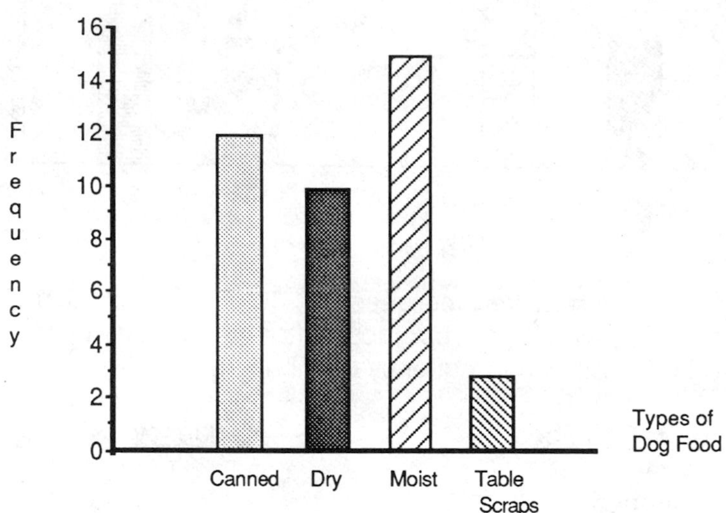

d) Represent the data with a pie chart.

Solution:

d) Because the pie chart is based on the relative frequency distribution, we first divide each of the frequencies by 40, as indicated in formula [1], to obtain the following relative frequency distribution:

Type of Dog Food	Relative Frequency
Canned	.300
Dry	.250
Moist	.375
Table Scraps	.075

Hint: Be sure the relative frequencies add to 1. Also, three decimal places were kept here to eliminate round-off error since these values will be used with multiplication to draw the pie chart.

To identify the sector corresponding to each of the classes, multiply each of the relative frequencies by 360° to obtain the following:

Canned	.300(360)	$= 108^{\circ}$
Dry	.250(360)	$= 90^{\circ}$
Moist	.375(360)	$= 135^{\circ}$
Table Scraps	.075(360)	$= 27^{\circ}$.

Draw a circle and measure with your protractor from a zero point (chosen anywhere on the rim of the circle) an angle of 108° :

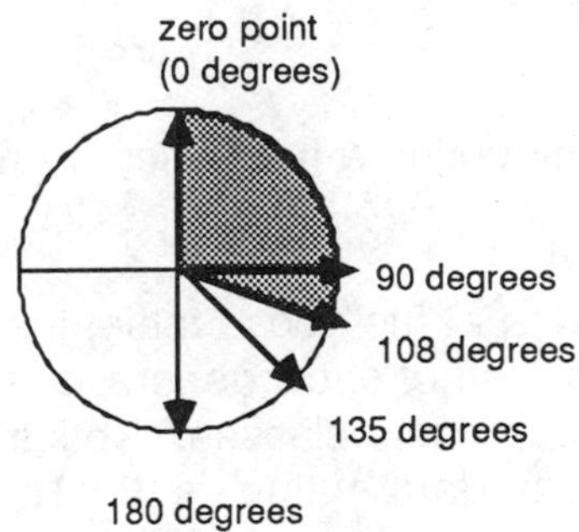

Measure the other sectors in similar manner to obtain the finished pie chart:

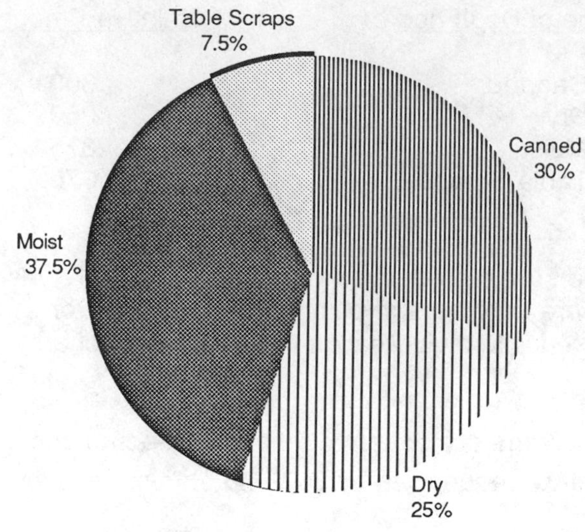

5. The following data represent the amounts of regular unleaded gasoline (rounded off to the nearest gallon) purchased by 40 customers at a local service station:

14	10	9	10	28
16	24	5	10	15
13	14	23	8	12
2	19	26	10	17
20	18	17	6	18
21	14	13	25	14
18	14	16	20	15
10	13	23	26	14

a) Summarize the data by constructing a frequency distribution:

<u>Solution</u>:

a) As you can see by looking at the above table, the data now is simply a mass of numerical values that do not show general characteristics. To summarize the data, we should group it into classes. Notice that the largest data value is 28 and the smallest data value is 2. To construct the frequency distribution for this quantitative data, we must first decide on the approximate width of each of the classes. If we pick, say, a class width of 10, formula [2] gives the approximate number of classes as

$(28-2)/10 = 2.6$ which is rounded up to a value of 3.

Using three classes is probably grouping the data too much, losing many of the patterns in the data that a frequency distribution can show. Thus, by trial

and error, let us choose a class width of 5.
Then, formula [2] gives the approximate number of classes as

(28–2)/5 = 5.2 which is rounded up to a value of 6.

Using 6 classes, we are satisfying the guideline of choosing between 5 and 20 classes for the frequency distribution.

Tip: Do not forget to round the value obtained in fromula [2] as the approximate number of classes up. If you do not round this value up to the next highest value, you will probably not include the highest data values in your classes.

Next, we determine the class limits for the distribution. Choose a convenient starting point as the lower limit of the first class, making sure to include the lowest value. (Do not go too far below this lowest value, or your last class may end before including the largest data value.) Arbitrarily choosing 1 as the lower limit of the first class, we obtain the following classes: 1-5, 6-10, 11-15, 16-20, 21-25, and 26-30. Remember that the classes must be nonoverlapping and of equal width. Thus, if the first class ends with 5, the second class cannot begin at 5, for then the value of 5 could possibly be put in both classes! Also notice that the class width is the difference between successive lower (or upper) class limits. Tally the data into the classes, making sure the sum of the frequencies equals the total number of data values, to obtain the following:

Frequency Distribution

Number of Gallons of Gasoline Purchased	Frequency
1 - 5	2
6 - 10	8
11 - 15	12
16 - 20	10
21 - 25	5
26 - 30	3

b) Construct a relative frequency distribution for this data:

Solution:

(b) Using formula [1] to obtain the relative frequencies from the frequencies, we obtain the relative frequency distribution:

Relative Frequency Distribution

Number of Gallons of Gasoline Purchased	Relative Frequency
1 - 5	.050
6 - 10	.200
11 - 15	.300
16 - 20	.250
21 - 25	.125
26 - 30	.075

c) What are the real class limits for this data?

Solution:

c) The apparent class limits are the upper and lower class limits shown in the frequency distribution. Because this data was obtained by rounding to the nearest gallon, the real class limits are not the same as the apparent class limits. For instance, the data value of 16 may have actually been 15.85 gallons which was rounded off to 16 gallons. This "real" value of 15.85 is not included in any of the classes given in the frequency distribution. To obtain the real class limits, we use formulas [3] and [4] with a unit difference of 1 gallon (since the data was rounded off to the nearest gallon). Thus, the real class limits are: 0.5-5.5, 5.5-10.5, 10.5-15.5, 15.5-20.5, 20.5-25.5, 25.5-30.5.

d) Summarize the data by constructing a cumulative frequency distribution:

Solution:

d) Recall that the cumulative frequency distribution contains the same number of classes as the frequency distribution, but the cumulative frequency distribution shows the total number of data items with value less than or equal to the real upper limit for the class. Thus, using the real upper limits determined in part c) and accumulating (summing) the frequencies as we proceed from class to class, we obtain the following:

Number of Gallons Purchased	Cumulative Frequency
Less than or equal to 5.5	2
Less than or equal to 10.5	10
Less than or equal to 15.5	22
Less than or equal to 20.5	32
Less than or equal to 25.5	37
Less than or equal to 30.5	40

6. The weights of 60 students in the seventh grade at Syracuse Junior High School are summarized in the following frequency distribution. (The weights have been rounded to the nearest pound.)

Weight of student	Frequency
45 - 52	2
53 - 60	5
61 - 68	9
69 - 76	13
77 - 84	13
85 - 92	10
93 - 100	8

(a) What is the width of each class in this frequency distribution?

Solution:

(a) The width of each class is the difference in successive lower class limits (that is, 53 – 45 = 61 – 53 = etc.) or the difference in successive upper class limits (that is, 60 – 52 = 68 – 60 = etc.). Thus the width of each of the equal classes is 8.

(b) What would the real class limits be for the class 69 - 76?

Solution:

(b) Because this data has been rounded to the nearest pound, the unit difference is one pound. Thus, using formulas [3] and [4] and the apparent class limits given in the frequency distribution, we find:

Real Lower Limit = 69 – (1/2)(1) = 68.5 and
Real Upper Limit = 76 + (1/2)(1) = 76.5.

(c) Construct a histogram for this frequency distribution.

Solution:

(c) The real limits for the classes are determined as in part b) of this problem. These real class limits are 44.5-52.5, 52.5-60.5, 60.5-68.5, 68.5-76.5, 76.5-84.5, 84.5-92.5, 92.5-100.5. Thus, in drawing the histogram, the base for the rectangle for the class interval 45-52 must begin at 44.5 and end at 52.5, and so on. Using these real class limits on the horizontal axis and the frequencies on the vertical axis, we obtain the histogram for this frequency distribution. Note that the class width in the frequency distribution is the same as the width of each of the rectangles and that the rectangles are adjacent since the real class limits have no "gap" between the upper limit of one class and the lower limit of the next class.

Histogram for problem 6:

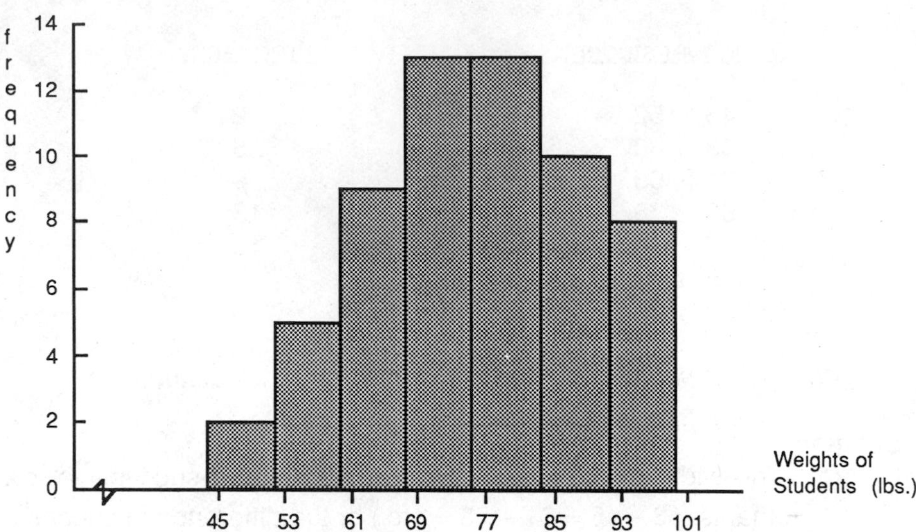

d) Represent the frequency distribution with a frequency polygon.

Solution:

d) To construct the frequency polygon, we find the midpoints of each of the class intervals by averaging the class limits. It does not matter whether we average the apparent or the real limits. For instance, the midpoint of the first class is:

$$(52 + 45)/2 = (52.5 + 44.5)/2 = 48.5 .$$

The midpoints of the other classes can be found in the same manner, or they can be found by adding the class width the the midpoint of the preceeding class. To draw the frequency polygon, plot the class midpoints on the horizontal axis versus the frequencies on the vertical axis and connect these points with straight line segments.

Don't forget to add classes of zero frequency at each end of the frequency distribution so that the frequency polygon touches the horizontal axis at both ends of the graph.

Note: The " ⩘ " symbol on the horizontal axis is standard notation used to show an interruption in the scale. That is, the distance shown from 0 to 45 is not the same as the distance shown from 45 to 53.

Frequency Polygon for Problem 6:

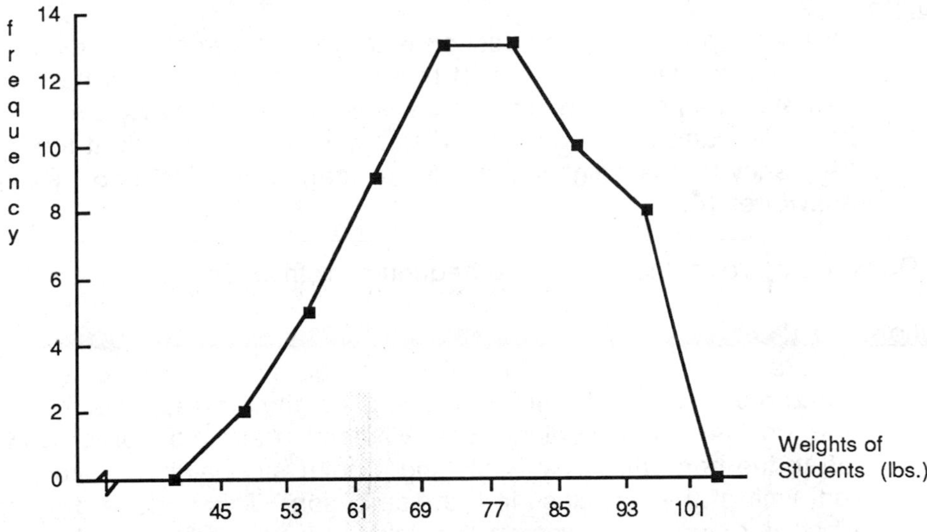

7. (a) Give the cumulative frequency distribution for the data in problem 6.

Solution:

(a) Using the real upper limits of each of the classes in the frequency distribution and accumulating the frequencies as we go from class to class, we have the following as the cumulative frequency distribution for this data:

Weight of Student	Cumulative Frequency
Less than or equal to 52.5	2
Less than or equal to 60.5	7
Less than or equal to 68.5	16
Less than or equal to 76.5	29
Less than or equal to 84.5	42
Less than or equal to 92.5	52
Less than or equal to 100.5	60

Hint: As a check on your addition, remember that the last class cumulative frequency must equal to the total number of data values considered in the problem.

b) How many of the students weigh less than 69 pounds?

Solution:

b) One way to answer this question is to go to the frequency distribution and sum the frequencies of the first three classes. All weights from 45 through 68 have been recorded in these classes. An easier way, however, since we have the cumulative frequency distribution, is just to look at the cumulative frequency for the weights that are less than or equal to 68.5. This gives the answer of 16.

c) Draw the ogive for the cumulative frequency distribution:

Solution:

c) To draw the ogive, we plot the upper real limits of the classes (on the horizontal axis) at heights equal to the corresponding cumulative frequencies (on the vertical axis). Remember to "tie the graph down" on the left to the horizontal axis by plotting a point with height of zero at the lower real limit of the first class in the distribution. This is done only on the left since if it were done also on the right , it would indicate a decrease in the cumulative frequencies which would be impossible.

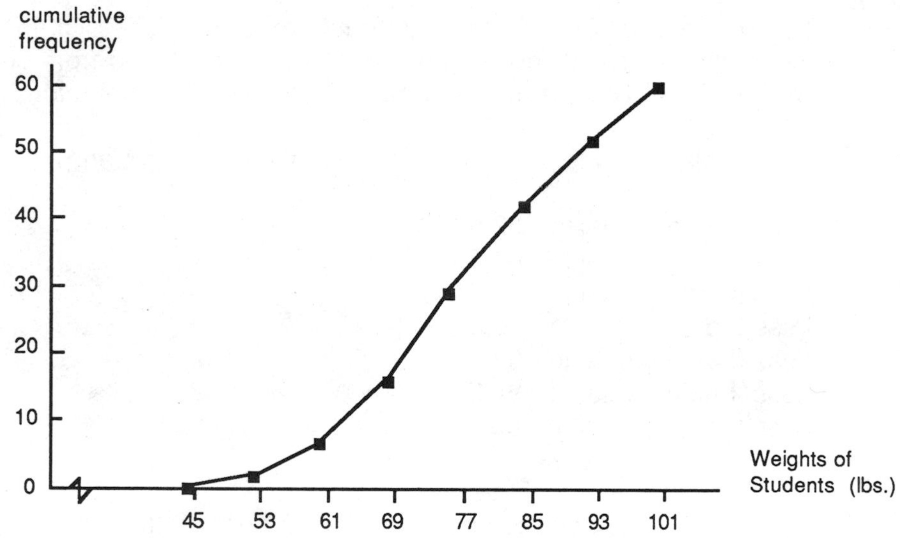

8. The following data show the IQ scores of 25 second-grade students. Construct a stem-and-leaf display of the data using leaves consisting of one digit.

128	100	115	82	99
142	98	152	100	105
110	114	86	124	102
125	107	94	128	133
128	113	99	111	103

Solution:

Since the leaves, which are the individual pieces of information on the stems, are to consist of one digit, we arrange the first digit(s) of each item, in order from smallest to largest, to the left of a vertical line. The units digit is then placed on the horizontal line corresponding to the first digit(s). Reading the IQ scores from left to right, we obtain:

```
 8 | 2 6
 9 | 9 8 4 9
10 | 0 0 5 2 7 3
11 | 5 0 4 3 1
12 | 8 4 5 8 8
13 | 3
14 | 2
15 | 2
```

We then order by rank, from smallest to largest, the units digits on each horizontal line to obtain the required stem-and-leaf display.

```
 8 | 2 6
 9 | 4 8 9 9
10 | 0 0 2 3 5 7
11 | 0 1 3 4 5
12 | 4 5 8 8 8
13 | 3
14 | 2
15 | 2
```

Chapter 2

HAVE I LEARNED THE MATERIAL?

Problems

1. Reread the last sentence in the summary of Chapter 2 in the textbook (page 45):

   "The purpose of the descriptive statistical procedures presented in this chapter is to provide tabular and graphical approaches that facilitate the interpretation of data."

   (a) Do a frequency distribution for the vowels (a, e, i, o, u) appearing in this sentence.

   (b) Which vowel occurs most frequently in this sentence?

2. Classify the data obtained from the answers to the following as "nominal", "ordinal", "interval", or "ratio". Also, classify each as "qualitative" or "quantitative".

   (a) What is your height?

   (b) What is your shoe size?

   (c) What is your telephone number?

   (d) How many years have you lived at your present address?

   (e) Do you own a calculator?

3. Name five things that are wrong or misleading in the following bar chart:

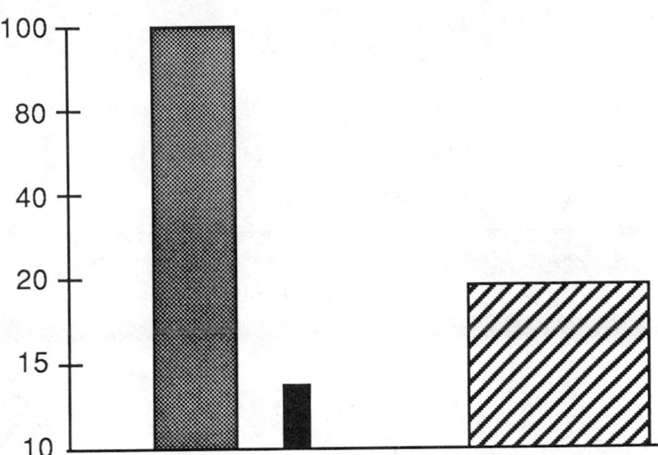

4. Professor Pringle examined his records and formed the following frequency distribution for the reorded number of absences for 20 students completing his two week course in investment analysis:

Number of Absences	Frequency
0	10
1	4
2	4
3	2

(a) Do a relative frequency distribution for this data:

(b) Display Professor Pringle's summary data with a bar graph.

(c) Represent the data with a pie chart:

5. The following data are the percentage scores (rounded to the nearest percent) on the third major test for 36 students enrolled in a certain section of the introductory statistics course at Clemson University:

65	53	95	87	78	82
70	75	68	50	64	77
72	83	62	75	80	58
85	70	76	85	75	78
56	78	87	67	86	69
79	98	71	70	75	70

(a) Summarize this data by constructing a frequency distribution: (use a class width of 10)

(b) Summarize this data by constructing a histogram:

(c) Draw a frequency polygon for this data:

(d) Summarize these test scores by constructing a cumulative frequency distribution:

(e) Give the cumulative relative frequency distribution for these test scores:

(f) Draw an ogive for the cumulative relative frequency distribution.

6. Answer the following questions relating to problem 5:

   (a) How many students made a score of 75% on the test?

   (b) What class occurs most frequently for these grades?

   (c) What percent of the students made below 80% on this test?

7. Referring again to the data of test scores in problem 5, suppose the teacher's grading scale is:

90 - 100%	A
80 - 89%	B
70 - 79%	C
60 - 69%	D
0 - 59%	F

(a) If you wished to summarize the data of test scores in this problem with a graph using the above grading scale, would you use classes with the numerical values (quantitative data with a histogram) or use the classes as the obtained letter grade (qualitative data with a bar graph) ? Why?

(b) Draw the graph mentioned in part a):

8. Again refer to the data of test scores in problem 5.

(a) Construct a stem-and-leaf display for the data.

(b) Rotate your stem and leaf diagram counterclockwise and compare its shape to the histogram obtained in problem 5b). Comment.

9. The following frequency distribution is a summary of the amount of money (rounded to the nearest dollar) spent on textbooks during the fall term by 50 freshmen at Ding-Bat College:

Dollar Amount Spent on Textbooks	Frequency
41 - 60	2
61 - 80	3
81 - 100	5
101 - 120	20
121 - 140	15
141 - 160	5

Draw the ogive for the cumulative frequency distribution.

10. Consider the following histogram showing the frequency distribution for the amount of time (rounded to the nearest hour) spent sleeping recorded for each of 25 students in one particular 24 hour period. (The frequencies have been placed on the top of each rectangle for easy reference.)

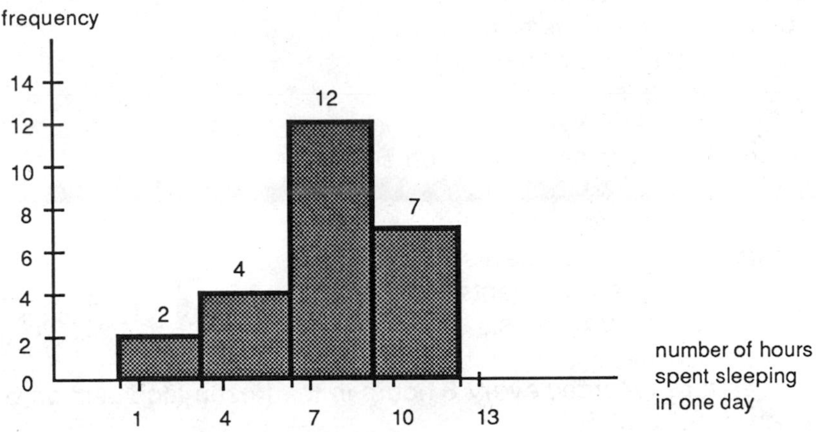

Answer the following questions:

(a) What is the most frequent interval for the number of hours spent sleeping?

(b) How many of the students spent less than 7 hours sleeping?

(c) What percent of students spent more than 6 hours sleeping?

(d) What fraction of the students spent between 7 and 9 hours sleeping that day?

Chapter 2

Multiple Choice Questions

1. The ranks of servicemen in the U.S. Air Force would be classified as

   (a) nominal level measurements
   (b) ordinal level measurements
   (c) interval level measurements
   (d) ratio level measurements.

2. The channel numbers on a television set are

   (a) nominal level measurements
   (b) ordinal level measurements
   (c) interval level measurements
   (d) ratio level measurements.

3. The temperature recorded every 8 hours in the frozen food section of a supermarket is an example of a(n)

   (a) nominal level measurement
   (b) ordinal level measurement
   (c) interval level measurement
   (d) ratio level measurement.

4. In determining the approximate number of classes to use in a frequency distribution for quantitative data, we

   (a) judiciously choose a value
   (b) take the square root of the total number of observations
   (c) round off the quotient: (smallest data value - largest data value)/class width
   (d) round up the quotient: (largest data value - smallest data value)/class width.

5. In the frequency distribution for a certain quantitative variable (rounded off to the nearest whole number), the first interval has the apparent class limits of 50-54. The width of this class interval is

   (a) 5
   (b) 5.5
   (c) 4
   (d) 4.5.

6. A frequency distribution is:

Class	Frequency
Freshman	21
Sophomore	15
Junior	14
Senior	10

The cumulative relative frequency of the class "Junior" is

(a) .14
(b) .23
(c) .83
(d) none of the above.

7. To graphically summarize quantative data, we can draw

(a) pie charts and bar charts
(b) histograms, frequency polygons, and ogives
(c) bar charts and histograms
(d) pie charts and frequency polygons.

8. When constructing a histogram, it is best to use equal class intervals, if possible, since

(a) it really looks nice
(b) this is the only way we can see all the individual data values on the graph
(c) then the heights of the rectangles are proportional to the frequencies
(d) by doing this, we can avoid classes with zero frequencies.

9. In plotting the ogive for a cumulative frequency distribution, the cumulative frequency is plotted as the height of each point corresponding to the horizontal value of

(a) the lower real limit of each class
(b) the lower apparent limit of each class
(c) the upper real limit of each class
(d) the upper apparent limit of each class.

10. In the "bonus round" on Wheel of Fortune, the contestants consistantly pick the consonants S, R, T, N, L and the vowel E as the letters to use as an aid in solving the word puzzle. Why should they?

(a) the host of the show told them to
(b) everyone else picks these letters
(c) these are the only letters available
(d) these consonants and vowel are probably the ones that occur most frequently in phrases in the English language.

Chapter 2

Answers to Problems

1. (a)

Vowels in Sentence	Frequency
a	16
e	17
i	13
o	8
u	3

(b) The vowel occurring most frequently in this set of 57 vowels is "e".

2. (a) ratio; quantative
(b) ordinal; qualitative
(c) nominal; qualitative
(d) ratio; quantative
(e) nominal; qualitative

3. The following lead to visual distortion and/or misrepresentation of the information:
(a) The vertical scale starts at 10, not 0.
(b) The numbers on the vertical axis are not "to scale"; that is, the distance shown between 15 and 20 is not the same as the distance shown between 40 and 80.
(c) The bars are not all of the same width.
(d) The axes are not labeled.
(e) No labels have been assigned to the bars, and without the data, there is no way of knowing what the graph represents.

4. (a)

Number of Absences	Relative Frequency
10	0.5
4	0.2
4	0.2
2	0.1

(b)

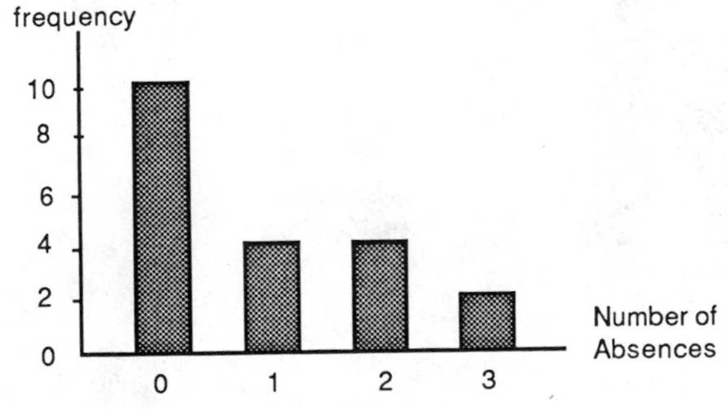

(c)

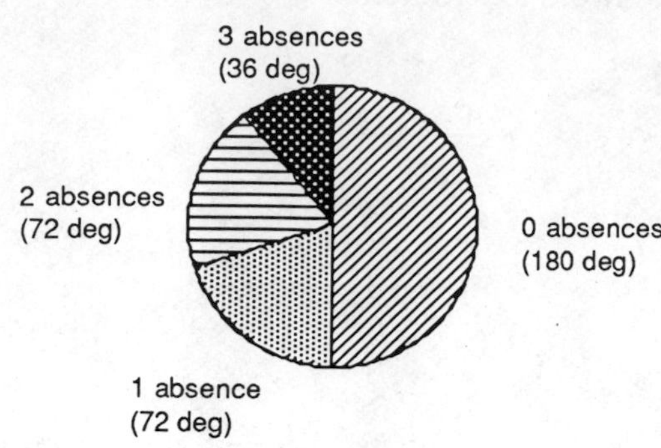

5. (a)

Percentage Score on Test 3	Frequency
50 - 59	4
60 - 69	6
70 - 79	16
80 - 89	8
90 - 99	2

(b)

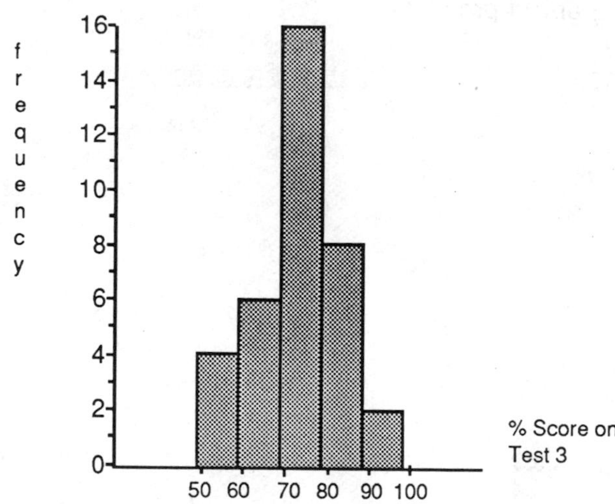

c)

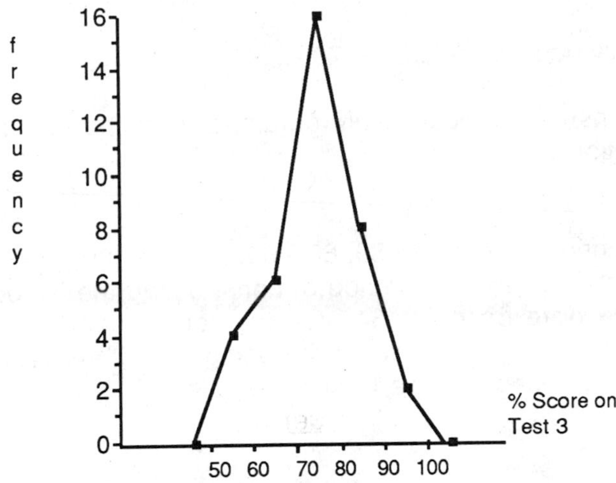

d) and e)

% Score on Test 3	Cumulative Frequency	Cumulative Relative Frequency
Less than or equal to 59.5	4	.11
Less than or equal to 69.5	10	.28
Less than or equal to 79.5	26	.72
Less than or equal to 89.5	34	.94
Less than or equal to 99.5	36	1.00

(f)

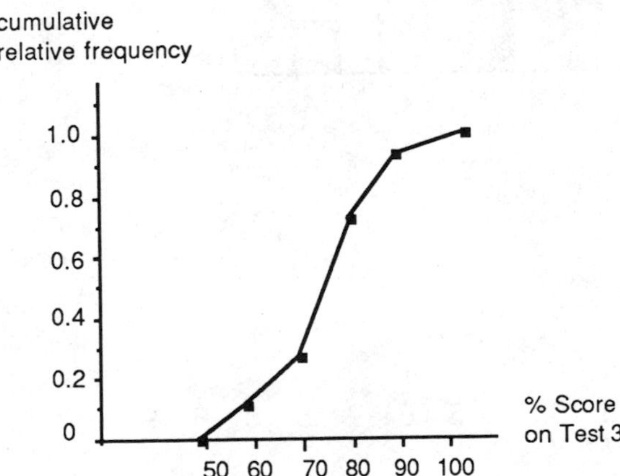

6. (a) You must look at the original data, not the summary data, to obtain the answer of 4.

   (b) The most frequently occurring class is 70 - 79.

   (c) 72% (This answer is most easily obtained from the cumulative relative frequency distribution.)

7. (a) If you use the numerical values (0 - 59, 60 - 69, ..., 90 - 100), the class intervals are of unequal width. Thus, the method of constructing the histogram must be modified (see the note on page 34 of Anderson/Sweeney/Williams). This problem can be taken care of, however, by using the letter grades (qualitative data) to obtain the following bar chart:

   (b)

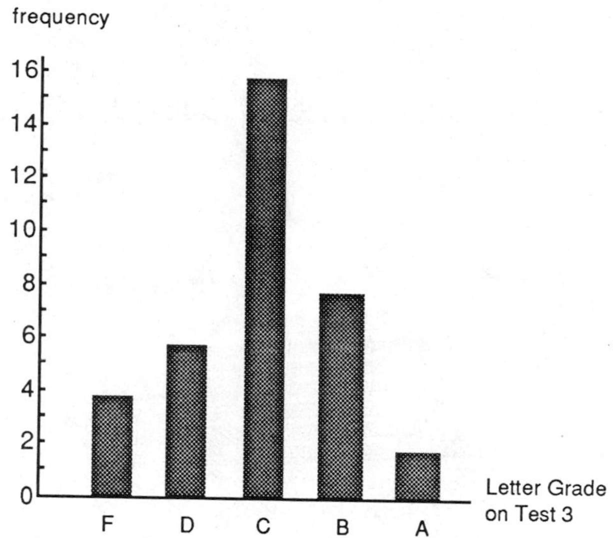

8.

```
5 | 0 3 6 8
6 | 2 4 5 7 8 9
7 | 0 0 0 0 1 2 5 5 5 5 6 7 8 8 8 9
8 | 0 2 3 5 5 6 7 7
9 | 5 8
```

9. The cumulative frequency distribution must be obtained in order to draw the ogive. It is:

Dollar Amount Spent on Textbooks	Cumulative Frequency
Less than or equal to 60.5	2
Less than or equal to 80.5	5
Less than or equal to 100.5	10
Less than or equal to 120.5	30
Less than or equal to 140.5	45
Less than or equal to 160.5	50

Thus, the ogive for the cumulative frequency distribution is:

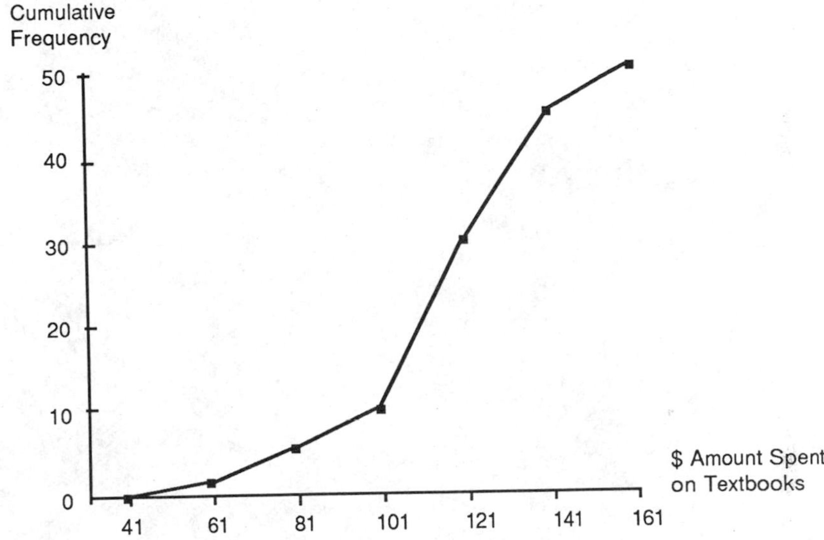

10. (a) 7 - 9 hours

(b) 6

(c) 19/25 = 76%

(d) 0.48 (the relative frequency of the interval 7 - 9)

Chapter 2

Answers to Multiple Choice Questions

1. a
2. b
3. c
4. d
5. a
6. c
7. b
8. c
9. c
10. d

Chapter 3
DESCRIPTIVE STATISTICS II: MEASURES OF LOCATION AND DISPERSION

WHAT AM I LEARNING?

Chapter Outline and Summary

The tools and techniques of descriptive statistics can be tabular, graphic, or numeric. Most of the more commonly used tabular and graphic methods of descriptive statistics were discussed in Chapter 2. Chapter 3 is concerned with the *numeric* methods of describing statistical data. Any numerical value used as a summary measure for a population value is called a *parameter.* If the numerical value is used as a summary measure for a sample, it is called a *statistic.* Population parameters are denoted by letters in the Greek alphabet while sample statistics are symbolized with lower case English alphabet letters.

This chapter considers the numeric summary measures for characterizing individual data values and data values which have been grouped in a frequency distribution. The descriptive methods will be discussed for measures of central location and measures of variability in sets of both population and sample data.

There are three principal numeric measures of the central location, or average, of a set of data values. These measures serve to locate the "middle" of the set of data. The most common of these, which involves summing all the data values and then dividing by the total number of values, is called the *mean.* The mean of a population of size N is denoted by μ while the mean of a sample of size n is symbolized by $\bar{x}$.

A second measure of central location is the *median.* (There are no specific symbols used to represent the median.) If there are an odd number of data values, the value that falls in the middle when the measurements are arranged in order of magnitude is called the median. If there are two middle values (that is, when the number of observations is odd), the median is the mean of these two middle values.

While the mean and the median are unique values, the *mode*, which is the data value that occurs with the highest frequency, is not necessarily a single number and may not even exist. When two data values occur with equal frequency and that frequency is more than the frequency of any of the other data values, these two values are both modes and the data are *bimodal*. If a data set has more than two modes, it is said to be *multimodal* . When no value or values occur with highest frequency (that is, all data values are different), we say the data has no mode. Unless there is a unique value the mode is not really an appropriate measure of the center of a set of data.

While these three numerical values, mean, median, and mode, are all measures of the central location or average of a set of data, the mean is the one most often referred to as "the average". Sometimes the median is the preferred measure (when there are extreme values in the set of observations), and sometimes the mode is the only useful measure of the center (when working with nominal data).

Data sets with the same central location can be quite different. Thus, a measure of variability is necessary since a measure of central tendency does not alone adequately describe a set of data. Percentiles are useful in describing the variability (spread, dispersion) of the data in that they partition the data into a specific number of parts, each containing the same number of values. The *pth percentile* of a data set is a value such that at least (that many or more) p percent of the items take on this value or less and at least (100-p) percent of the items take on this value or more. The median divides the data into two equal sections, so it is the 50th percentile. The *first quartile* is the 25th percentile, and the *third quartile* is the 75th percentile.

Other measures of variability include the range and the interquartile range. The *range* is the difference between the largest data value and the smallest data value. The *interquartile range* , sometimes used to overcome the sensitivity of the numeric measures to extreme values, is the difference between the third and first quartiles.

Two other measures of the spread of the data which will be used quite a bit in inferential statistics are the variance and the standard deviation. The *variance*, which takes into account all the data values in the set, involves the *deviation about the mean* which is the difference between each observation in the set of data and the mean of the data set. Because the sum of the deviations about the mean for any set of data is always zero, the variance is defined as the *average squared deviation.* The symbol for the variance of a population is σ^2 while the symbol for population variance is s^2. Very often, the positive square root of the variance, denoted by σ for the population and s for the sample, is more convenient to use. This quantity is expressed in the same units as the original data and is called the *standard deviation.*

One of the ways to describe a set of data using both the mean and standard deviation is given by *Chebyshev's theorem.* It is used to give a very conservative estimate of the fraction or percentage of the data values which are expected to fall within a particular number of standard deviations on either side of the mean. Chebyshev's theorem states:

> For any set of data and any value of k greater than or equal to 1, at least $1 - (1/k^2)$ of the data must be within $\pm$ k standard deviations of the mean.

This theorem makes a statement about only the data set itself, not an inference about some larger population. Thus, we use the population standard deviation formula when computing the standard deviation mentioned in Chebyshev's theorem whether the data involved is a sample or a population.

The variance and standard deviation are measures of absolute measure of dispersion. When the means of two or more data sets differ greatly, an accurate picture of their relative variability cannot be obtained by comparing the variances or standard deviations. For such comparisons, the coefficient of variation can be used. The *coefficient of variation* expresses the standard deviation as a percent of the mean for a set of data. Large coefficients of variation would indicate highly variable data sets, while small coefficients of variation indicate less dispersion within the data set.

To summarize these numerical measures used in descriptive statistics, we have:

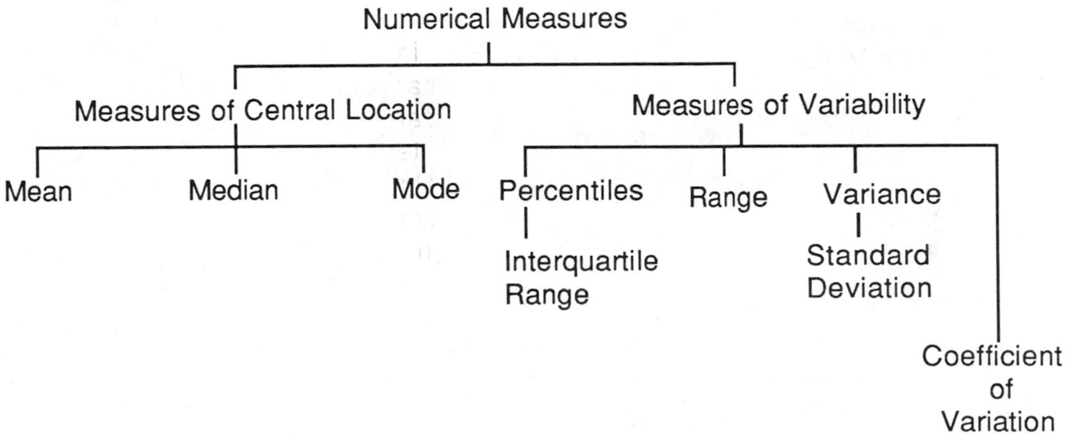

When the data is presented in the form of a frequency distribution, approximations of the mean, variance, and standard deviation for the original data can be given treating the midpoint of each class as if it were the mean of the items in the class. The mean and variance will not be the same as for the original data because in the *grouped data* (that is, the data in the summary form of the frequency distribution) each data value is assumed to be at the class midpoint. The difference between the mean calculated from the original data and the mean calculated from the grouped data is called the *grouping error.*

Techniques of exploratory data analysis presented in this chapter are 5-number summaries and box-and-whisker plots. These methods provide information about the location, dispersion, and shape of the distribution of data sets. The median and first and third quartiles, together with the smallest and largest data values, give the five numbers that make up the *5-number summary* of a set of data. The following differences can also be computed: median - lowest value = *lowspread*; upper hinge - lower hinge = *midspread*; highest value - median = *highspread*. These three values are also called the *half-ranges.*

A graphical representation of the five numbers in the 5-number summary is called a *box-and-whisker plot.* This plot is obtained by filling in the numerical values in the diagram shown on the next page.

Box-and-Whisker Plot of the 5-Number Summary:

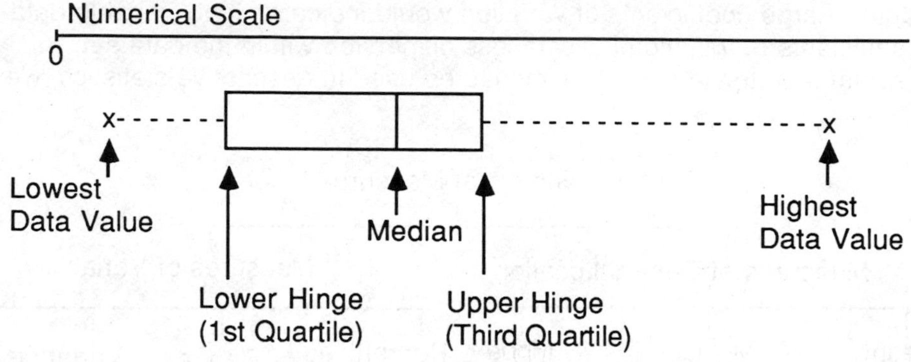

Chapter 3

WHICH FORMULA SHOULD I USE?

Formulas

When:

finding the <u>mean of a sample</u> consisting of n numerical data items x,

Use:

Sample Mean

$$\bar{x} = \frac{x_1 + x_2 + \ldots + x_n}{n} = \frac{\Sigma x}{n} \qquad [1]$$

When:

finding the <u>mean of a population</u> consisting of a set of N data items x,

Use:

Population Mean

$$\mu = \frac{x_1 + x_2 + \ldots + x_n}{N} = \frac{\Sigma x}{N} \qquad [2]$$

When:

calculating the <u>pth percentile</u> of a set of n data values,

Use:

Step 1: Arrange the data values in ascending order (from smallest to largest).

Step 2: Compute the index $i = np/100$ where p is the desired percentile. [3]

Step 3: (a) If i is <u>not</u> an integer, the next integer value greater than i denotes the <u>position</u> of the pth percentile.

(b) If i is an integer, the pth percentile is the average (mean) of the data values in <u>positions</u> i and i + 1.

When:

calculating the variance of a sample consisting of n numerical data items x,

Use:

Definition of Sample Variance

$$s^2 = \frac{\Sigma (x - \bar{x})^2}{n - 1} \qquad [4]$$

When:

calculating the variance of a sample consisting of n numerical data items x,

Use:

Shortcut Formula for Sample Variance

$$s^2 = \frac{\Sigma x^2 - (\Sigma x)^2 / n}{n - 1} \qquad [5]$$

When:

calculating the variance of a population consisting of N numerical data items x,

Use:

Definition of Population Variance

$$\sigma^2 = \frac{\Sigma (x - \mu)^2}{N} \qquad [6]$$

When:

calculating the variance of a population consisting of N numerical data items x,

Use:

Shortcut Formula for Population Variance

$$\sigma^2 = \frac{\Sigma x^2 - (\Sigma x)^2 / N}{N} \qquad [7]$$

When:

finding the standard deviation,

Use:

Sample standard deviation $= s = \sqrt{s^2}$ [8a]

Population standard deviation $= \sigma = \sqrt{\sigma^2}$ [8b]

When:

computing the coefficient of variation for data sets involving positive values,

Use:

coefficient of variation for the sample $= (s/\bar{x})100\%$ [9a]

coefficient of variation for the population $= (\sigma/\mu)100\%$ [9b]

When:

finding the sample mean for a set of n data items in a frequency distribution (grouped form) where M_i is the midpoint of each class i and f_i is the frequency of class i,

Use:

$$\bar{x} = \frac{\Sigma f_i M_i}{n} \quad [10]$$

When:

finding the sample variance for a set of n data items in a frequency distribution (grouped form) where M_i is the midpoint of each class i and f_i is the frequency of class i,

Use:

$$s^2 = \frac{\Sigma f_i M_i^2 - (\Sigma f_i M_i)^2/n}{n - 1} \quad [11]$$

When:

finding the population mean for a set of N data items in a frequency distribution (grouped form) where M_i is the midpoint of each class i and f_i is the frequency of class i,

Use:

$$\mu = \frac{\Sigma f_i M_i}{N} \qquad [12]$$

When:

finding the sample variance for a set of n data items in a frequency distribution (grouped form) where M_i is the midpoint of each class i and f_i is the frequency of class i,

Use:

$$\sigma^2 = \frac{\Sigma f_i M_i^2 - (\Sigma f_i M_i)^2 / N}{N} \qquad [13]$$

HERE'S HOW IT'S DONE!

Examples

1. Consider the following data sets. Compute the mean, median, and mode of each set, and tell which of the three is the preferred measure of central location of the data set.

(a) The set of heights (in inches) of a sample of six children:

38 44 52 37 40 50

Solution:

(a) Adding the values together, we get $\Sigma x = 261$. Using formula [1] with $n = 6$, we obtain a sample mean of $\bar{x} = 261/6 = 43.5$.

Since $n = 6$ is even, to obtain the median, we average the two middle values when the data is arranged in ascending order.

37 38 40 | 44 50 52
median

Thus, the median is $(40 + 44)/2 = 42$.

To find the mode, we find the value or values in the data set that occur most often. Since each value in this data set occurs with equal frequency (once), there is no mode.

Either the mean or the median would be a good measure of the center.

(b) The set of annual salaries of a sample of five lawyers:

\$55,000 \$45,000 \$40,000 \$200,000 \$40,000

Solution:

(b) Using formula [1], we find $\bar{x} = \Sigma x/n = 380000/5 = \$76{,}000$.

Since there are 5 data values (an odd number), the median is the value of the middle item when the data is arranged in order of magnitude from smallest to largest. Thus, the median is \$45,000.
The value that occurs most frequently (twice) is the mode of \$40,000.

Here, the extreme value of \$200,000 affects the mean but not the median. The mode is at the lower end of the distribution of the data. Thus, the median is the best measure of the central location of this data.

(c) The set of shoe sizes of the Edwards College basketball team is

12 13 10 13 14 9 10 13 14 9.

Solution:

(c) Assuming there are 10 players on the Edwards College basketball team, the shoe sizes constitute data items of a population of size N = 10. Thus, to find the population mean, we use formula [2], obtaining $\mu = \Sigma x/N = 117/10 = 11.7$.

Arranging the shoe sizes in order from smallest to largest we have:

9 9 10 10 12 | 13 13 13 14 14
median

Thus, the median is (12 + 13)/2 = 12.5.

The mode is 13 since the value of 13 occurs three times and no other value is repeated this many times or more.

The best measure of the central location of this set of data is probably the the mode since we are dealing with qualitative data. (There is no such shoe size as 11.7.)

2. The number of correct answers on a twenty question true-false competency test for a population of twenty applicants for a job were recorded as follows:

2	1	3	0	3
1	3	3	5	2
1	2	2	4	4
3	0	1	2	0

(a) Compute the mean of this data.

Solution:

(a) Using formula [2], we obtain $\mu = \Sigma x/N = 42/20 = 2.10$.

(b) Compute the median of this data.

Solution:

(b) Arranging the data in order of magnitude, we have
0, 0, 0, 1, 1, 1, 1, 2, 2, 2, 2, 2, 3, 3, 3, 3, 3, 4, 4, 5.
Since N = 20 is even, the median is the average of the 10th and 11th data values which gives the median = (2 + 2)/2 = 2.

(c) Compute the mode of this data.

Solution:

(c) Looking at the data which has been arranged in order of magnitude, we see that both 2 and 3 occur more frequently than the other values. Thus, the data is bimodal with modes of 2 and 3.

(d) For which value will at least 10% of the data items be this value or less and at least 90% of the data items be this value or more?

Solution:

(d) The question asks for the 10th percentile of the data. Using formula [3] with the data arranged in ascending order, we obtain the index i = (20)(10)/100 = 2. Since this index is an integer, we go to step 3b in formula [3] finding the 10th percentile as the mean of the data values in the second and third positions. Thus the 10th percentile is (0 + 0)/2 = 0.

3. For the data set 20, 10, 18, 16, 22, 32, 27, 30, 22, 14, 15, 21

(a) Find the 20th percentile.

Solution:

(a) Following the steps outlined for calculating the pth percentile in formula [3], we first arrange the 12 data items from the smallest value to the largest value: 10, 14, 15, 16, 18, 20, 21, 22, 22, 27, 30, 32 . Next, computing the index i, we have i = (12)(20)/100 = 2.4. Going to step 3(a) since i = 2.4 is not an integer, we have the next integer value greater than 2.4, or 3, denoting the position of the 20th percentile. Thus, the 3rd data value in the ascending set of values, 15, is the 20th percentile.

(b) Find and interpret the third quartile.

Solution:

(b) The third quartile is the 75th percentile. Again using formula [3], we have the index i = (12)(75)/100 = 9. Since this value is an integer, step 3(b) gives the 75th percentile as the average of the data values in the 9th and 10th positions. Therefore, the third quartile = (22 + 27)/2 = 24.5.

The interpretation of this value is: "75% (three-fourths) of the data items are less than 24.5, and 25% (one-fourth) of the data items are more than 24.5".

4. A group of 15 policemen each shot 6 times at a target. The number of bullseyes were recorded for each policeman. They were:

4	3	1	4	2
1	2	5	3	5
3	3	4	6	4

(a) Considering this as a sample chosen from the population of policemen, compute the mean.

Solution:

(a) Using formula [1], we add all the data values to obtain $\Sigma x = 50$. Thus, $\bar{x} = 50/15 = 3.33$ (rounded to the nearest hundredth for convenience).

(b) Compute the sample variance.

Solution:

(b) Either formula [4] or formula [5] could be used. Formula [4] involves subtracting the (rounded) mean 15 times and squaring each of these 15 decimal values which leads to more rounding error. Thus, since formula [5], the shortcut formula, involves fewer calculations and less chance of rounding error, it is the more advantageous one to use. We need the following:

																Totals
x	4	3	1	4	2	1	2	5	3	5	3	3	4	6	4	50
x^2	16	9	1	16	4	1	25	25	9	25	9	9	16	36	16	196

Substituting in formula [5], we obtain

$$s^2 = \frac{\Sigma x^2 - (\Sigma x)^2/n}{n-1} = \frac{196 - (50)^2/15}{14} = \frac{196 - 166.67}{14} = 2.10.$$

(c) Compute the coefficient of variation for this data.

Solution:

(c) First, we find the standard deviation of the data using formula [8a]: $s = \sqrt{s^2} = \sqrt{2.10} = 1.45$. Then, using formula [9a], we obtain the sample coefficient of variation equal to

$$(s/\bar{x})100\% = (1.45/3.33)100\% = 43.5\%.$$

5. A manufacturer of watch batteries reports the mean lifetime of their batteries is 14 months. Past experience has shown that the population variance for the lifetimes of this type of battery is 4 months. Use Chebyshev's theorem to answer the following questions:

   (a) What can be said about the fraction of batteries that will last betwen 10 and 18 months?

   Solution:

   (a) Using Chebyshev's theorem for $\bar{x} = 14$ and $\sigma = \sqrt{4} = 2$, we see that the interval 10 to 18, or (10,18), has a center at 14 with the value 10 being 2 standard deviations (4) to the left of the center and 18 being 2 standard deviations (4) to the right of the center of 14.

   Thus, the "k" in Chebyshev's theorem is 2 giving $1-(1/k)^2 = 3/4$. Therefore, we can say "at least 3/4 of the batteries will last between 10 and 18 months".

   (b) What can be said about the percentage of batteries that will last between 8 and 20 months?

   Solution:

   (b) Using the same reasoning as above, we find the value of 8 being 3 standard deviations to the left of $\bar{x}$ and 20 being 3 standard deviations to the right of $\bar{x}$. Thus, the interval (8,20) is the interval containing values within 3 σ of $\bar{x} = 14$. So, for $k = 3$, $1 - (1/k)^2 = 8/9$ or 88.9%.

   "At least 88.9% of the batteries will last between 8 and 20 months."

   (c) Develop an interval within which at least 93.75% of the lifetimes of the batteries can be expected to fall.

   Solution:

   (c) 93.75% = 15/16. Thus, $1 - (1/k)^2 = 15/16$ giving $1/k^2 = 1/16$ or $k = 4$. The required interval is 14 - 4(2) to 14 + 4(2) or 6 to 22 months.

6. Suppose we have two populations consisting of the following data:

Population 1: 16, 14, 12, 13, 15, 18, 24, 8, 10, 4
Population 2: 1, 3, 3, 5, 5, 5, 7, 7, 7

Compare the variability in these two populations by computing the coefficient of variation for each.

Solution:
From the data given above, we find:

$$\Sigma x_1 = 134 \qquad \Sigma x_1{}^2 = 2070 \qquad N_1 = 10$$
$$\Sigma x_2 = 43 \qquad \Sigma x_2{}^2 = 241 \qquad N_2 = 9.$$

Using formula [2], we calculate $\mu_1 = 134/10 = 13.40$ and $\mu_2 = 43/9 = 4.78$.

Using formula [7], we calculate

$$\sigma_1^2 = \frac{2070 - (134)^2/10}{10} = 27.44 \quad \text{giving} \quad \sigma_1 = \sqrt{27.44} = 5.24$$

$$\sigma_2^2 = \frac{241 - (43)^2/9}{9} = 3.95 \quad \text{giving} \quad \sigma_2 = \sqrt{3.95} = 1.99$$

Thus the coefficient of variation for the first population equals (5.24/13.4)100% = 39.1%, and the coefficient of variation for the second population equals (1.99/4.78)100% = 41.6%.

Note that the two populations are approximately the same size. The means are different, and it is fairly difficult to look at the data and compare the dispersions. We might be led astray by the fact that the variance of the first population is nearly seven times as large as the variance of the second population.

However, by comparing the coefficients of variation, we see that the relative variability in the two populations is fairly close.

7. Consider the following frequency distribution for a set of qualitative sample data:

Class	Frequency
0 - 2	10
3 - 5	20
6 - 8	30
9 - 11	40

Find the mean and variance of the grouped data.

Solution:

Looking at formulas [10] and [11], we see that we need the following quantities:

Class	Frequency f_i	Midpoint M_i	f_iM_i	M_i^2	$f_iM_i^2$
0 - 2	10	1	10	1	10
3 - 5	20	4	80	16	320
6 - 8	30	7	210	49	1470
9 -11	40	10	400	100	4000
Totals:	n =100		Σf_iM_i =700		$\Sigma f_iM_i^2$=5800

Tip: Notice that the last column in the above table ($f_iM_i^2$) uses only the square of the class midpoints M_i. The frequency f_i is not squared.

Then, using formula [10],

$$\bar{x} = \frac{\Sigma f_i M_i}{n} = \frac{700}{100} = 7.$$

Using formula [11], we get

$$s^2 = \frac{\Sigma f_i M_i^2 - (\Sigma f_i M_i)^2/n}{n-1} = \frac{5800 - 700^2/100}{99} = \frac{900}{99} = 9.09$$

8. A charitable organization raised funds to purchase 35 bicycles for needy children. The following table shows the distribution of times (rounded off to the nearest minute) for 35 volunteers to each assemble one of the bicycles.

Assembly Time	Frequency
30 - 39	1
40 - 49	0
50 - 59	2
60 - 69	6
70 - 79	12
80 - 89	7
90 - 99	5
100 - 109	2

Considering this a population (since all the bicycles were assembled), find the mean and variance of the frequency distribution.

Solution:

Setting up a table as in example 7, we find the following totals for the class limits M: 34.5, 44.5, 54.5, 64.5, 74.5, 84.5, 94.5, and 104.5.

Also, $N = 35$ $\quad \Sigma f_i M_i = 2697.5$ $\quad \Sigma f_i M_i^2 = 215168.75$

Substituting in formula [12], we obtain

$$\mu = \frac{\Sigma f_i M_i}{N} = \frac{2697.5}{35} = 77.07$$

To find the variance, we use formula [13].

$$\sigma^2 = \frac{\Sigma f_i M_i^2 - (\Sigma f_i M_i)^2/N}{N} = \frac{215168.75 - (2697.5)^2/35}{35} = 207.67$$

9. Twenty students in a dormitory were each asked how many plants were in their room. The answers were

1 3 0 2 1 0 4 5 0 3 2 6 2 1 0 2 3 5 4 1.

Develop a 5-number summary and associated box-and-whisker plot for these data.

Solution:

For the 5-number summary, we need these five numerical values:

(1) the lowest value in the data set - an inspection of the data shows the lowest value is 0.

(2) the first quartile (25th percentile) or lower hinge - analyzing the data in order of magnitude: 0, 0, 0, 0, 1, 1, 1, 1, 2, 2, 2, 2, 3, 3, 3, 4, 4, 5, 5, 6, we have step 2 in formula [3] giving i = 5. Thus the lower hinge is the average of the data values in positions 5 and 6. The first quartile is (1+1)/2 = 1.

(3) the median - since there are an even number of data values, the median is the average of the data values in the 10th and 11th positions. Therefore, the median equals 2.

(4) the third quartile (75th percentile) or upper hinge - step 2 in formula [3] gives i = 15, so the 75th percentile is the average of the data values in the 15th and 16th positions. The upper hinge is (3+4)/2 = 3.5.

(5) the largest value inthe data set - an inspection of the data shows the highest value is 6.

Thus, the 5-number summary of the number of plants in the dormitory rooms for the 20 people is:

0 1 2 3.5 6.

The box-and-whisker plot of this 5-number summary is constructed by placing vertical bars at the lower hinge and upper hinge and connecting them to form the "box". A vertical bar is also placed in the box at the median. Dashed lines (the "whiskers") are drawn from each hinge to the lowest and highest values in the data set. Thus, the box-and-whisker plot for the number of plants in the dormitory rooms for the 20 students is

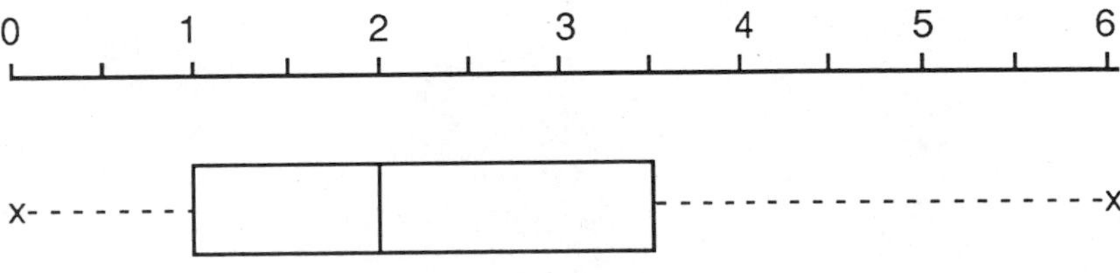

10. Professor Hardnose recorded the scores for the test he gave on the Monday following the homecoming game in the form of the following stem-and-leaf diagram:

4	1 2
5	3 4 5 6 7 7
6	0 1 4 5 6 8
7	0 3 3 6 6
8	0 2 5 7 9
9	5

Construct the box-and-whisker plot for the distribution of the test scores.

Solution:

Finding the 5-number summary by the same procedure used in example 9, we find the following:

(1) lowest value = 41
(2) lower hinge is the 7th data value = 57 since the index i = 6.25
(3) median is the 13th data value = 66
(4) upper hinge is the 19th data value = 76 since the index i = 18.75
(5) highest value = 95.

Thus, the graphical display is

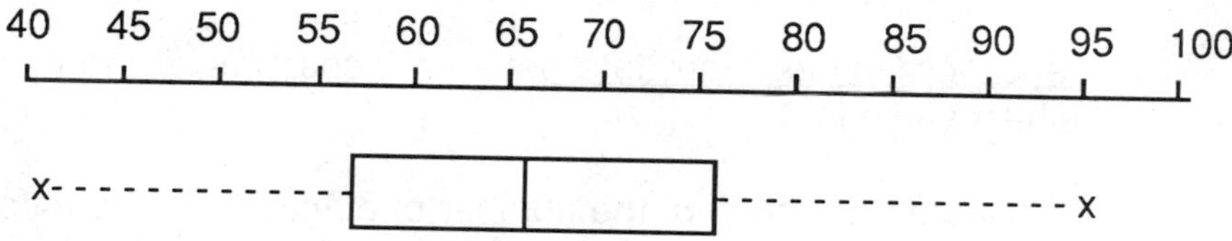

Chapter 3

HAVE I LEARNED THE MATERIAL?

Problems

1. For the set of sample data 3, 12, 15, 7, 9, 20, compute the mean, median, mode, the first quartile, and the interquartile range.

2. Molly Jones is staying with her grandchildren while their parents are away. Molly is 61 and the children's ages are 2, 2, 5, and 8.

   (a) Find the mean, median, and mode of the ages of the people in the house.

   (b) Which of the above three values is the better measure of the central location of the ages in this problem? Why?

3. The lengths of large-mouth bass (rounded to the nearest inch) caught in Lake Hartwell the first day of a three day fishing tournament are

9	20	15	16	12
11	12	14	6	18
8	17	20	11	16
23	23	14	12	20
10	18	22	15	10

(a) Find the mean length, in inches, of the fish caught that day.

(b) Find the variance of the lengths of the fish. Give units with your answer.

(c) Find the coefficient of variation. If possible, give units with your answer.

4. A frequency distribution for the data in problem 3 on the lengths of the large-mouth bass is as follows:

Length (inches)	Frequency
6 - 8	2
9 - 11	5
12 - 14	5
15 - 17	5
18 - 20	5
21 - 23	3

(a) Find the mean length using the grouped data.

(b) Compare the mean length found using the grouped data to the mean length found (in problem 3) using the ungrouped (raw) data. What is the grouping error?

(c) Using the grouped data, find the sample variance.

5. A large appliance center records, for each of 15 consecutive days, the number of new refrigerators sold. These data are 2, 4, 0, 1, 3, 5, 8, 2, 4, 6, 3, 4, 7, 3, 2.

   (a) Compute the mean, median, and mode for the number of new refrigerators sold.

   (b) Compute and interpret the 80th percentile for this data.

6. Ben's mother asked him how he did on his math test. Ben boasted "I am in the first quartile of my class" . Comment.

7. Mill Junction College has a faculty consisting of 20 teachers. Here are their ages (in years):

35	43	38	25	29
41	68	52	37	43
51	48	47	56	50
39	60	27	43	48

(a) Find the mean age of this population of teachers.

(b) What is the range of the distribution of ages?

(c) Find the standard deviation of the ages.

(d) Using Chebyshev's theorem, find an interval containing at least 8/9 of the ages.

(e) Using the original data, verify your answer to part d).

8. The ages of the teachers at Mill Junction College are summarized with the frequency distribution shown below:

Ages	Frequency
25 - 34	3
35 - 44	8
45 - 54	6
55 - 64	2
65 - 74	1

(a) Find the mean age of this population using the grouped data.

(b) Compare the mean age found above to the mean age found for the individual data values found in problem 7. Why is there a difference, and what is this difference called?

(c) Find the standard deviation of the ages using the grouped data.

9. First year sales for textbooks in marketing have had an average (mean) volume of 1200 books and a standard deviation of 500 books.

(a) What can be said about the fraction of marketing texts which have had first year sales between 450 and 1950 books?

(b) Develop an interval within which at least 75% of all first year sales of marketing texts would be expected to fall.

10. Refer to the box and whisker plot below:

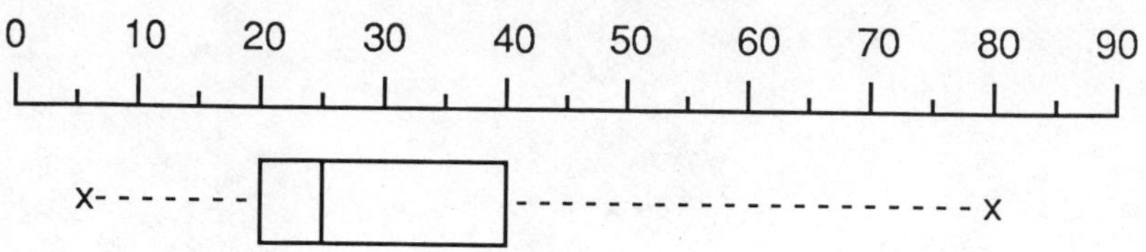

(a) What is the range of the data?

(b) What is the interquartile range of the data?

(c) What value is the upper hinge?

(d) What value is the median?

(e) What value is the mean?

(f) What values are the lowspread, midspread, and highspread?

Chapter 3

Multiple Choice Questions

1. For a set of ungrouped data, which of these three: mean, median, or mode, must be one of the data values?

   (a) mean
   (b) median
   (c) mode
   (d) none of these.

2. Which of the following statements about the median is not true?

   (a) It is more affected by extreme values than the mean.
   (b) It is the 50th percentile.
   (c) It is between the lower and upper hinges.
   (d) It is a measure of central location of a data set.

3. A sample of six compact automobiles were tested to measure miles per gallon. The results were

   38.7 35.4 32.6 42.7 40.0 36.2

   What is the median miles per gallon?

   (a) 37.60
   (b) 37.65
   (c) 37.45
   (d) none of these.

4. For the data items 8, 10, 7, 4, 3 , the 80th percentile is

   (a) 4.5
   (b) 7
   (c) 8
   (d) 9.

5. Harry remembers that his mean score on the four tests in his algebra class is 80. He has, however, lost one of the tests and does not remember the score he made on it. If the tests he has show grades of 75, 82, and 78, what is the score he made on the test he lost?

   (a) 85
   (b) 94
   (c) 79
   (d) none of these.

6. For a set of sample data items with mean of 60 and variance of 36, the coefficient of variation is

   (a) 60%
   (b) 90%
   (c) 1000%
   (d) 10%

7. For the data items 3, 4, 13, 26, 35, 4, 12, 14, 15, 33, the interquartile range is

   (a) 32
   (b) 29
   (c) 22
   (d) none of these.

8. If the variance of a set of ten data items is zero, then all the individual data items must equal to

   (a) zero
   (b) one
   (c) the range of the data set
   (d) the mean of the data set

9. The mean of the following frequency distribution, done for a set of sample data, is 10.

Classes	Frequency
5 - 9	1
10 - 14	2
15 - 19	3
20 - 24	1

   The variance of this grouped data, rounded to the nearest tenth, is

   (a) 338.7
   (b) 23.8
   (c) 20.4
   (d) none of these.

10. Which of the following numerical measures is not expressed in the same units as the original data?

    (a) standard deviation
    (b) mean
    (c) median
    (d) variance.

Chapter 3

Answers to Problems

1. mean $\bar{x}$ = 11, median = 10.5, There is no mode.
   first quartile = 7, interquartile range = 15 - 7 = 8

2. (a) mean μ = 78/5 = 15.6 , median = 5, mode = 2

   (b) The median is the better measure of the center of location since it is not affected by the extreme value 61.

3. (a) Σx = 372 giving $\bar{x}$ = 372/25 = 14.88 inches.

   (b) Σx^2 = 6088 giving s^2 = 23.03 inches squared.

   (c) The coefficient of variation is (4.80/14.88)100% = 32.25%. Because both s and $\bar{x}$ are measured in inches, the coefficient of variation is a unitless quantity.

4. (a) $\Sigma f_i M_i$ = 370 and Σf_i = n = 25 giving $\bar{x}$ = 14.8.

   (b) Using the ungrouped data, $\bar{x}$ = 14.88 while using the grouped data, $\bar{x}$ = 14.80. The grouping error is 14.88 - 14.80 = 0.08.

   (c) Also, $\Sigma f_i M_i^2$ = 5980 giving s^2 = 21.0.

5. (a) mean = 54/15 = 3.6, median = 3, and the data is multimodal with modes 2, 3, 4.

   (b) The 80th percentile is 6. The interpretation is: "At least 80% of the number of refrigerators sold per day are 6 or less and at least 20% of the number of refrigerators sold per day are 6 or more."

6. Ben could be "at" the first quartile (25th percentile), but not "in" it. Also, he shouldn't boast if his score is better than only approximately one-fourth of the scores and less than approximately three-fourths of the other student's scores.

7. (a) $\Sigma x = 880$ with $N = 20$ giving $\mu = 880/20 = 44$.

   (b) range $= 68 - 25 = 43$.

   (c) $\Sigma x^2 = 40964$ giving $\sigma^2 = 112.20$. Thus, $\sigma = 10.59$.

   (d) For $k = 3$, $1 - (1/k^2) = 8/9$. Thus, the interval containing at least 8/9 of the data values is $44 - 3(10.59)$ to $44 + 3(10.59)$ or (12.23, 75.77).

   (e) Looking at the original data, we see that all (100%) of the data values are in this interval.

8. (a) For the midpoints M_i: 29.5, 39.5, 49.5, 59.5, and 69.5, $\Sigma f_i M_i = 890$ and $\Sigma f_i = N = 20$ giving $\mu = 44.5$.

   (b) Using the ungrouped data, $\mu = 44.0$, while using the grouped data, $\mu = 44.5$. These values are different because when the grouped data is used all values in a particular class are assumed to be at the midpoint of that class. The difference is called the grouping error. The grouping error here is $44.5 - 44 = 0.05$.

   (c) $\Sigma f_i M_i^2 = 41705$ giving $\sigma^2 = 105$ and $\sigma = 10.25$.

9. (a) The fraction is at least 5/9.

   (b) 200 to 2200

10. (a) $80 - 5 = 75$

    (b) $40 - 20 = 20$

    (c) 40

    (d) 25

    (e) You cannot determine the mean without knowing all the individual data values which are not given in the box-and-whisker plot.

    (f) lowspread $= 25 - 5 = 20$; midspread $= 40 - 20 = 20$, and highspread $= 80 - 25 = 55$.

Chapter 3

Answers to Multiple Choice Questions

1. c
2. a
3. c
4. d
5. a
6. d
7. c
8. d
9. b
10. d

Chapter 4
DESCRIPTIVE STATISTICS III: DATA ANALYSIS INVOLVING MORE THAN ONE VARIABLE

WHAT AM I LEARNING?

Chapter Outline and Summary

Many statistical problems are concerned with the relation, if one exists, between two or more variables of interest. Up to this point, we have been interested in using the methods of descriptive statistics to analyze values of a single variable. In this chapter we wish to answer the following questions:

1) Are the variables being considered related?
2) If the variables are related, what is the nature of the relationship?
3) If the variables are related, can information about one be used to predict the other?

When the analysis involves two variables, we have a *bivariate* data set. When there are more than two variables involved, we have a *multivariate* data set. In this chapter, we will consider bivariate data and see how to determine the extent to which the two variables are *linearly related* (that is, where the relationship between the variables can be described as a straight line).

The statistical techniques in this chapter deal with regression and correlation analysis. The purpose of *regression analysis* is to estimate the value of one variable given knowledge of another quantitative variable. The purpose of *correlation analysis* is to measure the degree of the relationship (association) between the variables. When two variables are being used, the variable that is being predicted is called the *dependent variable.* The variable being used to predict the value of the dependent variable, that is, the variable we know the values of, is called the *independent variable.*

When the values of the two variables are plotted, the resulting graph is called a *scatter diagram.* The independent variable, usually denoted by x, is measured along the horizontal axis, and the dependent variable, denoted by y, is measured along the vertical axis. The resulting points compose the scatter diagram of the data.

A measure of the linear association between two variables is the *covariance.* The covariance tells us how the variables vary together and can be computed for sample values as well as population values. Sample covariance is denoted by s_{xy} and is an estimate of the population covariance, denoted by σ_{xy}. To interpret the sample covariance, we use the following:

a) If s_{xy} is positive, there is a positive linear association between x and y; that is, as the value of x increases, the value of y increases.
b) If s_{xy} is negative, there is a negative linear association between x and y; that is, as the value of x increases, the value of y decreases.
c) If s_{xy} equals zero, there is no linear association between x and y.

One problem with the covariance is that it depends on the unit of measurement of the variables being considered. A measure that avoids this difficulty is the *correlation coefficient* , a quantity which expresses the extent to which two variables are related. The correlation coefficient we will use is the *Pearson Product Moment correlation coefficient* (commonly referred to for sample values as the sample correlation coefficient). It is computed by dividing the sample covariance by the product of the sample standard deviation of x and the sample standard deviation of y. The symbol for the sample correlation coefficient is r , while the symbol for the population correlation coefficient is ρ. These correlation coefficients will always range between -1 and 1. To interpret the sample correlation coefficient, we use the following:

a) If $r = 1$, there is a perfect positive linear association between x and y with all the data points falling on a straight line with positive slope.
b) If $r > 0$, there is a positive linear association between x and y that gets stronger as r gets closer to 1.
c) If $r = 0$, there is no <u>linear</u> relationship between between x and y.
d) If $r < 0$, there is a negative linear association between x and y that gets stronger as r gets closer to -1.
e) If $r = -1$, there is a perfect negative linear association between x and y with all the data points falling on a straight line with negative slope.

A graphical summary of scatter diagrams as related to covariance and correlation coefficients is given at the end of this section.

When interpreting the correlation coefficients, a word of warning is necessary. When values of r close to zero are found, it it tempting to conclude that there is little or no relationship between the variables under consideration. However, you must remember that the Pearson Product Moment correlation coefficient measures only the linear relationship between the values. Even if $r = 0$, there could still be a relationship, possibly strong, between the variables, but it would be nonlinear. Also, even if two variables show a high correlation (whether positive or negative) , this does not imply a cause-and -effect relationship between them. These methods measure the strength of a relationship - they do not prove that such a relationship exists.

A second objective in analyzing bivariate data is to use information about one variable to predict another through a linear equation relating the two variables. In regression analysis, we fit a straight line to the data of a scatter diagram. The *estimated regression line,* or the line which "best fits" the data, is the line obtained through the *least squares method.* This method provides formulas for calculating the y-intercept of the line, denoted by b_0, and the slope of the line, denoted by b_1. The equation of the estimated regression line is $\hat{y} = b_0 + b_1 x$. This estimated regression line is determined from the sample points, and it should not be used to predict values of the dependent variable outside the range of the data. Chapter 16 of the text goes into greater detail of the issues in regression analysis.

A descriptive procedure that is effective with two or more qualitative variables is *crosstabulation* in a contingency table. A *contingency table* is a two-dimensional table in which data is classified on two scales. The boxes, or cells, in the contingency table consist of the frequencies or relative frequencies of the data. Row and column totals are given, but these are not counted in giving the size of the contingency table. Contingency tables are given for qualitative variables. Quantitative data can also be analyzed using crosstabulation procedures by considering a frequency distribution for the quantitative variable(s).

Interpretation of Sample Covariance and Correlation:

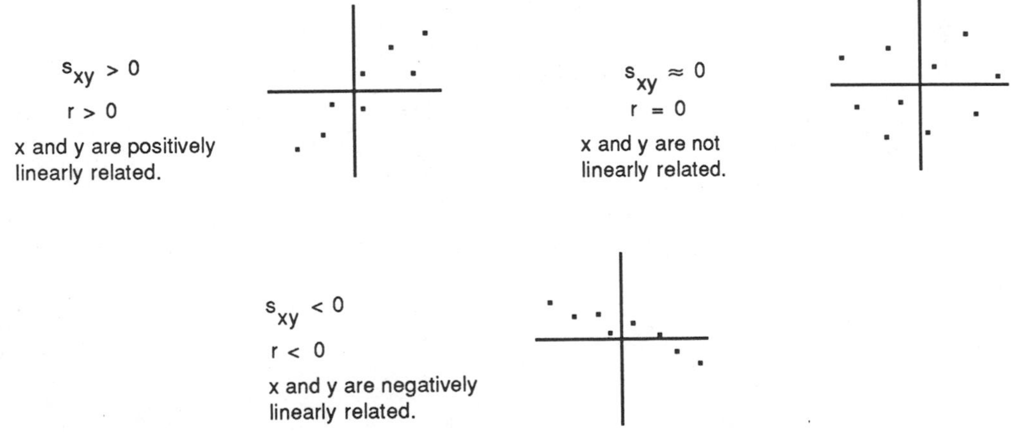

WHICH FORMULA SHOULD I USE?

Formulas

When:

computing the sample covariance s_{xy} for a set of n data points (x,y) where the mean of the x values is $\bar{x}$ and the mean of the y values is $\bar{y}$,

Use:

$$s_{xy} = \frac{\sum (x - \bar{x})(y - \bar{y})}{n - 1} \qquad [1]$$

When:

computing the population covariance σ_{xy} for a set of N data points (x,y) where the mean of the population of x values is μ_x and the mean of the population of y values is μ_y,

Use:

$$\sigma_{xy} = \frac{\sum (x - \mu_x)(y - \mu_y)}{N} \qquad [2]$$

When:

<u>defining</u> the Pearson Product Moment Correlation Coefficient for sample data where s_{xy} is the sample covariance obtained in formula [1], s_x is the sample standard deviation of x and s_y is the sample standard deviation of y,

Use:

$$r = \frac{s_{xy}}{s_x s_y} \qquad [3]$$

When:

computing the Pearson Product Moment Correlation Coefficient (sample correlation coefficient) for a set of n data points (x,y),

Use:

$$r = \frac{\Sigma xy - (\Sigma x \Sigma y)/n}{\sqrt{\Sigma x^2 - (\Sigma x)^2/n}\ \sqrt{\Sigma y^2 - (\Sigma y)^2/n}} \qquad [4]$$

When:

defining the Pearson Product Moment Correlation Coefficient for population data where σ_{xy} is the population covariance obtained in formula [2], σ_x is the population standard deviation for x and σ_y is the population standard deviation for y,

Use:

$$\rho = \frac{\sigma_{xy}}{\sigma_x \sigma_y} \qquad [5]$$

When:

calculating the least squares values for the slope b_1 and the y-intercept b_0 of the estimated regression line for a set of sample data points (x,y) where $\bar{x}$ is the mean of the x values and $\bar{y}$ is the mean of the y values,

Use:

$$b_1 = \frac{\Sigma xy - (\Sigma x \Sigma y)/n}{\Sigma x^2 - (\Sigma x)^2/n} \qquad [6]$$

$$b_0 = \bar{y} - b_1\bar{x} \qquad [7]$$

When:

calculating the estimated regression with y-intercept b_0 and slope b_1,

Use:

$$\hat{y} = b_0 + b_1 x \qquad [8]$$

HERE'S HOW IT'S DONE!

Examples

1. A plant manager wishes to study the relationship between the time required for an employee to complete a certain task and the noise level at the work station. His data on a group of 5 employees is:

Noise Level	0	0.5	2	2.5	3
Time required to complete task	2	1	3	4	5

(a) Which variable would more logically be the independent variable?

Solution:

(a) If the plant manager is interested in predicting the time required for an employee to complete the task, the noise level would be the independent variable. If the noise is coming from machinery, for instance, it would not be feasible to try to predict this variable.

(b) Develop a scatter diagram for these data with the independent variable on the horizontal axis.

Solution: (b)

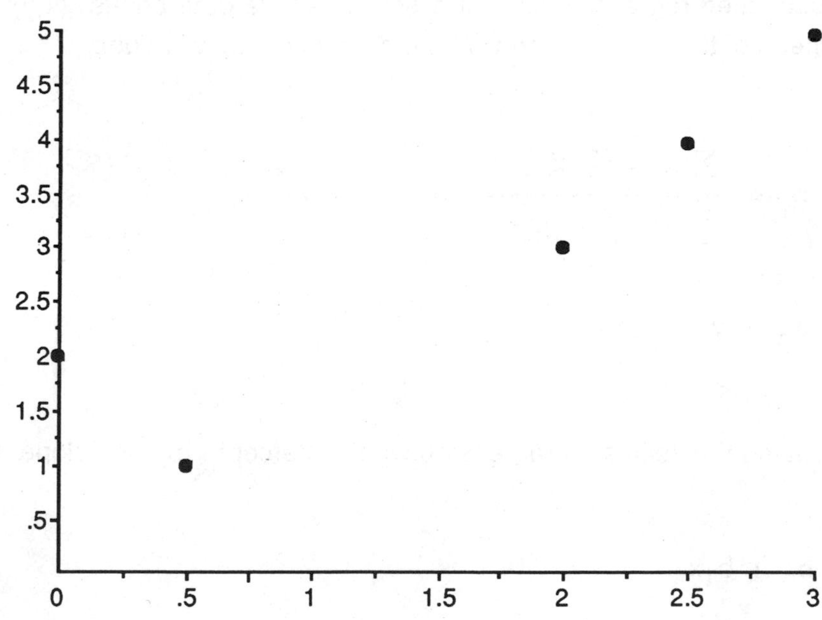

(c) Does there appear to be any relationship between the noise level and the time required to complete the task? Explain.

Solution:

(c) The scatter diagram seems to indicate that there is an increasing linear relationship between x and y. That is, in general, it appears that as the noise level increases, the time required to complete the job also increases. Visually, this increase seems to be in the form of (approximately) a straight line.

(d) Compute and interpret the sample covariance for these data.

Solution:

(d) To compute the sample covariance s_{xy} using formula [1], we first need to compute $\bar{x}$ and $\bar{y}$ using the formula for the mean of a sample from Chapter 3. Thus, $\bar{x} = \Sigma x/n = 8/5 = 1.6$ and $\bar{y} = \Sigma y/n = 15/5 = 3$.

We also need the following quantities:

	x	y	$(x - \bar{x})$	$(y - \bar{y})$	$(x - \bar{x})(y - \bar{y})$
	0	2	-1.6	-1	1.6
	0.5	1	-1.1	-2	2.2
	2	3	0.4	0	0
	2.5	4	0.9	1	0.9
	3	5	1.4	2	2.8
Totals:	8	15	0	0	7.5

Substituting in formula [1], we have

$$s_{xy} = \frac{\Sigma (x - \bar{x})(y - \bar{y})}{n - 1} = \frac{7.5}{4} = 1.875 .$$

The interpretation of the correlation coefficient is: "Since s_{xy} is positive, there seems to be a positive linear association between x and y; that is, as the noise level (x) increases, the time required to complete the task (y) increases."

2. Find and interpret the sample correlation coefficient for the data in Example 1.

<u>Solution</u>:

To compute the sample correlation coefficient, r, either formula [3] or formula [4] could be used. The computation with a calculator is easier using formula [4] (even though it doesn't appear that way when you look at the formula!)

Formula [4] requires the following:

	x	y	xy	x^2	y^2
	0	2	0	0	4
	0.5	1	0.5	0.25	1
	2	3	6	4	9
	2.5	4	10	6.25	16
	3	5	15	9	25
Totals:	8	15	31.5	19.5	55

Substituting in formula [4], we have

$$r = \frac{\Sigma xy - (\Sigma x \Sigma y)/n}{\sqrt{\Sigma x^2 - (\Sigma x)^2/n}\ \sqrt{\Sigma y^2 - (\Sigma y)^2/n}} = \frac{31.5 - (8)(15)/5}{\sqrt{19.5 - \frac{64}{5}}\ \sqrt{55 - \frac{225}{5}}}$$

$$r = \frac{31.5 - 24}{\sqrt{19.5 - 12.8}\ \sqrt{55 - 45}} = \frac{7.5}{(2.5884)(3.1623)} = .916 .$$

<u>Tip</u>: As a rough check, recall that $-1 \leq r \leq 1$.

Recall that a value of 0 for r indicates that there is no linear relationship between x and y and a value of 1 for r means that there is a perfect positive linear association between x and y.

Thus, this value of r = .916 indicates that "there is a very strong positive linear association between x and y. As the noise level (x) increases, the time required to complete the task also increases, and this increase follows the model of a straight line."

<u>Note</u>: Compare this interpretation of r to the interpretation of the covariance in Exercise 1.

3. (a) For the data in Exercise 1, develop the estimated regression line that relates noise level to the time required to complete the task.

Solution:

(a) In the calculation of b_0 and b_1, the following quantities, calculated in Exercise 2, are needed: $\Sigma x = 8$, $\Sigma y = 15$, $\Sigma xy = 31.5$, $\Sigma x^2 = 19.5$, and $n = 5$.

Then, substituting in formulas [6] and [7], we have:

$$b_1 = \frac{\Sigma xy - (\Sigma x \Sigma y)/n}{\Sigma x^2 - (\Sigma x)^2/n} = \frac{31.5 - (8)(15)/5}{19.5 - 64/5} = \frac{31.5 - 24}{19.5 - 12.8} = 1.1194$$

$$b_0 = \bar{y} - b_1\bar{x} = 3 - (1.1194)(1.6) = 3 - 1.7910 = 1.209.$$

Substituting in formula [8], we obtain the equation of the estimated regression line as

$$\hat{y} = 1.21 + 1.12x.$$

Tip: As a check on your calculations of b_0 and b_1, recall that the regression line must pass through the point whose coordinates are $(\bar{x},\bar{y})$.

Here, $(\bar{x},\bar{y}) = (1.6,3)$ and 3 must equal $1.21 + 1.12(1.6) = 3.002$. (ok)

Note: The slight difference in the above is due to round-off error. Even though we kept the recommended number of decimal places (4) in intermediate calculations, the final values were rounded.

(b) Use the line developed in a) of this problem to estimate the time required to complete the task for a person subjected to a noise level of 1.

Solution:

(b) Substituting in the estimated regression line $\hat{y} = 1.21 + 1.12x$, we have

$\hat{y} = 1.21 + 1.12(1) = 2.33$. Thus, we predict a time of 2.33 minutes for a person to complete the task when the noise level is 1.

(c) Plot this estimated regression line on the scatter diagram you obtained in Exercise 1a). (Does the line visually appear correct?)

Solution:

(c) Using any two points on the line, we connect them to draw the line.

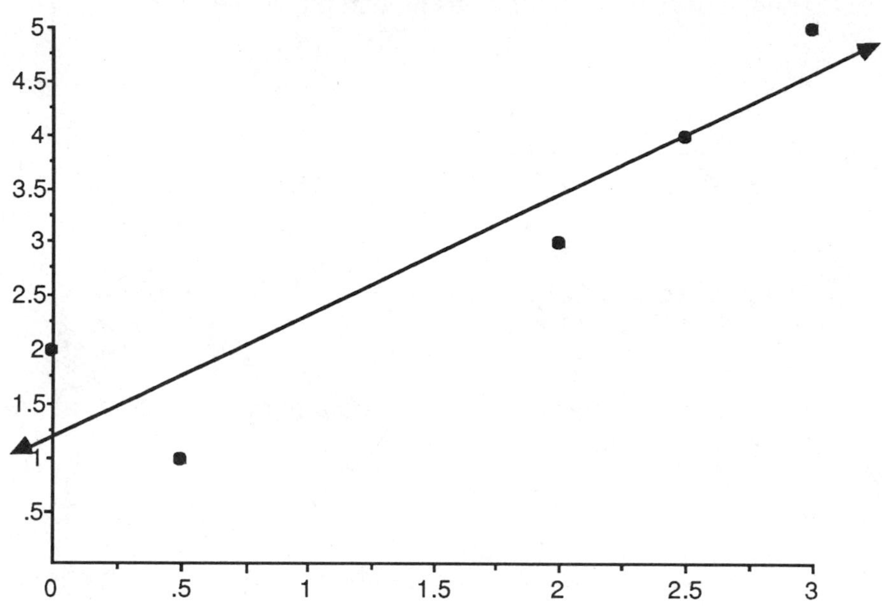

Visually, the line seems appropriate.

4. For the sample data points

x	0	2	4	6	8	10
y	9	7	3	1	-2	-3

,

(a) Develop a scatter diagram with x on the horizontal axis. What does the scatter diagram indicate about the relationship between the two variables?

Solution:

(a) The scatter diagram is obtained by plotting the above data points. The scatter diagram suggests that the relationship between the two variables is linear. (It also looks like we should expect y to decrease as x increases.)

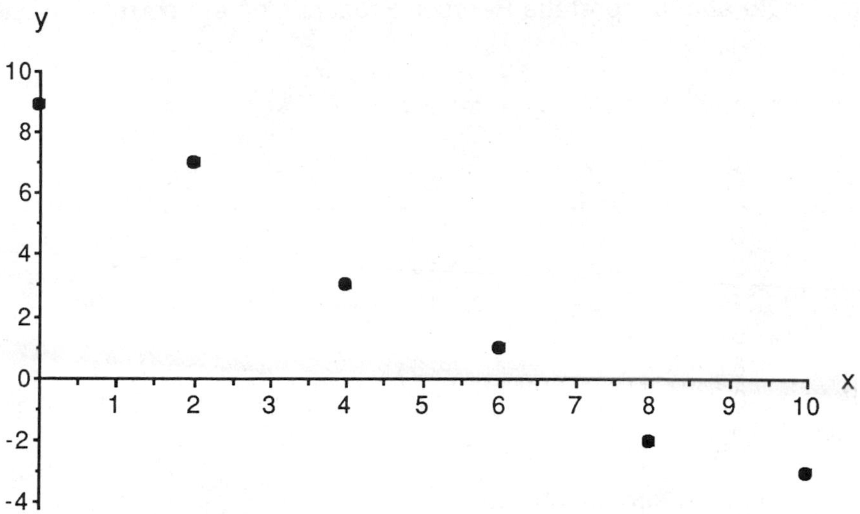

(b) Compute and interpret the sample covariance for these data.

Solution:

(b) To compute the sample covariance s_{xy} using formula [1], we first need to compute $\bar{x}$ and $\bar{y}$: $\bar{x} = \Sigma x/n = 30/6 = 5$ and $\bar{y} = \Sigma y/n = 15/6 = 2.5$.

We also need the following quantities:

	x	y	$(x - \bar{x})$	$(y - \bar{y})$	$(x - \bar{x})(y - \bar{y})$
	0	9	-5	6.5	-32.5
	2	7	-3	4.5	-13.5
	4	3	-1	0.5	-0.5
	6	1	1	-1.5	-1.5
	8	-2	3	-4.5	-13.5
	10	-3	5	-5.5	-27.5
Totals:	30	15	0	0	-89.0

Substituting in formula [1], we have

$$s_{xy} = \frac{\Sigma (x - \bar{x})(y - \bar{y})}{n - 1} = \frac{-89}{5} = -17.8 .$$

The negative value of s_{xy} is indicative of a negative linear association between x and y (as we expected from the scatter diagram). Remember that the value obtained for the covariance depends on the unit of measurement of the variable. This might explain the large negative value.

(c) Compute and interpret the Pearson Product Moment correlation coefficient.

<u>Solution</u>:

(c) Formula [4] requires the following:

	x	y	xy	x^2	y^2
	0	9	0	0	81
	2	7	14	4	49
	4	3	12	16	9
	6	1	6	36	1
	8	-2	-16	64	4
	10	-3	-30	100	9
Totals:	30	15	-14	220	153

Substituting in formula [4], we have

$$r = \frac{\Sigma xy - (\Sigma x \Sigma y)/n}{\sqrt{\Sigma x^2 - (\Sigma x)^2/n}\sqrt{\Sigma y^2 - (\Sigma y)^2/n}} = \frac{-14 - (30)(15)/6}{\sqrt{220 - \frac{900}{6}}\sqrt{153 - \frac{225}{6}}}$$

$$r = \frac{-89}{\sqrt{220\text{-}150}\sqrt{153\text{-}37.5}} = \frac{-89}{(8.3666)(10.7471)} = \frac{-89}{89.9167} = -.99 .$$

(d) Develop the estimated regression line that relates x to y.

<u>Solution</u>:

(d) In the calculation of b_o and b_1, the following quantities, calculated in c), are needed: $\Sigma x = 30$, $\Sigma y = 15$, $\Sigma xy = -14$, $\Sigma x^2 = 220$, and $n = 6$.

Then, substituting in formulas [6] and [7], we have:

$$b_1 = \frac{\Sigma xy - (\Sigma x \Sigma y)/n}{\Sigma x^2 - (\Sigma x)^2/n} = \frac{-14 - (30)(15)/6}{220 - 900/6} = \frac{-14 - 75}{220 - 150} = -1.2714$$

$$b_0 = \bar{y} - b_1\bar{x} = 2.5 - (-1.2714)(5) = -8.8570.$$

Substituting in formula [8], we obtain the equation of the estimated regression line as $\hat{y} = 8.86 - 1.27x$.

(e) Does it appear that you could use this line to predict the value of y at x = 5? If your answer is "yes", give the prediction.

Solution:

(e) Yes, the scatter diagram, s_{xy}, and r indicate that there is a negative linear association between x and y. (In fact, the value of r = -0.99 is extremely close to -1, the perfect negative linear association.) Substituting in the equation of the estimated regression line, we have $\hat{y}$ = 8.86 -1.27(5) = 2.51.

(f) Draw the estimated regression line obtained in part d) on the scatter diagram obtained in part a):

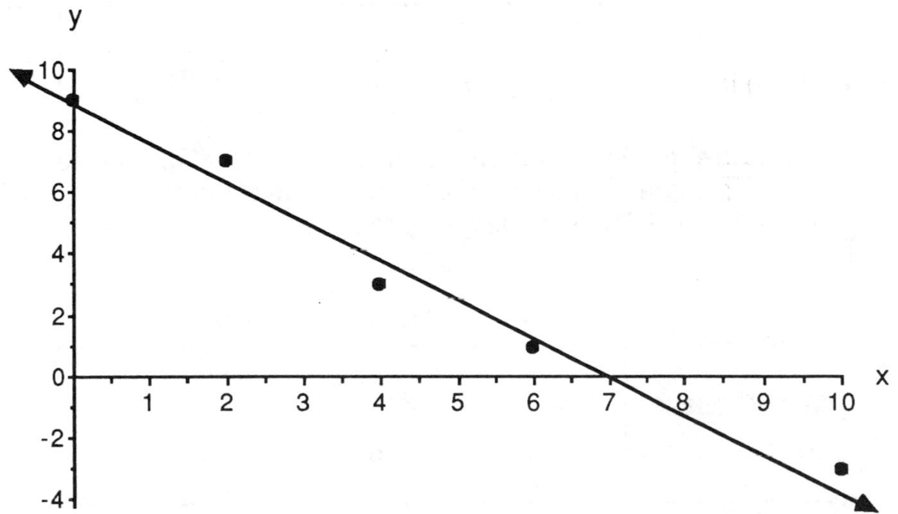

5. An optician wishes to determine if there is a relationship between certain occupations and wearing glasses. It is found that, among 336 lawyers, 182 wear glasses and 154 do not. 215 of 351 doctors wear glasses while 136 do not. Among 313 teachers, 203 wear glasses and 110 do not.

(a) Summarize this data by developing a contingency table.

Solution:

(a) The contingency table contains 6 cells to list the possible combinations of occupation and wearing or not wearing of glasses. A row is added at the bottom of the table and a column is added on the right of the table for the totals. The data (here the number of people in each category) is then entered into the table and the totals are computed.

Tip: The sum for the row totals must equal the sum for the column totals.

	OCCUPATION			
	Lawyer	Doctor	Teacher	Total
Wear Glasses	182	215	203	598
Do Not Wear Glasses	154	136	110	402
Total	336	351	313	1000

Next, the percentages of each cell relative to the total number of observations are calculated and entered into the table for easy reference. The final result is the contingency table:

	OCCUPATION			
	Lawyer	Doctor	Teacher	Total
Wear Glasses	182 (18.2)	215 (21.5)	203 (20.3)	598 (59.8)
Do Not Wear Glasses	154 (15.4)	136 (13.6)	110 (11.0)	402 (40.2)
Total	336 (33.6)	351 (35.1)	313 (31.3)	1000 (100.0)

(b) What preliminary conclusions can be drawn from a careful inspection of this table?

Solution:

(b) We see that a higher percentage (almost 2-1) of teachers and doctors wear glasses than do not. The percentage of lawyers who wear glasses is not much more than the percentage of lawyers who do not wear glasses.

HAVE I LEARNED THE MATERIAL?

Problems

1. (a) Complete the following table:

x	y	xy	x^2	y^2
1	1			
2	1			
3	2			
4	2			
5	4			

(b) Find the following:

n Σx Σy Σxy Σx^2 Σy^2 $(\Sigma x)^2$

$(\Sigma y)^2$ $\Sigma xy - (\Sigma x \, \Sigma y)/n$ $\sqrt{\Sigma x^2 - (\Sigma x)^2/n}$

$\sqrt{\Sigma y^2 - (\Sigma y)^2/n}$ r .

2. Twenty people are surveyed and asked whether or not they have a (at least one) pet. They were also asked if they were a parent or not. The results were:

Person	Have Pet?	Parent?	Person	Have Pet?	Parent?
1	Yes	Yes	11	No	No
2	No	Yes	12	Yes	Yes
3	Yes	No	13	No	No
4	No	No	14	No	Yes
5	No	Yes	15	Yes	Yes
6	No	No	16	No	No
7	Yes	Yes	17	No	No
8	No	Yes	18	No	No
9	Yes	Yes	19	No	No
10	Yes	No	20	Yes	Yes

(a) Develop a contingency table for these data.

(b) What preliminary conclusions can be drawn from a careful inspection of this table?

3. Six children of various ages are involved in an experiment. The number of mistakes made by each child while performing the required task is recorded.

Child	Age	Number of mistakes
Mary	1	6
Bill	2	3
Sue	4	2
Lee	8	1

(a) Plot these points on a scatter diagram with age on the horizontal axis.

(b) What, if anything, does this scatter diagram indicate about the relationship between the two variables?

(c) Compute and interpret the sample covariance for these data.

(d) Compute and interpret the sample correlation coefficient for these data.

4. (a) Using the data on ages and number of mistakes from problem 3, develop the estimated regression line that relates age to number of mistakes.

(b) Plot the estimated regression line on the scatter diagram drawn in problem 3a).

(c) Use the estimated regression line to predict the number of mistakes that Jared, who is 6 years old, would make while performing the task.

(d) Should you use the estimated regression line to predict the number of mistakes that Darian, who is 14 years old, would make while performing the task? Why or why not?

5. The following observations were made for two variables:

x	y
1	1
2	3
3	4
4	4
5	2

(a) Comment on the relationship between these two variables.

Chapter 4

Multiple Choice Questions

1. In a contingency table, the number of rows and columns

   (a) must always be equal
   (b) cannot be more than two each
   (c) can never be found for quantitative data
   (d) none of the above.

2. If the sample correlation coefficient r equals 1, then

   (a) there is a perfect negative linear association between x and y
   (b) the y-intercept of the estimated regression line must equal zero
   (c) there is a perfect positive linear association between x and y
   (d) the slope of the estimated regression line must equal one.

3. The sample correlation coefficient r for an independent variable x and a dependent variable y equals $^{-}0.8$. This implies that, for the data in the sample, as x increases

   (a) y increases
   (b) y decreases
   (c) y remains the same
   (d) y first increases, then decreases.

4. What information about the variables is given by the correlation coefficient?

   (a) strength of relationship only
   (b) strength and direction of the relationship
   (c) direction of relationship only
   (d) none of the above.

5. The estimated regression line for a particular set of data is found to have a slope of 3 and a y-intercept of −1. When the independent variable $x = 5$, what is the estimated value of y?

   (a) 14
   (b) −2
   (c) 8
   (d) none of these.

6. Which of the following statements are true?

   (a) The higher the absolute value of the correlation coefficient, the stronger the linear association between the variables they are measuring.
   (b) Covariance depends on the units of the variable being measured.
   (c) The sample correlation coefficient will always be between -1 and 1.
   (d) All of the above are true.

7. A set of 7 data points yielded the following information:

   $\Sigma x = 35$ $\quad \Sigma y = 28$ $\quad \Sigma xy = 103$

   $\Sigma x^2 = 209$ $\quad \Sigma y^2 = 166$

   The sample correlation coefficient is computed to be

   (a) $-.8635$
   (b) $.8739$
   (c) $-.8739$
   (d) none of these.

8. For the data in problem 7, the estimated least squares regression line is computed to be

   (a) $\hat{y} = 1.09 - 9.45x$
   (b) $\hat{y} = 9.45 + 1.09x$
   (c) $\hat{y} = 9.45 - 1.09x$
   (d) $\hat{y} = 1.09 + 9.45x$.

9. The number of cells in a contingency table with 3 rows and 6 columns is

   (a) 9
   (b) 6
   (c) 18
   (d) 20.

10. Using the criterion of least squares, which of the lines, $y = 1 + .9x$ or $y = x$, "best fits" set of data points $\{(1,2), (2,3), (3,3), (4,5)\}$?

   (a) $y = 1 + .9x$
   (b) $y = x$
   (c) neither of these lines - the best fit is obtained by using $\bar{y} = 3.25$
   (d) none of these - the fit is not linear.

Chapter 4

Answers to Problems

1. (a)

x	y	xy	x^2	y^2
1	1	1	1	1
2	1	4	1	2
3	2	9	4	6
4	2	16	4	8
5	4	25	16	20

(b)

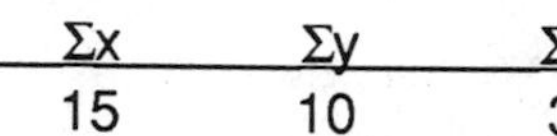

n	Σx	Σy	Σxy	Σx^2	Σy^2	$(\Sigma x)^2$	$(\Sigma y)^2$
5	15	10	37	55	26	225	100

$\Sigma xy - (\Sigma x\, \Sigma y)/n$	$\sqrt{\Sigma x^2 - (\Sigma x)^2/n}$	$\sqrt{\Sigma y^2 - (\Sigma y)^2/n}$	r
7	3.1623	2.4495	0.904

2. (a)

	Have Pet	No Pet	Total
Parent	6 (30)	4 (20)	10 (50)
Non Parent	2 (10)	8 (40)	10 (50)
Total	8 (40)	12 (60)	20 (100)

(b) Pertaining to this sample data, we see that a higher percentage of people with children have pets (3 times as many) and that people who are not parents prefer not having a pet by a 2-to-1 ratio.

3. (a)

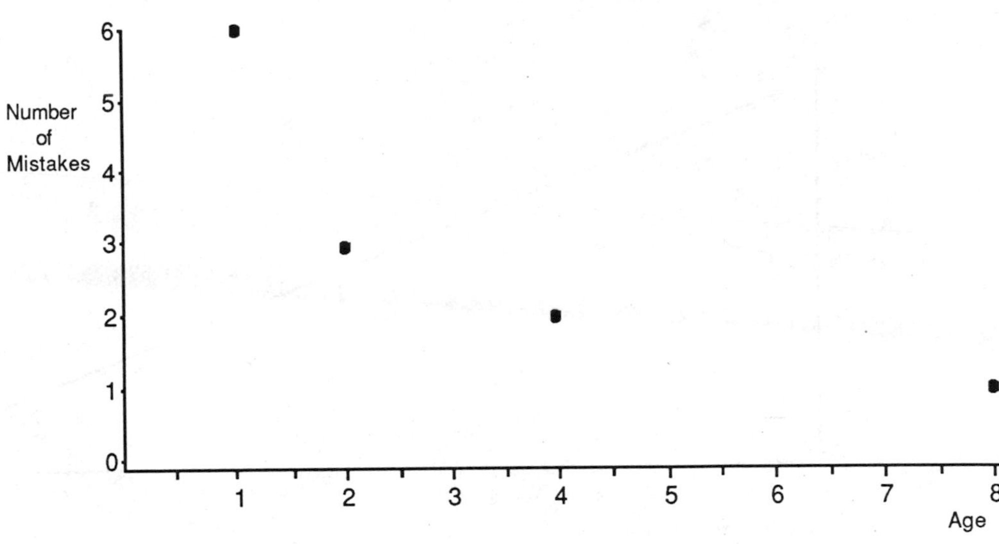

(b) There appears to be a negative association between age (x) and number of mistakes (y), and it may be linear.

(c) $\bar{x} = 3.75$, $\bar{y} = 3$, $n = 4$ giving $s_{xy} = -5.667$.

This negative value of sxy is indicative of a negative linear association between x and y; that is, as x increases, the value of y decreases.

(d) $\Sigma x = 15$, $\Sigma x^2 = 85$, $\Sigma y = 12$, $\Sigma y^2 = 50$ $\Sigma xy = 28$ giving $r = -0.847$.

There appears to be a negative linear association between x and y; that is, as the child's age increases, the number of mistakes made in performing the task decreases.

4. (a) $\hat{y} = 5.22 - .59x$

(b)

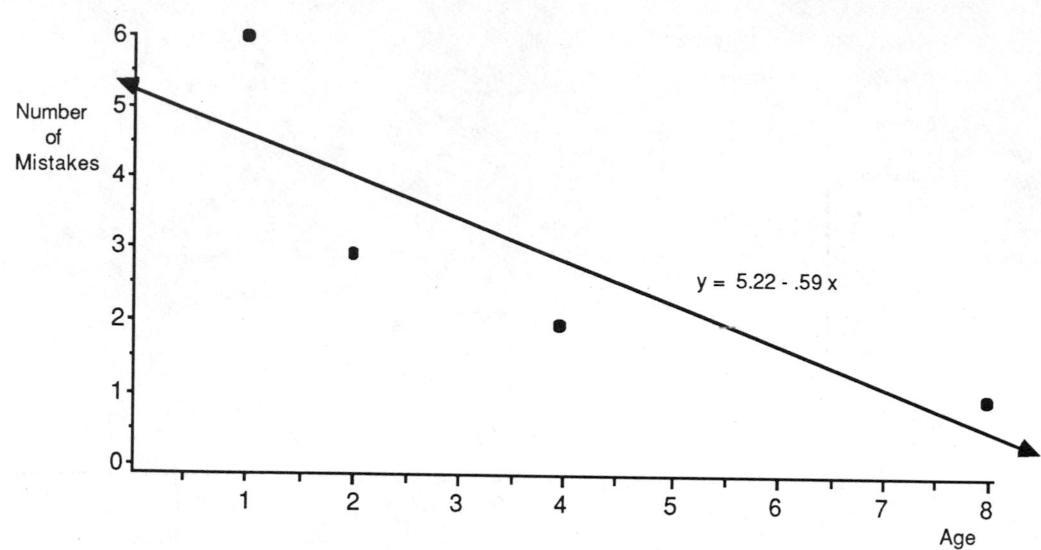

(c) Using the estimated regression line $\hat{y}$ = 5.22 - .59x, we predict Jared (x=6) will make 1.68 mistakes.

(d) X = 14 is outside of the range of data that the sample in this problem covers. No, we should not use this line to predict y at a value of x = 14. (Note that at x = 14 the value of y is negative. A negative number of mistakes doesn't even make sense for the problem.)

5. Analyzing the data, we find:

$\bar{x} = 3$, $\bar{y} = 2.8$, $n = 5$ giving $s_{xy} = 0.75$. Looking at this value of s_{xy}, we may be tempted to say there is a positive linear association between x and y.

$\Sigma x = 15$, $\Sigma x^2 = 55$, $\Sigma y = 14$, $\Sigma y^2 = 46$, $\Sigma xy = 45$ giving $r = 0.36$.

Remembering that a value of r = 1 indicates a perfect positive linear association between x and y and a value of r = 0 indicates no linear association between x and y, we may be tempted to say there is a "weak" linear association between x and y.
To make a decision on the type of association between x and y, if any, we should look at the scatter diagram of the data. It shows that a relationship other than a straight line is probably the one that should be used. Chapter 16 will further explore how to tell conclusively if the relationship is linear or not.

Scatter diagram for Problem 5:

(A curve that appears to fit the data is drawn for purposes of illustration.)

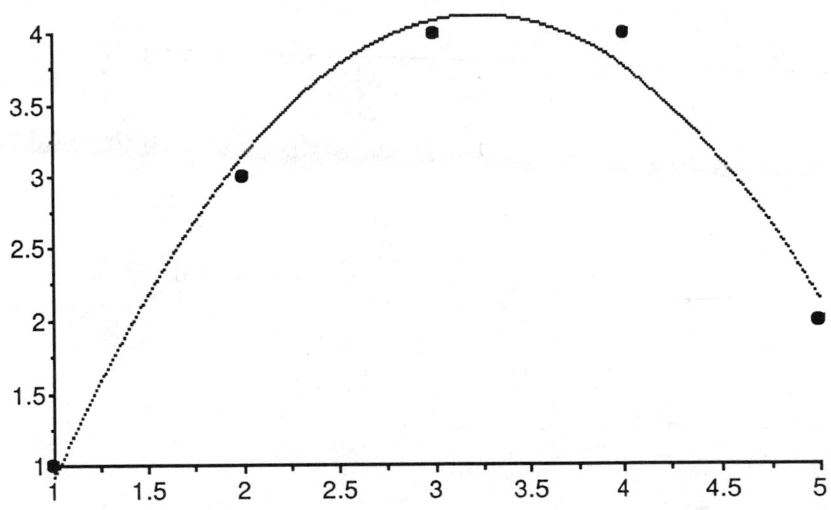

Chapter 4

Answers to Multiple Choice Questions

1. d
2. c
3. b
4. b
5. a
6. d
7. a
8. c
9. c
10. a

Chapter 5
INTRODUCTION TO PROBABILITY

WHAT AM I LEARNING?

Chapter Outline and Summary

One of the main reasons for studying statistics and the closely related field of probability is to aid us in making decisions and/or predictions about experiments whose individual outcomes cannot be determined with certainty. An understanding of basic probability theory will help us to give an estimate of the reliability of our statistical conclusions.

Probability may be regarded as a numerical measure of the chance that a certain event will happen. These events that are assigned probabilities are the outcomes of what are called experiments. In probability theory, an *experiment* is any process that generates outcomes that are well-defined. On any single repetition of the experiment, one and only one of the outcomes will occur. The *sample space* for an experiment is the set of all possible outcomes, and each outcome in a sample space is called a *sample point.* In defining a sample space for an experiment, be sure that it is not possible for any of the sample points to overlap (that is, occur simultaneously) and that all possible sample points are included.

In probability theory, an *event* is a collection of sample points. The probability of any event is a number between 0 and 1. If an event has a probability of 0, then this event is called the impossible event and it will never occur. If an event has a probability of 1, it is called the certain or sure event and will occur with absolute certainty. Events with probabilities between 0 and .5 are more likely to not happen than happen, and events with probabilities between .5 and 1 are more likely to occur than not.

Many probability experiments involve two or more steps, each of which can result in any number of different outcomes. There are several ways we can determine the total number of sample points for such experiments. One such way is the *Counting Rule for Multiple-Step Experiments* (given in formula [5] of this Guide). Another method to determine the sample points is a graphical aid called a *tree diagram.* The various paths of the tree give the distinct sample points for the experiment. A path is made up of its component branches obtained from the various stages (called nodes on the diagram) of the experiment.

Reading the notation P(A) as "the probability of event A", the *two basic requirements of probability* that must be satisfied for any approach that is taken to assign probabilities to experimental outcomes are:

1. The probability values assigned to each experimental outcome (sample point) must be between 0 and 1, inclusive. That is, $0 \le P(E_i) \le 1$ for all i.
2. The sum of the probabilities for all the experimental outcomes must equal 1. That is, if a sample space S has k sample points, we must have
$$P(E_1) + P(E_2) + \cdots + P(E_k) = P(S) = 1.$$

The concept of probability can be approached from three different viewpoints. The *classical* definition looks at probabilities as identified for sample points prior to the availability of specific sample data related to the event. It is based on the assumption that all outcomes are equally likely. When each of the n sample points is just as likely to occur as any other one, the probability of each sample point is assigned a value of 1/n.

The second approach to probability is based on actual experimentation. This *relative frequency* method defines probability as the proportion of time (relative frequency) the outcome occurs when the experiment is identically repeated a large number of times.

The third approach assigns a probability to an experimental outcome based on the decision maker's degree of confidence in the likelihood of the occurrence of that outcome. Because this definition of probability assigns values that are the result of individual judgments based on the person's prior knowledge and experience, it is called the *subjective* method. Probabilities assigned to the same outcome by the subjective approach will vary from individual to individual. Take care to remember that regardless of the approach, the two basic requirements of probability must still be satisfied.

In any particular experiment all events under consideration will be within a specific sample space. The relationship between the events and their corresponding sample space can be illustrated graphically using a *Venn diagram.* In a Venn diagram a rectangle is normally used to represent the sample space and events are shown as circles inside the rectangle.

One event associated with any particular event, say A, is its complement. The *complement* of event A is denoted by $\bar{A}$ and is the event consisting of all sample points in the sample space that are not in A. Note that $P(A) + P(\bar{A}) = 1$.

There are certain operations with events that will result in the formation of new events. Also, it is often easier to determine the probability of an event by first finding the probability of other events. The *union* of two events A and B, written $A \cup B$, is the event containing all sample points belonging to either A or B or both A and B. The associated probability statement can be written P(A or B) as well as $P(A \cup B)$. When determining

$P(A \cup B)$, we may use the *Addition Rule*. (See formula [6] in this Guide.)

Another way of combining events is referred to as the intersection of the events. The *intersection* of two events A and B, written $A \cap B$, is the event containing the sample points in both (common to) A and B. The associated probability statement can be written P(A and B) as well as $P(A \cap B)$. Statements used to represent the probability that two events will both occur are referred to as *joint probability* statements. When summarized in table form, these probabilities of intersection give a *joint probability table.* In this table, the entries in the margins (that is, in the "total" row and column) are referred to as *marginal probabilities.*

One of the types of relationship that can exist between events is that they have no sample points in common. Such events are called *mutually exclusive*. For mutually exclusive events A and B, $P(A \cap B) = 0$.

We may be interested in determining the probability of some event, say A, knowing that another related event, say B, has already happened. This is called the *conditional probability* of the event and is denoted by $P(A|B)$.

Events may be related in such a way that the occurrence or nonoccurrence of one event has an influence on the probability of another event occurring. When the probability of an event, say A, is affected by the occurrence of another event, B, events A and B are called *dependent* (that is, $P(A|B) \neq P(A)$). However, if the occurrence of an event, say R, has not changed the probability of event A, then A and R are called *independent* events (that is, $P(A|R) = P(A)$).

It is often true that conditional probabilities are known. In this case it is possible to calculate the probability of the intersection of certain events using the *Multiplication Rule* (formulas [11] and [12] in this Guide). When it is known that the two events are independent, the Multiplication Rule gives formula [13] of this Guide. (This formula may also be used to see whether or not the two events are independent.)

One of the applications of the concepts of probability theory involves estimating unknown probabilities determined before *(prior)* sample information is taken into account and then revising or updating these probabilities when given new information. The updated, or revised, probabilities are called *posterior* probabilities. *Bayes' Theorem* (formulas [14] and [15] of this Guide) provide a means for computing these (conditional) posterior probabilities. In using Bayes' Theorem, we wish to determine the probability of some event given that another event will be observed. To conduct the calculations involved in using Bayes' Theorem, a tabular approach is helpful.

Chapter 5

WHICH FORMULA SHOULD I USE?

Formulas

When:

determining the number of sample points for an experiment consisting of a sequence of k multiple steps in which there are n_1 possible outcomes on the first step, n_2 possible outcomes on the second step, . . . , n_k possible outcomes on the last step

Use:

total number of sample points $= (n_1)(n_2)\cdots(n_k)$ [1]

When:

assigning probabilities to k sample points for experimental outcomes E_i

Use:

the two basic requirements that must always be true for any probability values

$0 \leq P(E_i) \leq 1 \quad \text{for all} \quad 1 \leq i \leq k$ [2]

$P(E_1) + P(E_2) + \cdots + P(E_k) = 1$ [3]

When:

assigning probabilities to n sample points where all sample points are equally likely (classical method)

Use:

$P(E_i) = 1/n$ [4]

When:

determining the probability of an event A using the complement of the event

Use:

$P(A) = 1 - P(\bar{A})$ [5]

When:
determining the probability that at least one of two events occurs

Use:
Addition Rule: $P(A \text{ or } B) = P(A \cup B) = P(A) + P(B) - P(A \cap B)$ [6]

When:
determining the probability that at least one of two mutually exclusive events will occur

Use:
Addition Rule for Mutually Exclusive Events

$$P(A \text{ or } B) = P(A \cup B) = P(A) + P(B) \qquad [7]$$

When:
determining the conditional probability $P(A|B)$ (that is, the probability of event A knowing that event B has happened)

Use:

$$P(A|B) = P(A \cap B)/P(B) \qquad [8]$$

When:
determining the conditional probability $P(B|A)$ (that is, the probability of event B knowing that event A has occurred)

Use:

$$P(B|A) = P(A \cap B)/P(A) \qquad [9]$$

When:
determining whether or not two events A and B are independent or if you know that two events A and B are independent

Use:

$$P(A|B) = P(A) \qquad [10a]$$

or

$$P(B|A) = P(B) \qquad [10b]$$

When:

determining the probability of the intersection of two events (joint probability) when conditional probabilities are known

Use:

Multiplication Rule: $P(A \cap B) = P(B)\,P(A|B)$ [11]

or

$P(A \cap B) = P(A)\,P(B|A)$ [12]

When:

determining the probability of the intersection of two events (joint probability) when it is known that the two events are independent or to determine if the two events are independent

Use:

Multiplication Rule for Independent Events: $P(A \cap B) = P(A)P(B)$ [13]

When:

determining the posterior probability $P(A_i|B)$, $i = 1,2$, for two mutually exclusive outcomes A_1 and A_2 that represent the only possible outcomes in a situation

Use:

Bayes' Theorem:

$$P(A_1|B) = \frac{P(B|A_1)\,P(A_1)}{P(B|A_1)\,P(A_1) + P(B|A_2)\,P(A_2)} \qquad [14]$$

and

$$P(A_2|B) = \frac{P(B|A_2)\,P(A_2)}{P(B|A_1)\,P(A_1) + P(B|A_2)\,P(A_2)} \qquad [15]$$

When:

determining the posterior probability $P(A_i|B)$, $i = 1,2,\cdots,n$, for n mutually exclusive outcomes $A_1, A_2, \ldots, A_n$ that represent the only possible outcomes in a situation

Use:

Bayes' Theorem (general case):

$$P(A_i|B) = \frac{P(B|A_i)\,P(A_i)}{P(B|A_1)\,P(A_1) + P(B|A_2)\,P(A_2) + \cdots + P(B|A_n)\,P(A_n)} \qquad [16]$$

Chapter 5

HERE'S HOW IT'S DONE!

Examples

1. Consider the following experiments, and answer the related questions:

Experiment 1: In the "bargain basket" at the local supermarket are 5 unlabeled cans. You are told that three of the cans contain peas and 2 of the cans contain corn, but you do not know which vegetable is in which can. You are to choose 1 can out of the group of 5 cans.

(a) What is the sample space for this experiment?

Solution:

(a) Since we may choose any one of the 5 cans, the sample space must consist of 5 sample points. Labeling the cans with subscripts and referring to the cans by the contents, we have the sample space, written in set form, as $S = \{P_1, P_2, P_3, C_1, C_2\}$.

Note: The order in which the sample points are written does not matter.

(b) If all the cans are of the same size and shape, what is the probability that you will choose a can of corn?

Solution:

(b) The fact that the cans are unlabeled and of the same size and shape tells us that we are just as likely to choose any one can as any other can (that is, the cans are equally likely to be chosen). Thus, using formula [4] with n = 5, we have the probability of each can being chosen equal to 1/5. Then, using formula [3], we have

$$P(\text{Corn}) = P(C_1) + P(C_2) = 1/5 + 1/5 = 2/5 \quad \text{or} \quad .40.$$

(c) What event corresponds to the statement: "A can of peas is chosen" ?

Solution:

(c) The event that corresponds to this statement is the collection of sample points in the sample space corresponding to "peas" : $E = \{P_1, P_2, P_3\}$.

Experiment 2: There are 3 people in a room, Micki, Jack, and Otis, and 3 chairs in the room. One person is to sit in any one of the chairs, then the second person sits in one of the remaining chairs, and then the last person is seated.

(a) How many sample points are there for this experiment?

Solution:

(a) Because this is a multiple-step experiment, we use the Counting Rule, formula [1], to determine the number of possibilities (sample points). There are any of three chairs in which the first person can be seated. There are only two remaining chairs in which the second person can sit, and finally, just one chair left for the third person. Thus, by formula [1], we have

the number of sample points = (3)(2)(1) = 6.

(b) Develop a tree diagram for this experiment.

Solution:

(b) Letting each node represent the seating of a different person, we have

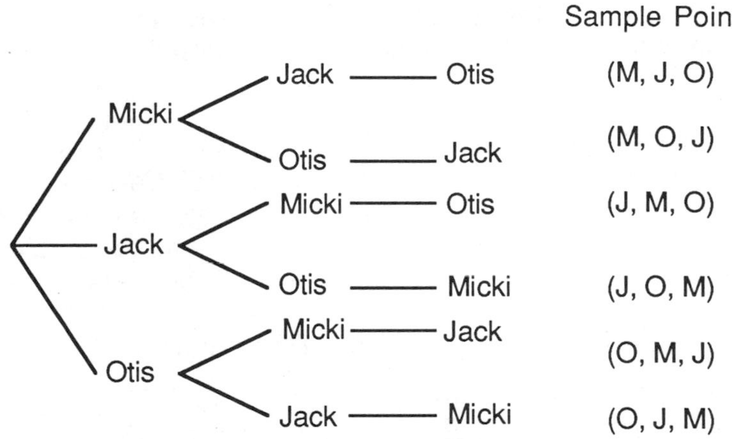

Experiment 3: A coin is thrown. If a head turns up, a die is rolled. If a tail is on the upturned face of the coin, the coin is thrown again. Draw a tree diagram to find the sample space for this experiment.

Solution:

Letting the first branches in the tree represent outcomes of the first part of the experiment, tossing the coin, and letting the second branches represent the results of the second stage of the experiment, we have

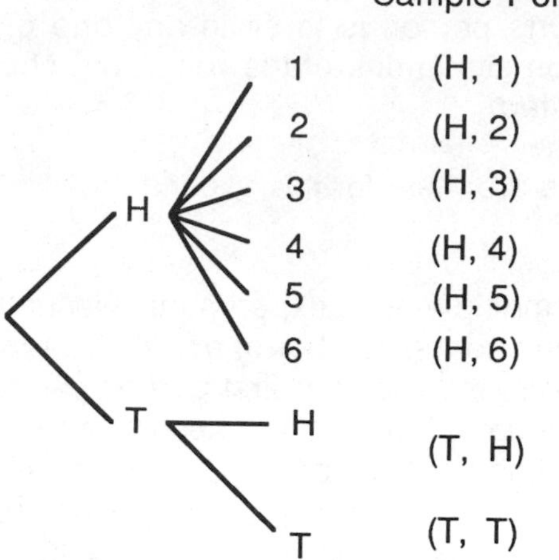

2. Sam is taking a true-false test consisting of 3 questions. Unfortunately, Sam has not attended class or studied the material. Thus, Sam simply guesses at the answer to each of the 3 questions.

   (a) How many experimental outcomes are possible? Interpret what is meant by "experimental outcome" in the context of this problem.

   Solution:

   Since this experiment consists of multiple-stages (that is, answering the 3 questions), and there are two choices of answers at each stage (true or false), the Counting Rule (formula [1]) gives the number of sample points as (2)(2)(2). Here, an experimental outcome would be a choice of answers to the 3 questions on the test. Thus, there are 8 possible answers for the test itself.

   (b) Give the sample space for this experiment in set form:

   Solution:

   (b) Because the order in which the answers appear is important in this problem (that is, a test answer of TTF is not the same as an answer of FTT since different questions are being assigned different answers), t o get the 8 sample points, we must consider all arrangements of the possible answers to each question. Thus, the sample space is

$$S = \{TTT, TTF, TFT, FTT, TFF, FTF, FFT, FFF\}.$$

   Note: The answers could have also been listed with the notation using parentheses. For example, write TFT as (T, F, T), etc.

(c) What is the probability Sam gets lucky and gets all the answers correct?

Solution:

(c) Since Sam is only guessing at the answer to each question, each of the 8 sample points for this experiment is just as likely to occur as any of the others. Thus, using formula [4], we assign each one of the test answers the probability of 1/n = 1/8. Now, there is only one of the sample points that represent the correct answers to the 3 questions on the test. Thus, the probability that Sam chooses that set of correct answers is 1/8 = .125.

3. There are 4 different routes between positions A and B and 3 distinct routes between positions B and C.

(a) In how many different ways it is possible to go from A to C by way of B?

Solution:

(a) Since this is a multiple-step experiment with two stages (going from A to B and then going from B to C), we use the Counting Rule, formula [1], to determine the total number of experimental outcomes as (4)(3) = 12.

(b) In how many different ways is it possible to make a roundtrip from A to C by way of B if one cannot use the same route more than once?

Solution:

(b) Again using the Counting Rule, we have the stages: go from A to B by any of 4 routes, go from B to C by any of 3 routes, go back from C to B by any of 2 routes, and go back from B to A by any of 3 routes. Thus, the total number of different ways (experimental outcomes) is (4)(3)(3)(2) = 72.

4. For each of the following experiments,
   (a) How many sample points are possible?
   (b) Which method (classical, relative frequency, or subjective) would you recommend for assigning probabilities to the sample points?
   (c) Show that your probability assignments satisfy the two basic requirements for assigning probabilities.

Experiment 1: One ball is drawn out of a bag containing 2 white, 3 red, and 4 blue balls. All balls are identical except for color.

Solution:

(a) Since we may choose any of the 9 balls, there are 9 sample points.

(b) Due to the fact that all balls are identical for color, we have the situation where any one ball is just as likely to be chosen as any other. Thus, the classical approach is recommended.

(c) Using formula [4], each of the sample points (that is, each of the individual balls) is assigned a probability of 1/9. If we are considering what color ball is chosen from the bag, we have

P(W) = 2/9, P(R) = 3/9 and P(B) = 4/9.

The two basic requirements of probability are given in formulas [2] and [3]:

$0 \leq P(W) = 2/9 \leq 1$, $0 \leq P(R) = 3/9 \leq 1$, and $0 \leq P(B) = 4/9 \leq 1$

Also, P(W) + P(R) + P(B) = 2/9 + 3/9 + 4/9 = 9/9 = 1.

Note: Instead of considering colors, we could have considered the individual balls and seen that the two basic requirements are still satisfied.

Experiment 2: During the month of December, 50 cars were inspected at a local service station. Of these, 5 had faulty brakes, 2 had broken headlights, and 6 had tail lights that were not working properly. The rest of the cars passed the inspection satisfactorily.

Solution:

(a) There are 4 experimental outcomes here: faulty breaks, broken headlights, tail lights not working properly, and passed satisfactorily.

(b) Because we are working with data from an experiment that is repeated a large number of times (all cars need to be inspected), the relative frequency approach is recommended. (Note that the four sample points above are not equally likely.)

(c) Assigning probabilities as the proportion of the time the experimental outcome occurs, we have

P(faulty breaks) = 5/50 = .10, P(broken headlights) = 2/50 = .04, P(tail lights not working properly) = 6/50 = .12, and P(passed satisfactorily) = 37/50 = .74.

The two basic requirements of probability are given in formulas [2] and [3]:

$0 \leq$ P(faulty breaks) = .10 ≤ 1, $0 \leq$ P(broken headlights) = .04 ≤ 1,
$0 \leq$ P(tail lights not working properly) = .12 $\leq$, and
$0 \leq$ P(passed satisfactorily) = .74 ≤ 1.

Also, .10 + .04 + .12 + .74 = 1.

Experiment 3: What is the probability that you will pass the next test in the statistics course you are taking?

Solution:

(a) There are two possible outcomes (pass or fail), so the number of sample points is 2.

(b) To assign probabilities to these sample points, we hope that the two outcomes are not equally likely! Also, you have not taken many tests like the next test in your course, so there are no relative frequency data available. Thus, you must assign a probability for passing the test based on your individual judgment, including such factors as how much you have studied, how well you have listened in class, etc. Therefore, you are using the subjective method.

(c) Suppose you decide that the probability you will pass the test is .90. Then, using formula [5], you determine the probability of not passing, that is, failing, is 1 - .90 = .10.

The two basic requirements of probability are given in formulas [2] and [3]:

$0 \leq P(\text{passing}) = .90 \leq 1$, and $0 \leq P(\text{not passing}) = .10 \leq 1$

Also, $P(\text{passing}) + P(\text{not passing}) = .9 + .1 = 1$.

5. Out of 200 students surveyed, 150 are taking mathematics (M), 105 are taking English (E), and 75 are taking both mathematics and English. What is the probability that one of these students will be taking either mathematics or English?

Solution:

By the relative frequency approach, we have $P(M) = 150/200 = .750$, $P(E) = 105/200 = .525$ and $P(M \cap E) = 75/200 = .375$. We wish to obtain $P(M \cup E)$. Using formula [6], the Addition Rule, we have:

$$P(M \cup E) = P(M) + P(E) - P(M \cap E) = .750 + .525 - .375 = 1.275 - .375 = \underline{.90}.$$

Tip: The key words in the problem that let you identify what you are given and what you desire to find are the words "both" (meaning $\cup$) and "or" (meaning $\cap$).

6. A survey of 200 college students was conducted by a manufacturer of athletic equipment. The results of the study showing the type of sporting activity regularly engaged in by these students is summarized in the following table. (If a student participated regularly in more than one activity, he/she was asked to give the one with which the most time was spent.)

Sex	In which type of sporting activity do you regularly participate? Jogging	Tennis	Aerobics	Golf	None	Total
Male	50	10	5	20	15	100
Female	35	20	40	0	5	100
Total	85	30	45	20	20	200

(a) Show the joint probability table for the given data.

Solution:

(a) Summarizing the information available in the table, we have the following probability values: (for convenience in notation, refer to each category by the first letter of the word)

$P(M \cap J) = 50/200 = .25$ = probability that the person is a male and a jogger

$P(F \cap T) = 20/200 = .10$ = probability that the person is a female who plays tennis,

and so forth.

Since each of these is the probability of an intersection of two events, they are called joint probabilities and appear in the body of the table.

Now, $P(M) = 100/200 = .50$ = probability that the person selected is a man
$P(J) = 85/200 = .425$ = probability that the person selected jogs regularly
$P(A) = 45/200 = .225$ = probability that the person selected participates in aerobic exercise regularly, and so forth. These values in the margins provide the probability of each event separately and are called the marginal probabilities.

Filling these values in the table, we have the joint probability table

	Jogging	Tennis	Aerobics	Golf	None	Total
Male	.25	.05	.025	.10	.075	.50
Female	.175	.10	.20	0	.025	.50
Total	.425	.15	.225	.10	.10	1.00

(b) Use the marginal probabilities to comment on the athletic activities of the group.

Solution:

(b) It appears that jogging is the most popular activity for the group with a probability of .425. Next is aerobics, for the probability that a person selected from this group will have aerobic exercise as the preferred activity is .225. Golf and no preferred athletic activity are the least likely to find.

(c) What is the probability of finding a person who prefers aerobics and is a male?

Solution:

(c) Here we are asked for the joint probability $P(A \cap M) = P(M \cap A) = \underline{.025}$.

(d) If you know that the person chosen is a female, what is the probability that she chooses tennis as her preferred athletic activity?

Solution:

(d) The phrase "if you know" tells us that this is a problem involving conditional probability. Thus, we are asked to find P(person prefers tennis|person is a female) = P(T|F). Using formula [8], we have

$$P(T|F) = P(T \cap F) / P(F) = .10/.50 = \underline{.20}.$$

7. A fair die is rolled once. Answer the following questions.

   (a) Which of the following pairs of events, if any, are mutually exclusive?

   (b) Find the probability, in each case, of at least one of the two events happening.

Case 1: Event A: a 3 is on the upturned face; Event B: an odd number is on the upturned face.

Solution:

(a) For the experiment, S = {1, 2, 3, 4, 5, 6}. For events A and B to be mutually exclusive, they cannot have any sample points in common. Here we see that $A \cap B = \{3\}$ which is not empty. So, we conclude that A and B are not mutually exclusive.

(b) We are asked for the probability of at least one of the two events happening. For two events, "at least one" means one or the other or both. Thus, we need to find $P(A \cup B)$. Since the die is fair, each side has an equally likely chance of turning up. Thus, the probability of each of these 6 sample points is 1/6. Therefore, P(A) = P(3) = 1/6. Using this classical approach to probability, to find the probability of event B, we sum the probabilities of the sample points in B. Thus, P(B) = P(1, 3, 5) = 3/6 = 1/2. Also, $P(A \cap B)$ = P(3) = 1/6. Using the Addition Rule, formula [6], we have

$$P(A \cup B) = P(A) + P(B) - P(A \cap B) = 1/6 + 1/2 - 1/6 = \underline{1/2}.$$

Case 2: Event A: a 3 is on the upturned face; Event B: an even number turns up.

Solution:

(a) A = {3} while B = {2, 4, 6}. We see that events A and B have no sample points in common. Therefore, we conclude that A and B are mutually exclusive.

(b) Using the same reasoning as in the first case, P(A) = P(3) = 1/6 while P(B) = P(2, 4, 6) = 3/6 = 1/2. However, since the events are mutually exclusive, we go to formula [7], the Addition Rule for Mutually Exclusive Events, to find

$$P(A \cup B) = P(A) + P(B) = 1/6 + 1/2 = 4/6 = \underline{2/3}.$$

8. An experiment consists of tossing a fair coin twice. Let A be the event that the same side turns up on both flips, B be the event that at least one head turns up in the two flips, and C be the event that a head occurs on the first of the two flips.

   (a) You flip the coin twice (without looking at the results) and someone tells you that at least one head has turned up in the two flips. Find the probability that a head occurred on the first of your two flips.

<u>Solution</u>:

(a) The sample space for this experiment is S = {HH, HT, TH, TT}. If the coin is fair, each sample point is equally likely, so the probability of each of the 4 sample points is 1/4. Since you know that at least one head has turned up in the two flips, you are being asked to find the conditional probability P(C|B). Event B = {HH, HT, TH}, event C = {HH, HT}, and event $B \cap C$ = {HH, HT}. Using formula [9], you have

$$P(C|B) = P(B \cap C) / P(B) = 2/4 \div 3/4 = \underline{2/3}.$$

(b) Are events A and C independent? Why or why not?

<u>Solution</u>:

(b) A = {HH, TT} and C = {HH, HT} with P(A) = 1/2 and P(C) = 1/2. Using the definition of independence, formula [10a] (or [10b] which is the same except for the letters), we must see if P(A|C) = P(A).

$$P(A|C) = P(A \cap C) / P(C) \text{ (by formula [9])} = 1/4 \div 2/4 = 1/2.$$

Thus, since P(A|C) = P(A), <u>events A and C are independent</u>.

Note that another way to check for independence is given by formula [13]. We could have just as well answered the question using this formula:

$$P(A \cap C) = 1/4 = P(A)\,P(C) = (1/2)(1/2).$$

<u>Tip</u>: Do not confuse "mutually exclusive" with "independent". Notice that in this problem, A and C are independent events, but because they have a sample point in common, they are not mutually exclusive.

9. If R, S, and T are events in a sample space such that $P(R) = .3$, $P(T) = .5$, $P(S) = .1$, and $P(S|T) = .6$, find

(a) $P(S \cap T)$.

Solution:

(a) Using formula [11], we find $P(S \cap T) = P(T)P(S|T) = (.5)(.6) = \underline{.3}$.

(b) $P(R \cup S)$ if it is known that R and S are independent events.

Solution:

(b) Since R and S are independent events, formula [13] gives $P(R \cap S) = (.3)(.1) = .03$. We are asked to find $P(R \cup S)$. Using formula [6], we have:

$$P(R \cup S) = .3 + .1 - .03 = \underline{.37}.$$

10. A camera shop buys film from three different sources. Company X supplies 40% of the film, Company Y supplies 25% of their film, and Company Z supplies 35% of the film. Suppose it is known that 5% of the film supplied by Company X is defective, 2% of the film supplied by Company Y is defective, and 3% of Company Z's film is defective. A customer returns a roll of defective film and the camera shop is unable to identify the company from which it came. What is the probability it came from Company Y?

Solution:

Since we are asked for a posterior (after) probability knowing prior (before) probabilities, we will use Bayes' theorem. A tabular approach is helpful in organizing and conducting the calculations for Bayes's theorem. We need these 4 columns:

Column 1: The list of all mutually exclusive events that can occur in the problem. These are the events that the film came from one of the three companies which will be denoted by X, Y, and Z.

Column 2: The prior probabilities for the events. These are the probabilities that the film comes from one of the three companies - P(X) , P(Y), and P(Z). Note that since the companies in column 1 are all the events that can occur and are mutually exclusive, the sum of these probabilities in column 2 must be 1.

Column 3: The conditional probabilities of the new information (the event that the film is defective, denoted by D) given each of the mutually exclusive events (the companies) in column 1; that is, the probabilities $P(D|X)$, $P(D|Y)$, and $P(D|Z)$.

Column 4: The joint probabilities for each mutually exclusive event and the new information, event D. These joint probabilities are found from formula [12] - that is, $P(X \cap D) = P(X)P(D|X)$, $P(Y \cap D) = P(Y)P(D|Y)$, and $P(Z \cap D) = P(Z)P(D|Z)$. Next add these values in column 4 to obtain the probability that the film is defective - that is, $P(D)$.

Column 5: The posterior probabilities for the problem. These are found by using the definition of conditional probability (formula [8]) to obtain $P(X|D)$, $P(Y|D)$, and $P(Z|D)$ using the value of $P(D)$ found in column 4.

Filling in the table, we have

	Column 1	Column 2	Column 3	Column 4	Column 5
	X	.40	.05	(.4)(.05) = .02	.02/.0355 = .563
	Y	.25	.02	(.25)(.02) = .005	.005/.0355 = .141
	Z	.35	.03	(.35)(.03) = .0105	.0105/.0355 = .296
Totals		1.00		P(D) = .0355	1.000

Note: The sum of the values in column 5 must be 1 since they represent all the posterior probabilities for the experiment consisting of the mutually exclusive events in column 1. If you have rounded any of the values used in the calculation in column 5, round-off error will show up here.

Recall that we were asked to find $P(D|Y)$. This is the posterior probability found in column 5 for Company Y. Thus, the answer to the problem is .141.

Chapter 5

HAVE I LEARNED THE MATERIAL?

Problems

1. A box contains 3 coins - a penny, a nickel, and a dime. The penny and the dime are fair, but the nickel is two-headed. One coin is chosen from the box and tossed one time.

   (a) Develop a tree diagram for this experiment.

   (b) How many experimental outcomes are possible?

   (c) To which event in the sample space is the following statement referring? "The result of the toss is a head."

2. Suppose that A and B are two events in a sample space S. If P(A) = .4, P(B) = .5, and P(A and B) = .25,

   (a) Find P(A or B).

   (b) Are A and B independent or dependent events? Why?

   (c) Are A and B mutually exclusive events? Why or why not?

3. For each of the following experiments,
   (a) How many sample points are possible?
   (b) Which method (classical, relative frequency, or subjective) would you recommend for assigning probabilities to the sample points?
   (c) Show that your probability assignments satisfy the two basic requirements for assigning probabilities.

Experiment 1: A book store is trying to determine which types of books to stock for the next season. They have the following data which is based on the last five years' sales.

Type of book	Cookbook	Mystery	Science Fiction	Romantic Novel
Number sold	270	630	390	1710

(a) Number of sample points?

(b) Which method?

(c) Two basic requirements of probability:

Experiment 2: One letter is chosen from the letters in the word PURSE.

(a) Number of sample points?

(b) Which method?

(c) Two basic requirements of probability:

4. Mrs. Johnson is trying to decide whether or not to invest in Ransom Corporation stock. She feels that the probability the stock will go up is .45, the probability it will go down is .35, and the probability it will remain the same price is .25. Comment.

5. A four-digit numeral is to be formed by choosing four different numbers from the set {0,1,2,3,4,5,6,7,8,9}. How many such numerals are possible?

6. One day is selected from the days of the week in such a fashion that any day is an equally probable choice. Assuming the probability of rain on any day is .10 and that the choice of the day and the weather are independent of one another, find

   (a) the probability that a rainy Wednesday will be selected.

   (b) the probability that a dry Saturday will be chosen.

7. A survey of 200 people (with jobs outside the home) was taken in Atlanta, Georgia. The results will be used in a study of the city's public transportation system and are

	How do you get to work?		
Distance from work ?	Private Car	Public Transportation	Total
less than 10 miles	80	65	145
10 miles or more	25	30	55
Total	105	95	200

(a) Develop a joint probability table for the given data.

(b) Use the marginal probabilities to compare private and public transportation usage.

(c) What is the probability that a person uses public transportation to get to work?

(d) If a person lives 10 miles or more from work, what is the probability that he/she uses public transportation?

8. Joe buys only brown socks and black socks. Unfortunately, they are all mixed up in his dresser drawer. Joe gets up early one morning and doesn't want to put on the light and wake Mary. How many socks does he have to choose from his dresser drawer to be sure that he has a matching pair? (Hint: Develop a tree diagram.)

9. A traveler must go by taxicab from his hotel to the airport during the rush hour. There are 4 different routes, and the probabilities of completing the trip within an hour on the four routes are .45, .3, .1, and .05, respectively. Since he is not familiar with the city, the traveler enters a taxicab, tells the driver to take any of the four routes he desires, and arrives at the airport within an hour. What is the probability that the taxicab driver chose the second route?

10. Mrs. Pritch will buy a coat today with probability .6. The probability that she will not buy a pair of gloves today is .8. What is the probability that she will buy either a coat or a pair of gloves today if the probability that she buys a pair of gloves, having already bought a coat, is .1 ?

Chapter 5

Multiple Choice Questions

1. The I. C. U. Detective Agency assigns the following subjective probabilities:
   P(solving case A in less than one week) = .2
   P(solving case B in less than one week) = .1.
   What probability should be assessed that both cases will be solved in less than one week if the cases are solved independently of one another?

   (a) .30
   (b) .072
   (c) .02
   (d) none of these.

2. If one person is chosen from the group of people described below, what is the probability of that person being a female with blonde hair?

	Brown Hair	Blonde Hair	Red Hair
Male	10	15	22
Female	5	18	30

   (a) .33
   (b) .18
   (c) .53
   (d) .15.

3. If A and B are mutually exclusive events with P(A) = 0.3 and P(B) = 0.45, then the probability that either A or B occurs is

   (a) .135
   (b) .750
   (c) 0
   (d) none of these.

4. If Jane has a choice of 3 appetizers, 2 main courses, 4 desserts, and 3 drinks, how many different choices does she have for a complete dinner?

   (a) 12
   (b) 36
   (c) 64
   (d) 72.

5. 80% of all freshmen at Big City University take mathematics. 60% of all freshmen take both mathematics and English. The probability that a freshman who is taking math will also be taking English is

   (a) .75
   (b) .25
   (c) .33
   (d) .20.

6. Subjective probabilities are assigned to events A and B. These two events comprise the sample space for the experiment. Which of the following assignments of probabilities is not valid?

   (a) $P(A) = .3$, $P(B) = .7$
   (b) $P(A) = .7$, $P(B) = .5$, $P(A \cap B) = .4$
   (c) $P(A) = .2$, $P(B) = .9$, $P(A \cap B) = .1$
   (d) $P(A) = .5$, $P(B) = .5$, $P(A \cap B) = 0$.

7. If two events cannot occur simultaneously, they are called

   (a) equally likely events
   (b) independent events
   (c) conditional events
   (d) mutually exclusive events.

8. An experiment consists of rolling a die once and then flipping a coin twice in succession. How many sample points are there for this experiment?

   (a) 36
   (b) 10
   (c) 24
   (d) 3.

9. If A and B are events such that $P(A \cup B) = .65$, $P(A) = .5$, and $P(B) = .25$, then A and B are

(a) mutually exclusive events
(b) independent events
(c) dependent events
(d) sample points.

10. Which of the following statements is not true?

(a) Events that are mutually exclusive must be dependent.
(b) Dependent events need not be mutually exclusive.
(c) Independent events cannot be mutually exclusive.
(d) Events that are not mutually exclusive must be independent.

Chapter 5

Answers to Problems

1. (a)

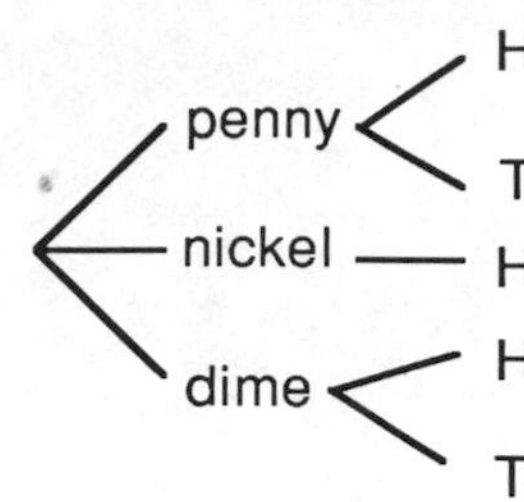

   (b) 5

   (c) {(penny, H), (nickel, H), (dime, H)}

2. (a) $P(A \cup B) = .4 + .5 - .25 = \underline{.65}$

   (b) A and B are <u>dependent</u> events. They are not independent since $.25 \neq (.4)(.5)$.

   (c) <u>No</u>, since $P(A \cap B) = .25$, A and B must have sample points in common.

3. Experiment 1: (a) 4

   (b) relative frequency method

   (c) Assigning the following probabilities for the books being sold: P(cookbook) = .09, P(mystery) = .21, P(science fiction) = .13, and P(romantic novel) = .57, we see that
   (1) each of the probabilities is between 0 and 1, and
   (2) .09 + .21 + .13 + .57 = 1.

   Experiment 2: (a) 5

   (b) classical method (assuming an equally likely choice of letters)

   (c) Assigning the probability of 1/5 to each letter, we see that
   (1) each of the probabilities (1/5) is between 0 and 1, and
   (2) 1/5 + 1/5 + 1/5 + 1/5 + 1/5 = 1.

4. S = {stock goes up, stock goes down, stock remains the same}. Rule 2 of the basic rules of probability states that P(stock goes up) + P(stock goes down) + P(stock remains the same) must equal 1. Here, the sum of these three is 1.05. Thus, these probabilities have not been assigned correctly.

5. By the Counting Rule, we have (9)(9)(8)(7) = <u>4536</u> different numerals. Note that there are not 10 choices for the first value in the numeral since if a number begins with 0, we would have a 3-digit, not a 4-digit numeral.

6. (a) P(rainy Wednesday) = P(rain and Wednesday) = (.10)(1/7) = <u>.014</u> by formula [13].

   (b) P(dry day) = 1 - P(rainy day) = .9 so P(dry Saturday) = (.9)(1/7) = <u>.129</u>.

7. (a)

	Private Car	Public Transportation	Total
less than 10 miles	.40	.325	.725
10 miles or more	.125	.15	.275
Total	.525	.475	1.000

   (b) The likelihood of a person using a private car rather than public transportation is a little more than one-half, actually .525.

   (c) P(public transportation) = .475

   (d) P(public transportation|distance from work is 10 miles or more) = .15/.275 = <u>.55</u>

8. We can see by the tree diagram that whenever he has chosen <u>3</u> socks, he is assured of having a matching pair.

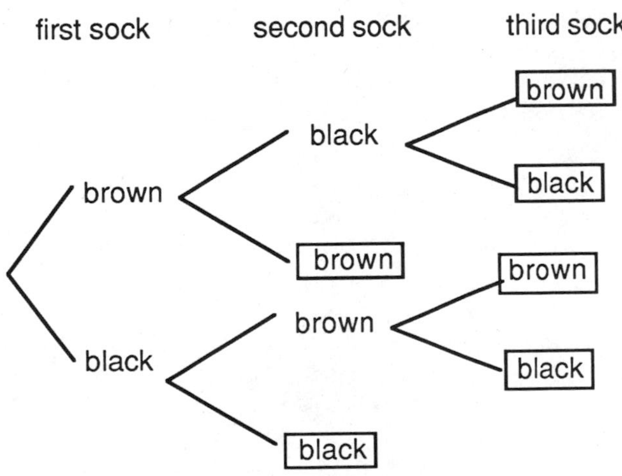

9. Using formula [16] with H representing the event he makes it within an hour and 1, 2, 3, and 4 representing the respective routes, we have

$$P(2|H) = \frac{P(H|2)P(2)}{P(H|1)P(1) + P(H|2)P(2) + P(H|3)P(3) + P(H|4)P(4)}$$

$$= \frac{(.3)(.25)}{(.45)(.25) + (.3)(.25) + (.1)(.25) + (.05)(.25)} = \frac{1}{3}$$

Note that the solution could have also been obtained from the tabular summary having 5 columns and 4 rows.

10. We are given $P(C) = .6$, $P(\bar{G}) = .8$ (so $P(G) = .2$), and $P(G|C) = .1$. Thus, by formula [11], we have $P(G \cap C) = (.6)(.1) = .06$. Then, using formula [6], we get $P(C \cup G) = .6 + .2 - .06 = \underline{.74}$.

Chapter 5

Answers to Multiple Choice Questions

1. c
2. b
3. b
4. d
5. a
6. b
7. d
8. c
9. c
10. d

Chapter 6
RANDOM VARIABLES AND DISCRETE PROBABILITY DISTRIBUTIONS

WHAT AM I LEARNING?

Chapter Outline and Summary

In this chapter we extend the study of probability by examining random variables, probability distributions, and a specific distribution - the binomial probability distribution.

A *random variable* is a numerical description of the outcome of an experiment. Values of random variables are assigned after the experimental outcomes are observed. If a random variable may assume only a finite or countable infinity of values, it is labeled a *discrete random variable.* If a random variable can assume any real number value in a certain interval or collection of intervals, it is referred to as a *continuous random variable.* In general, we will associate discrete random variables with the process of counting and continuous random variables with the process of measuring.

A *probability function,* denoted by f(x), gives the probabilities associated with the values of a discrete random variable. Since one and only one value of the random variable is assigned to each sample point of an experiment, the basic requirements of probability in Chapter 5 give us the two required conditions for a discrete probability function: $f(x) \geq 0$ and $\Sigma f(x) = 1$. A table, graph, or formula listing all possible values that a discrete random variable can take on, together with the associated probabilities (that is, the probability function) is called the *probability distribution.*

The *expected value* of a discrete random variable x with probability function f(x) gives us the average, or mean, value for the random variable. To compute this expected value, we multiply each value of the random variable by its respective probability function value and add the resulting products. A measure of the variability, or dispersion, of the random variable is its variance. The *variance* of a discrete random variable is computed by multiplying the square of the deviation of each value of the random variable from its mean by its corresponding probability function value and adding the resulting products. Because the mean and variance for a random variable are computed using the population of values of the random variable (that is, all values determined from the sample space), the symbol for the expected value, or mean, of a random variable is μ or E(x), and the symbol for the variance of a random variable is σ^2 or Var(x). The *standard deviation,* σ , is defined as the positive square root of the variance.

Many experiments exhibit essentially the same characteristics and involve the same type of probability functions. In such instances it is useful to apply the results of probability theory to obtain some general results about a probability distribution rather than re-deriving those characteristics for each specific problem. The general properties and form of one of the most widely used discrete probability distributions, the binomial probability distribution, is studied in this chapter.

The four defining characteristics of a *binomial experiment* are:

1. The experiment consists of a sequence of n identical trials.
2. There are only two possible outcomes on each trial, referred to as "success" and "failure".
3. The probability of success on each trial, denoted by p, remains constant from trial to trial.
4. The trials are independent.

Letting the random variable x be the *number of successes occurring in n trials,* the *binomial probability distribution* gives the probability distribution for this discrete random variable. The *binomial probability function* (given in formula [9] of this Guide) can be used to compute the probability of x successes in n trials for any binomial experiment. This probability can also be obtained from Table 5 of Appendix B of the Anderson/Sweeney/Williams text. This table is generally easier to use and quicker than formula [9], especially when the number of trials is large.

Chapter 6

WHICH FORMULA SHOULD I USE?

Formulas

When:

developing a probability function for a discrete random variable or deciding whether or not a function is a probability function of a discrete random variable x

Use:

the required conditions for a discrete probability function

$f(x) \geq 0$ for all values of the random variable x [1]

and

$\Sigma f(x) = 1$ [2]

When:

calculating the expected value, or mean, of a discrete random variable x with probability function f(x)

Use:

$E(x) = \mu = \Sigma x f(x)$ [3]

When:

<u>defining</u> the variance of a discrete random variable x with probability function f(x)

Use:

$Var(x) = \sigma^2 = \Sigma (x - \mu)^2 f(x)$ [4]

When:

<u>computing</u> the variance of a discrete random variable x with probability function f(x)

Use:

$Var(x) = \sigma^2 = \Sigma x^2 f(x) - \mu^2$ [5]

When:

determining the number of experimental outcomes providing exactly x successes in n trials of a binomial experiment

Use:

$$\text{number of outcomes} = \frac{n!}{x!\,(n-x)!} \quad [6]$$

where $n! = n(n-1)(n-2)\cdots(2)(1)$ for integers $n > 0$
and $0! = 1$ [7]

When:

determining the probability of a particular sequence of trial outcomes with x successes in n trials with probability p of success on each trial for a binomial experiment

Use:

$$\text{probability of sequence} = p^x\,(1-p)^{n-x} \quad [8]$$

When:

determining values of the binomial probability function f(x) = the probability of x successes in n trials with probability of success p on any one trial and probability of failure (1 - p) on any one trial

Use:

$$f(x) = \frac{n!}{x!\,(n-x)!}\,p^x\,(1-p)^{n-x} \quad [9]$$

When:

determining the expected value and variance for the binomial probability distribution where n is the number of trials and p is the probability of success on any one trial

Use:

$$E(x) = \mu = np \quad [10]$$

$$Var(x) = \sigma^2 = np(1-p) \quad [11]$$

HERE'S HOW IT'S DONE!

Examples

1. A bag contains 2 good apples (labelled G_1 and G_2) and 1 bad apple (B). One apple is chosen from the bag, put in Jimmy's lunchbox, and then another apple is chosen from the bag and put in Mary's lunchbox.

(a) List the experimental outcomes.

<u>Solution</u>:

(a) The experimental outcomes are the possibilities for the apples that are put in the two lunchboxes. Writing these as ordered pairs with the first position representing the apple that goes in Jimmy's lunchbox and the second position representing the apple that goes in Mary's lunchbox, the sample points for the experiment are

$$(G_1,G_2),\ (G_2,G_1),\ (G_1,B),\ (B,G_1),\ (G_2,B),\ (B,G_2).$$

<u>Note</u>: The counting rule of Chapter 5 gives the number of sample points as 3(2) = 6.

(b) Define a random variable that represents the number of good apples that are chosen for the lunchboxes. Is this a discrete or continuous random variable?

<u>Solution</u>:

(b) Let x = the number of good apples chosen to be put in the two lunchboxes. Then, x takes on the values 1 or 2. Since the values for x represent a finite set that is countable, x is <u>discrete</u>.

(c) Show what value the random variable will assume for each of the experimental outcomes.

<u>Solution</u>:

(c)

Experimental Outcome:	(G_1,G_2),	(G_2,G_1),	(G_1,B),	(B,G_1),	(G_2,B),	(B,G_2)
Value of x:	2	2	1	1	1	1

2. For the experiments listed below and the associated random variables, identify the value(s) that the random variable can assume and state whether the random variable is discrete or continuous.

(a) Experiment: Answer the 10 multiple choice questions at the end of this chapter. The random variable is the number of questions you answer correctly.

Solution:

(a) The values for x are 0, 1, 2, 3, 4, 5, 6, 7, 8, 9, 10. This is a discrete random variable since the values are countable.

(b) Experiment: Measure the time interval between arrivals at the bank teller's window. The random variable is the length of time between arrivals.

Solution:

(b) The values for x are the real numbers in a certain interval which could conceivably be any value between the time the bank opens and closes. Because time can be measured, theoretically to any real number, the variable is continuous.

(c) Experiment: Count the number of people attending a local college's basketball game. The random variable is the number of people in attendance.

Solution:

(c) The values for x are 0, 1, 2, · · ·, n where n is the capacity of the building where the game is being played. Because these values are countable, the variable is discrete.

(d) Experiment: Measure the low temperature on a particular day in Miami, Florida. The random variable is the observed low temperature.

Solution:

(d) The values for x are the real numbers in a certain interval which could conceivably be any real number (most logically, between 0 and 100 degrees). Given an accurate enough measuring device, this is a continuous random variable.

3. A fair coin is tossed twice. Let the random variable x be the number of tails observed on the two tosses.

 (a) Give the probability distribution for x in tabular form.

Solution:

(a) For this experiment, S = {HH, HT, TH, TT}. The associated values that the random variable x will take on for each sample point are 0, 1, 1, and 2, respectively. Since the coin is fair, each of these sample points is equally likely giving the probability distribution

x	f(x)
0	1/4
1	1/2
2	1/4

 (b) Show that this probability distribution satisfies the required conditions for a discrete probability function.

Solution:

(b) Each value of f(x), 1/4 and 1/2, is greater (or equal to) 0.
Over all values of x, $\Sigma f(x) = 1/4 + 1/2 + 1/4 = 4/4 = 1$.

4. Suppose a function is defined by the equation $f(x) = 1/x$ for $x = 2, 3,$ and 4. Is f(x) a probability function for the discrete random variable x? Why or why not?

Solution:

Looking at f(x) in tabular form, we have

x	f(x)
2	1/2
3	1/3
4	1/4.

Notice that each value of f(x) is between 0 and 1, so the first of the required conditions for a probability function is satisfied. However, looking at the second required condition, we find

$$\Sigma f(x) = 1/2 + 1/3 + 1/4 = 13/12 \neq 1.$$

Thus, because both of the requirements are not satisfied, f(x) is not a probability function for x.

5. The random variable x has the following discrete probability distribution:

x	f(x)
1	0.2
2	0.3
4	0.5

(a) Find the expected value of the random variable x.

Solution:

(a) Substituting in formula [3], we have

$$\mu = E(x) = \Sigma xf(x) = 1(.2) + 2(.3) + 4(.5) = \underline{2.8}.$$

(b) Find the variance of x.

Solution:

(b) Substituting in the computational formula for the variance of a discrete random variable, formula [5], we have

$$\text{Var}(x) = \sigma^2 = \Sigma x^2 f(x) - \mu^2 = 1^2(.2) + 2^2(.3) + 4^2(.5) - (2.8)^2$$
$$= .2 + 1.2 + .8 - 7.84 = \underline{1.56}.$$

A reminder: Only the values of x are squared in $\Sigma x^2 f(x)$. Do not square the f(x) values! Also, do not forget to subtract the value of μ^2 after finding this sum.

6. A game of chance is called a *fair game* if the player's net winnings are zero; that is, the expected net winnings for the player equals the price of playing the game.

Consider the spinner shown to the right with the payoff for each region written on the spinner. Should the owner of the spinner expect to make money over an extended period of time if the charge to play the game is $2.00 per spin?

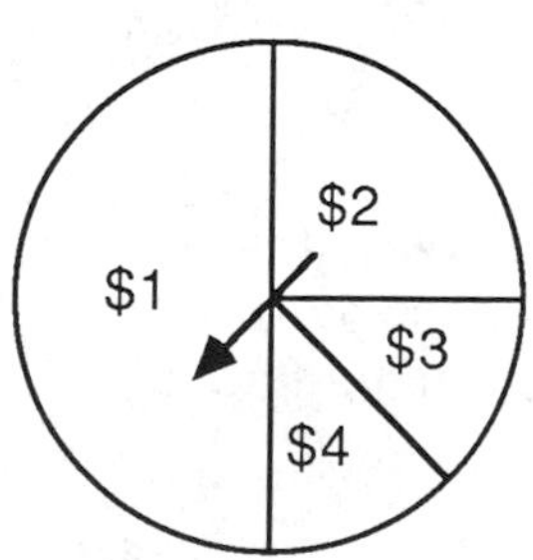

Solution:

Define a random variable x to be the player's net winnings (amount won – amount paid to play) on any particular play of the game. Assigning probabilities by the area of the region in which the spinner can land (landing on a line is not counted as a possibility), the probabilities for the various dollar amounts on the spinner are: P($1) = 1/2, P($2) = 1/4, P($3) = 1/8, and P($4) = 1/8. Thus, we have the following probability function for the discrete variable x:

x	f(x)
(1-2) = -1	1/2
(2-2) = 0	1/4
(3-2) = 1	1/8
(4-2) = 2	1/8

The expected value of the player's net winnings is

$$E(x) = -1(1/2) + 0(1/4) + 1(1/8) + 2(1/8) = -.125.$$

Thus, on each play of the game, the player can expect to lose $0.125 or approximately 13 cents.

Since the player stands to lose money, on the average, the owner should make a profit over a long period of time. This is not a fair game, but one biased in favor of the owner.

7. An experiment is to deal a five card poker hand from an unmarked deck of cards. The random variable of interest is the number of three's in the hand. Is this a binomial experiment? Why or why not?

Solution:

We must check to see if all the four properties of a binomial experiment are satisfied:

1. The experiment consists of n = 5 identical trials, where each trial involves the dealing of one card from the deck of cards. This condition is satisfied.
2. There are two outcomes possible for each trial. The possible outcomes are the card dealt is a three (success) and the card dealt is not a three (failure). This condition is satisfied.
3. The probability of a three being dealt must be the same for each card that is dealt. This condition is <u>not</u> satisfied, for the cards in poker are dealt from the deck without replacement - that is, once dealt, a card is not put back in the deck to possibly be dealt again. For instance, the probability a three is dealt as the first card is 4/52. The probability of a three being dealt for the second card will either be 3/51 or 4/51, depending on whether or not a three was the result of the first trial.

Thus, the probability of success is not the same from trial to trial and this is not a binomial experiment.

8. A restaurant owner has observed that 30% of the dinner bills are paid with a major credit card. Five bills are randomly chosen during a given evening, and the method of payment is noted.

(a) What are the trials of the experiment in this problem? How many trials are there?

Solution:

(a) Each trial involves noting the method of payment of the dinner bill. Since five bills are chosen for inspection, $n = 5$.

(b) How many outcomes are possible on each trial and what are they?

Solution:

(b) There are two outcomes possible for each trial - paying with major credit card and paying by some means other than a major credit card.

(c) What are the probabilities associated with the outcomes for each trial? Are these probabilities the same for each trial?

Solution:

(c) The probability of a customer paying with a major credit card is given as the constant value .30. The probability of the complement, not paying with a major credit card, is therefore .70. By the way the problem is stated, these values are given as constant from trial to trial.

(d) Are the trials independent? Why or why not?

Solution:

(d) The trials are independent since the bills are randomly chosen.

(e) What is the random variable of interest in this problem? What values can it assume, and is it discrete or continuous?

Solution:

(e) The random variable is x = number of bills paid with a major credit card. In this case, x can assume the values of 0, 1, 2, 3, 4, or 5. Because these values are countable, x is discrete.

(f) What is the probability that exactly two of these bills will be paid with a major credit card?

Solution:

(f) Since x is a binomial random variable, we substitute in formula [9] to obtain

$$f(2) = \frac{5!}{2!\,(5-2)!}\,(.3)^2\,(1-.3)^3 = \frac{5(4)(3)(2)(1)}{2(1)(3)(2)(1)}\,(.09)(.343) = 10(.0309) = \underline{.309}.$$

9. A bag contains 10 tennis balls, all identical except for color. Of these 10 balls, 4 are white, 5 are orange, and 1 is yellow. Eight balls are chosen from the bag, each ball being replaced before the next one is drawn.

(a) Find the probability of obtaining at least 5 white balls.

Solution:

(a) Since the balls are replaced, the properties of a binomial experiment are satisfied with the random variable x being the number of white balls drawn in the $n = 8$ trials.

The probability of obtaining a white ball on each draw is 4/10 since the balls are equally likely to be chosen.

Now, x can assume the values 0, 1, 2, 3, 4, 5, 6, 7, or 8. We are looking for

$P(x \geq 5) = P(5) + P(6) + P(7) + P(8)$.

Rather than working these values out individually by formula [9], it is easier to use Table 5. Looking in this table for $n = 8$, $p = 0.4$, we find

$P(x = 5) = P(5) = .1239$, $P(6) = .0413$, $P(7) = .0079$, and $P(8) = .0007$.

The answer is therefore

$$P(x \geq 5) = .1239 + .0413 + .0079 + .0007 = \underline{.1738}.$$

10. Use Table 5 to find each of the following probabilities for the binomial random variable x with the given values of n and p.

(a) Find the probability x is 4 or 5 for $n = 9$ and $p = .4$

Solution:

(a) $P(x = 4) + P(x = 5) = .2508 + .1672 = \underline{.4180}$.

(b) Find the probability $x = 4$ for $n = 8$ and $p = 1/3$

Solution:

(b) There is no value of $p = 1/3 \approx .33$ in Table 5. We may approximate this value by taking the value midway between the p values of .30 and .35, obtaining $P(x = 4) \approx (.1361 + .1875)/2 = \underline{.1618}$.

Note: This value may be obtained exactly by using formula [9].

(c) Find the probability $x = 6$ for $n = 10$ and $p = .7$

Solution:

(c) There is no column in Table 5 for $p = .7$. Thus we realize that $x = 6$ successes in the binomial experiment with probability of success being $p = .7$ means exactly the same thing as $n - x = 4$ failures with probability of failure being $1 - p = .3$. Looking in Table 5 under the .3 column for $n = 10$ and the row for the value 4, we find $P(x = 6) = \underline{.2001}$.

(d) Find the probability of at most 3 successes for $n = 20$ and $p = .10$.

Solution:

(d) The probability of at most 3 successes means

$$P(x \le 3) = P(0) + P(1) + P(2) + P(3) = .1216 + .2702 + .2852 + .1901$$

$$= \underline{.8671}.$$

HAVE I LEARNED THE MATERIAL?

Problems

1. A survey of people living in apartments in a certain city showed that 20% preferred a white telephone over any other color available. Let the random variable x be the number of apartment dwellers who prefer a white telephone.

   (a) Is the random variable x discrete or continuous?

   (b) Suppose an experiment is to select 20 people living in apartments and ask them what color is the main telephone in their apartment. Describe the conditions necessary for this to be a binomial experiment.

   (c) What is the probability that at least 11 of these 20 people will prefer white telephones?

2. Why is the following not a probability associated with a binomial experiment?

   An urn contains 3 green balls, 2 blue balls, and 4 red balls. If 5 balls are chosen at random with each ball being replaced, after its color is noted, before the next ball is drawn, find the probability that 2 green balls and 3 red balls are drawn.

3. Write "discrete" or "continuous" to describe each of the following random variables:

   (a) the length of time required to play 18 holes of golf

   (b) the number of eggs laid each month by one hen

   (c) the number of draws required to obtain a king from a standard deck of 52 playing cards

   (d) the actual weight of a box of chocolate chip cookies

4. Consider the discrete random variable x with probability distribution

x	1	3	4	5
f(x)	.1	.5	c	.2

   (a) Find the value of c for which f(x) is a probability distribution.

   (b) What is the probability that x is less than or equal to 3?

5. One word is chosen at random from the set {on, no, big, me, dime}. Assume each word is just as likely to be chosen as any other word. If the random variable x is the number of vowels in the chosen word, what is the expected value of x?

6. Consider the given probability distribution and find

x	f(x)
0	.2
1	.6
3	.1
4	.1

(a) μ

(b) σ^2

7. A machine that produces stampings for automobile engines is malfunctioning and produces 10% defectives. The defective and nondefective stampings proceed from the machine in a random, independent manner. If 5 stampings are chosen for inspection, find the probability that exactly 3 of them are defective using

(a) formula [9]:

(b) Table 5:

8. Five hundred questionnaires are mailed to randomly selected individuals. The probability of any one person not responding to the questionnaire is assumed to be 1/5. Assume the responses are independent of one another. Find the expected number of responses and the standard deviation of the number of responses.

9. A student must choose 3 electives from 7 courses being offered. In how many ways can he make his choice?

10. Suppose Jane has won an $800 oven on Let's Make A Deal. She has a choice of keeping the oven or trading it for a prize behind one of the doors. She is told behind one of the doors is a $2400 vacation prize, behind another is a $1200 living room set, and behind the third door is $90 worth of peanuts. If each door has the same chance of being chosen by Jane, should she trade her $800 oven for a door?

Chapter 6

Multiple Choice Questions

1. Which of these variables is discrete?

(a) the number of ships using the Suez Canal on any one day
(b) the hours of flight time for a jet flying from New York to Los Angeles
(c) the high temperature in Chicago any particular day
(d) none of the above.

2. Which of the following is a valid probability distribution for the given discrete random variable x?

(a)

x	f(x)
-5	-.3
-3	-.1
3	.8
6	.6

(b)

x	f(x)
0	.4
1	.3
2	.1
3	.1

(c)

x	f(x)
-1	.6
0	.1
1.5	.1
8	.2

(d)

x	f(x)
2	.5
4	.2
6	.3
8	.2

3. The random variable x has a probability function given by:

x	f(x)
8	.4
10	.3
15	.3

The mean of the random variable x is

(a) 10
(b) 10.7
(c) 11
(d) 9.1

4. A random variable has a probability function f(x) given by the formula

$f(x) = 1/5$ for $x = 1, 2, 3, 4, 5$.

The probability that x is an even number is

(a) .20
(b) .60
(c) .40
(d) .55.

5. Weight, height, temperature, and time are all examples of

(a) continuous random variables
(b) discrete random variables
(c) binomial random variables
(d) none of the above.

6. The value in the binomial table for $n = 11$, $x = 4$, and $p = .3$ is .2201. Which of the following is the equivalent expression for the binomial probability function?

(a) $\frac{11!}{7!\,4!}(.3)^7(.7)^4$

(b) $\frac{11!}{3!\,8!}(.4)^3(.6)^8$

(c) $\frac{11!}{8!\,3!}(.4)^8(.6)^3$

(d) $\frac{11!}{4!\,7!}(.3)^4(.7)^7$

7. Suppose that 20% of all people over age 40 smoke cigarettes. If 10 persons are selected from this population, what is the probability that less than 6 people in this sample smoke cigarettes?

(a) .0264
(b) .9936
(c) .0055
(d) .9991.

8. It is known that 60% of the students at a certain college pay for their lunch with a meal ticket rather than with cash. If 20 students in the cafeteria are sampled and the random variable of interest is the number of students that are using a meal ticket to buy their lunch, which of the following is not a true statement?

(a) The experiment consists of 20 identical trials where each trial involves checking the method of payment for the student's lunch.
(b) There are 2 possible outcomes for each trial: "the student pays with a meal ticket" and "the student pays cash".
(c) The probability of purchase with a meal ticket or cash are assumed to be the same for each student with $p = .40$ and $1 - p = .60$.
(d) The trials are independent since the method of payment for a particular student is not affected or influenced by the method of payment of any other student.

9. The expected value of a discrete random variable is its

(a) probability function
(b) probability distribution
(c) variance
(d) mean.

10. For the probability distribution of the random variable x given below, what is the variance of x if $E(x) = 6$?

x	f(x)
0	.2
5	.4
10	.4

(a) 14
(b) 10
(c) 8
(d) 9.6.

Chapter 6

Answers to Problems

1. (a) discrete

   (b) n = 20 and p = .2 are given as constant; success is an answer of "white" and failure is getting an answer that is a color other than white. We must assume the trials are independent (that is, the color of the telephone in one person's apartment is not affected or influenced by the color of the telephone in another person's apartment.)

   (c) .0006

2. In a binomial experiment, there must be one outcome called success on each trial. Here, more than one result is called success, for "success" is getting both red and green balls.

3. (a) continuous
   (b) discrete
   (c) discrete
   (d) continuous

4. (a) c = .2

   (b) $P(x \leq 3) = .6$

5.

x	f(x)
1	4/5
2	1/5

and $E(x) = 1(4/5) + 2(1/5) = 6/5 = \underline{1.2}$.

6. (a) $\mu = 1.3$

   (b) $\sigma^2 = 1.41$

7. (a)

$$\frac{5!}{3!\ 2!}(.1)^3(.9)^2 = 10(.001)(.81) = .0081$$

(b) Looking in Table 5 for n = 5, x = 3, and p = .10, we find the probability is .0081.

8. This is a binomial experiment with n = 500, success being a person responding and failure being the person not responding, and p = 4/5. Using formulas [10] and [11], we obtain

$$\mu = np = 500(4/5) = \underline{400} \text{ and } \sigma^2 = \sqrt{np(1 - p)} = \sqrt{400\ (.2)} = \sqrt{80} = \underline{8.9443}.$$

9. Formula [6] gives the number of ways as 7! / (3! 4!) = 35.

10. Letting the random variable x be Jane's (gross) winnings,

$$P(x = 2400) = 1/3, P(x = 1200) = 1/3, \text{ and } P(x = 90) = 1/3.$$

Thus, Jane's expected winnings are

$$2400(1/3) + 1200(1/3) + 90(1/3) = 1230.$$

Since she will expect to win \$1230 which is more than the \$800 she has now, she should go for a door.

Chapter 6

Answers to Multiple Choice Questions

1. a
2. c
3. b
4. c
5. a
6. d
7. b
8. c
9. d
10. a

Chapter 7
THE NORMAL PROBABILITY DISTRIBUTION

WHAT AM I LEARNING?

Chapter Outline and Summary

In this chapter we are introduced to two specific examples of continuous probability distributions, the normal and standard normal probability distributions.

Many sets of data that occur in practical situations follow the *normal probability distribution.* It is defined mathematically as

$$f(x) = \frac{1}{\sigma \sqrt{2\pi}} e^{-(x-\mu)^2/2\sigma^2} \qquad \text{for} \quad -\infty \leq x \leq \infty$$

The form, or shape, of the normal probability distribution is the *normal curve* which is a symmetrical, bell-shaped curve. Actually, the normal probability distribution is a family of curves with each particular curve differentiated from the others in the family by its mean and standard deviation. For all the normal curves, the highest point occurs at the mean (which equals the median and the mode in this situation). The standard deviation (or variance) determines the width (or spread) of the curve. Larger values of σ result in wider, flatter curves and smaller values of σ give taller, narrower curves. Since the normal probability distribution is a probability distribution function, the total area under the normal curve is 1.

Probability is defined for continuous random variables in terms of areas under the graph of the probability function. The probability of any specific value of a continuous random variable must be zero since single numeric values have no width. Therefore, probabilities for continuous random variables are calculated for intervals of real values.

The probability that a continuous random variable assumes any value in an interval between two specific points a and b is the area under the graph of the probability distribution between a and b. Probabilities for some commonly used intervals are

1. 68.26% of the time a normal random variables assumes a value within plus or minus one standard deviation of its mean.
2. 95.44% of the time, a normal random variable assumes a value within plus or minus 2 standard deviations of its mean.
3. 99.72% of the time, a normal random variable assumes a value within plus or minus 3 standard deviations of its mean.

It is easier to compare normal distributions having different values of μ and σ if these curves are transformed to one common form which is called the *standard normal probability distribution.* The standard normal variable, denoted by z, has a mean of zero and a standard deviation equal to one.

The area under the standard normal curve (or probability) between the mean, $z = 0$, and a specific value of z is recorded in Table I of Appendix B, as well as on the inside of the back cover, in the Anderson/Sweeney/Williams text. That is, the table gives the shaded area

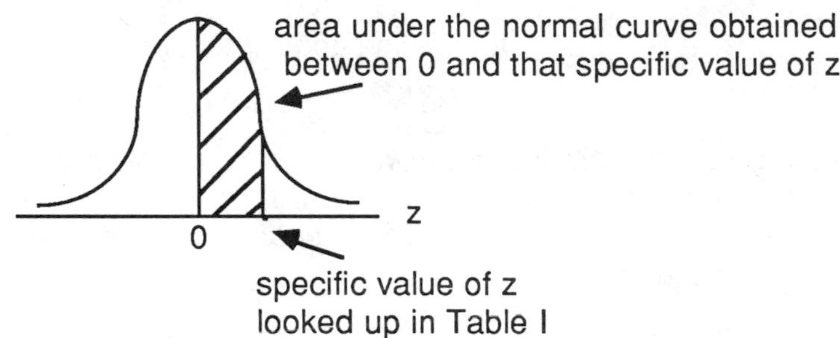

In general, since the normal distribution is symmetric and the total area under the normal curve is 1, half of the area will lie to the right of the mean and half to the left of the mean. Specifically, the areas for the standard normal distribution to the left of the mean of zero may be obtained by the symmetry of the distribution and are therefore, not recorded in Table I. Other related areas can be easily calculated by using the given area from the table and a reference sketch of the standard normal distribution. If given an area, or probability, this table and a reference sketch may also be used to determine the corresponding z-value.

In order to use Table I for normal distributions other than the standard normal distribution (z), it is necessary to convert any particular range of values of the normal variable x with mean μ and standard deviation σ to its equivalent z-value by using the formula $z = (x - \mu)/\sigma$. That is, we can interpret the z-value obtained from this formula as the number of standard deviations that the normal random variable, x, is from its mean μ. Since all values of x within an interval [a,b] have corresponding z-values in an interval $[z_1, z_2]$, the area under the normal curve for x, between a and b (that is,

$P(a \le x \le b) = P(a < x < b))$ is equal to the area under the standard normal curve between z_1 and z_2.

Under certain conditions (given in formula [2] of this Guide), the binomial distribution can be approximated by the normal distribution. It is logical to assume that the mean and variance used for the normal approximation should be the same as the mean and variance of the binomial distribution. Thus, the formula to find the equivalent z-value for the approximation is $z = (x - np)/\sqrt{np(1 - p)}$ for the binomial parameters n and p. To do this approximation requires the use of a continuous probability distribution to approximate the probability associated with a discrete probability distribution. In this situation, because of the differences between discrete and continuous random variables, we must include a *continuity correction* in the approximation procedure. This continuity correction involves adding 1/2 or subtraction 1/2, depending on the nature of the problem, to the x value(s) stated in the problem before converting to the corresponding z-value.

WHICH FORMULA SHOULD I USE?

Formulas

When:

converting a normal random variable x with mean μ and standard deviation σ to a standard normal random variable

Use:

$$z = \frac{x - \mu}{\sigma} \qquad [1]$$

When:

Both $np \geq 5$ and $n(1 - p) \geq 5$, the binomial variable, denoted by x_B, can be approximated by a normal variable, denoted by x_N. To do this approximation

Use:

Step 1: The continuity correction for either or both of the following, determined by the nature of the problem:

$$P(x_B \leq a) \approx P(x_N \leq a + 1/2)$$

$$P(x_B \geq b) \approx P(x_N \geq b - 1/2).$$

Step 2: The conversion of the above normal approximation(s) to the corresponding z-value(s) with the formula

$$z = \frac{(x - np)}{\sqrt{np(1 - p)}} \qquad [2]$$

Step 3: Look up the required area(s) in Table I and perform the necessary calculations determined from a reference sketch.

Chapter 7

HERE'S HOW IT'S DONE!

Examples

1. Weekly maintenance costs for the Widget Manufacturing Company, recorded since the factory opened and adjusted for inflation, have a normal distribution with mean of \$420 and a standard deviation of \$30.

   (a) Sketch a normal curve for the weekly maintenance costs.

<u>Solution</u>:

(a) The value of the mean and standard deviation given in the problem are population values since they represent values for all the weekly maintenance costs of the Widget factory. Using the fact that the normal distribution can be roughly drawn by placing the mean (μ = \$420) at the center of the symmetric curve and percentages of the total area of 1 estimated by the number of standard deviations (σ = \$30) the values of the variable are from the mean, we have

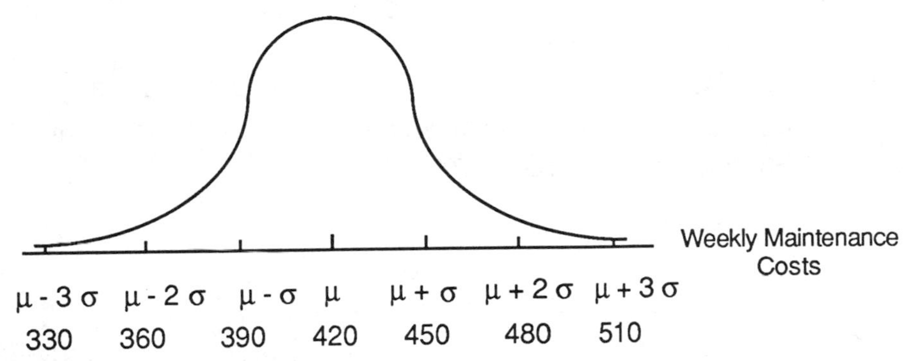

(b) What is the probability that the Widget's weekly maintenance costs are between \$390 and \$450?

<u>Solution</u>:

(b) We note the probabilities for the commonly used intervals given in the discussion of the normal variable, and we place these on the graph. It can be easily seen from the graph that 68.26% of the time, the weekly maintenance costs, (that is, the normal random variable) will assume values within $\pm$ 1 standard deviation of the mean.

Thus, the required probability is <u>.6826</u>.

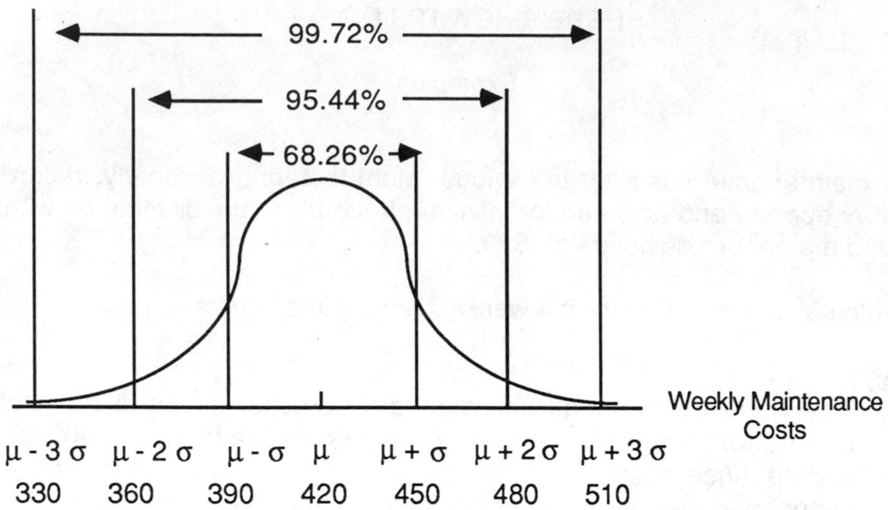

(c) What is the probability that a week selected at random will have maintenance costs greater than $480?

Solution:

(c) Since $480 = \mu + 2\sigma$, we again look at the graph above giving the probabilities for the commonly used intervals. Remembering that the total area under the normal curve is 1, we can place the following percentages on the graph:

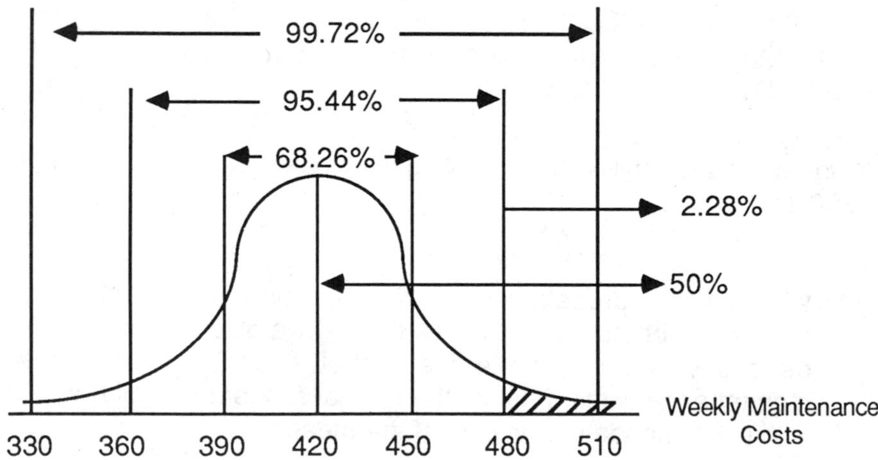

The value of 2.28% is obtained using the symmetry of the normal distribution in either of two ways:

$$(100\% - 95.44\%)/2 = 2.28\% \qquad \text{or}$$

$$50\% - [(1/2)(68.26\%) + (1/2)(95.44\% - 68.26\%)] = 2.28\%.$$

The percentage of weekly maintenance costs that are greater than $480 is 2.28%, so the required probability is .0228.

2. Use Table I to find each of the following probabilities for the standard normal distribution:

(a) $P(0 \le z \le 1.73)$

Solution:

(a)

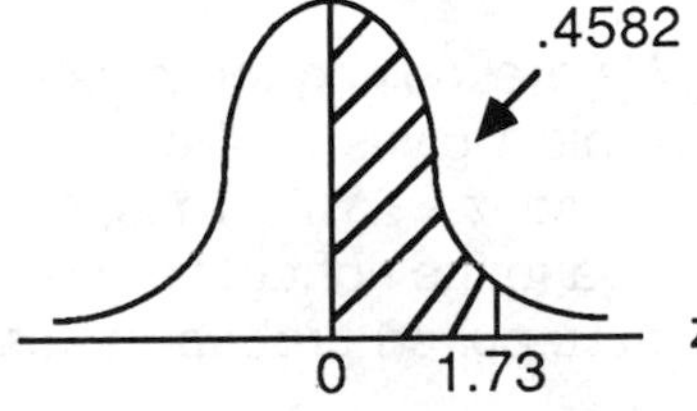

$P(0 \le z \le 1.73)$ is the shaded area on the graph. It is the same area that is given in Table 1 by looking up the value of $z = 1.73$. Thus, we have

$$P(0 \le z \le 1.73) = .4582.$$

(b) $P(-1.73 \le z < 0)$

Solution:

(b)

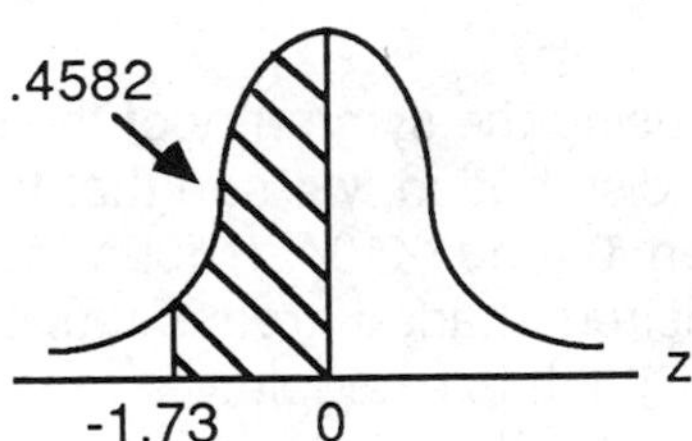

By the symmetry of the standard normal distribution, we see that this area is identical to the area in part a) of this problem. Thus,

$$P(-1.73 \le z < 0) = .4582.$$

(c) $P(-2 < z < 1.53)$

Solution:

(c)

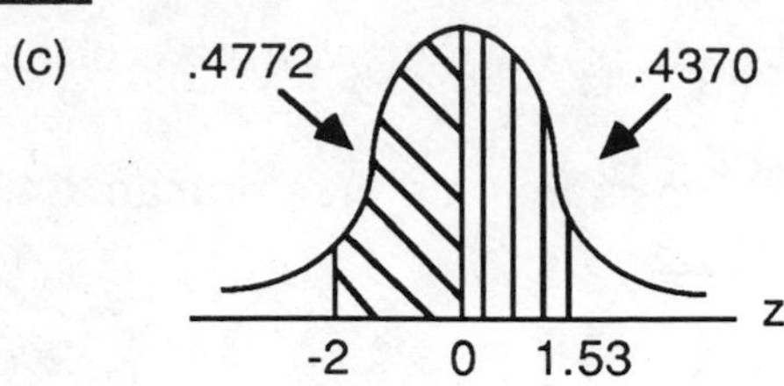

Obtain the area between 0 and -2 from Table I as .4772 since it is the same as the area between 0 and 2 by symmetry. Thus, we have

$P(-2 < z < 1.53) = .4772 + .4370$
$= .9142.$

(d) $P(z \geq 2.87)$

Solution:

(d)

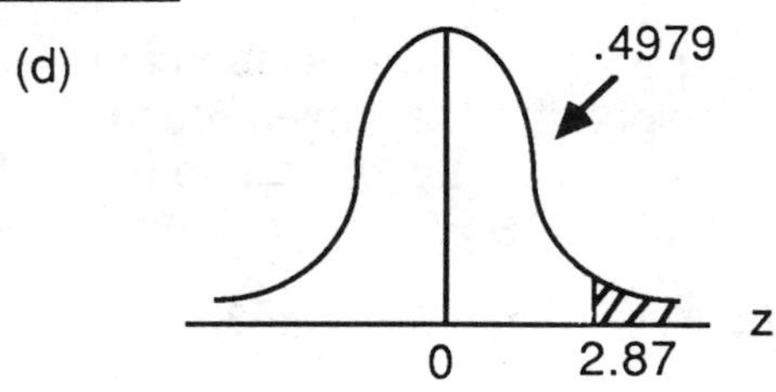

We are looking for the shaded area. Table 1 gives us the area between 0 and $z = 2.87$. Thus, since the total area to the right of zero is .5, we find the required probability as

$P(z \geq 2.87) = .5 - .4979 = .0021.$

(e) $P(z \leq -2.04)$

Solution:

(e)

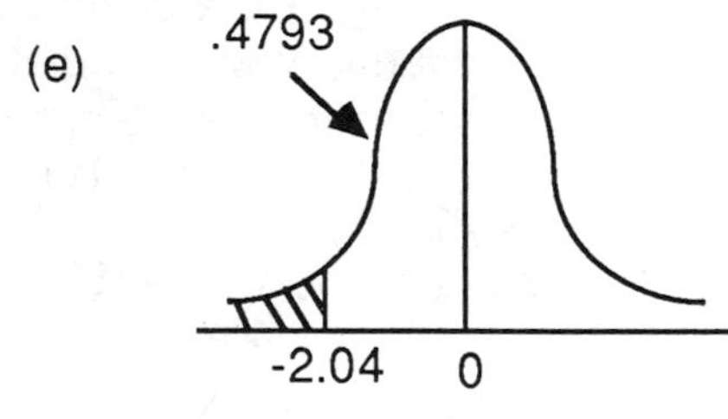

Again, using the symmetry of the standard normal distribution, we see that the area between 0 and -2.04 is found to be .4793. The desired shaded area is found as we did in part d) of this example.

$P(z \leq -2.04) = .5 - .4793 = .0207.$

(f) $P(1.7 \le z \le 2.83)$

Solution:

(f)

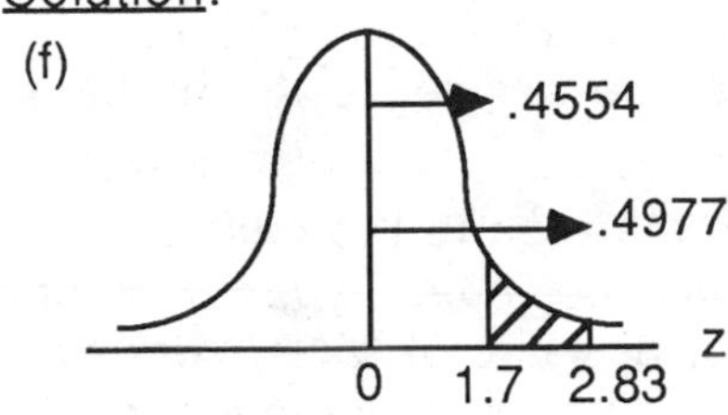

As seen in the graph, the shaded area is obtained by subtracting the areas corresponding to the z values of 2.83 and 1.70. Thus, we have

$$P(1.7 \le z \le 2.83) = .4977 - .4554 = .0423.$$

(g) $P(z < 1.18)$

Solution:

(g)

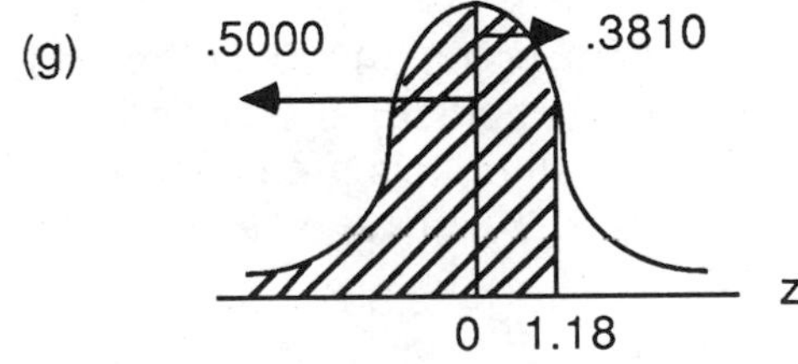

$P(z < 1.18) = P(-\infty < z < 1.18)$
Recall that by the symmetry of the normal distribution, the area to the left of the mean equals .5. Thus, we see by the graph, to obtain the shaded area, we find

$$P(z < 1.18) = .5 + .3810 = .8810.$$

3. Find the value of the standard normal distribution, say z_0, such that $P(z > z_0) = .0091$.

   Note: In working a problem of this type, that is, when you are given an area (probability) and wish to find the corresponding z-value, you must remember two things:

   (1) Table I gives you the area between 0 and a particular value of z,

   and

   (2) Table I gives areas for values of z between 0 and +3.09.

   Thus, you must answer two questions before being able to find a particular value of z, which here is called z_0 for the sake of having a name for it:

(1) Is the area I am given to the right of the point z_0 or to its left?
Answer: $P(z > z_0)$ means area to the right of z_0, and
$P(z < zo)$ means area to the left of zo.

(2) Will the value I find for z_0, that is, the answer to the problem, be positive or negative?
Answer: For the normal distribution, the area to the right of 0 is .5. The area to the left of 0 is .5. Thus, if you know that the area to the right of a particular value of z is more than .5, that value of z must be negative. If the area to the left of a particular value of z is more than .5, that value of z must be positive. Other cases may readily be evaluated by drawing a reference sketch, putting on the sketch the given area. In other words, *ALWAYS DRAW A PICTURE!*

Solution:

(a)

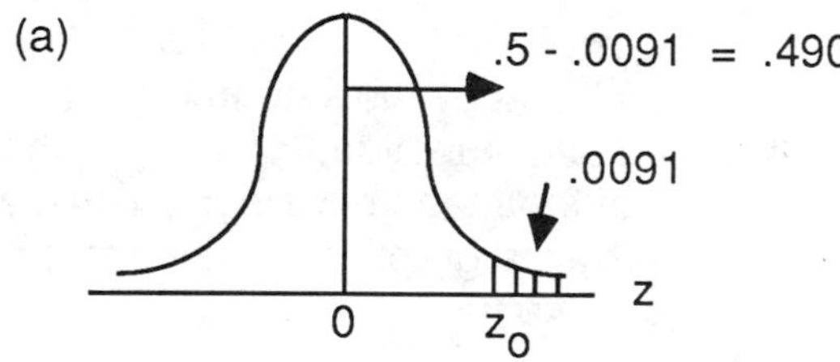

Looking up .4909 in the body (area portion) of Table I, we find that this area corresponds to 2.36. Thus,

$$z_0 = 2.36 .$$

Here, we were given $P(z > z_0) = .0091$. That is, we have the area to the right of the point z_0 being a value less than .5. The only way this can happen is if the point is positive. Table I does not give us the area to the right of a positive point, but the area between 0 and that point. Thus, the above subtraction was necessary.

(b) Find the value of z, say z_0, such that $P(z \geq z_0) = .8643$.

Solution:

(b)

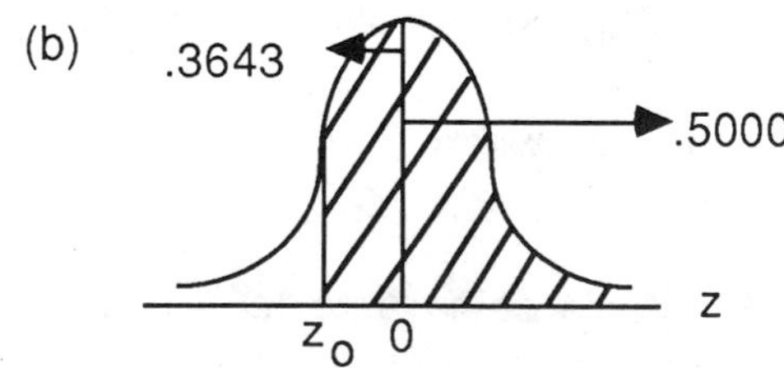

The area between 0 and the point we are looking for, z_0, is $.8643 - .5 = .3643$. Looking this area up in the main body of Table I, we see it corresponds to a z-value of 2.36. Thus, we have

$$z_0 = -2.36.$$

Since we were give the area to the right of the point as a value greater than .5, the point must be negative. A reference sketch quickly tells us which value to look for in Table I.

4. Find P(x > 55) if x has a normal distribution with mean of 45 and variance of 16.

<u>Solution</u>:

Here the variable x has a normal distribution, but it is not the standard normal distribution. Thus, we must convert the range of values (x > 55) to a range of z-values in order to find the required answer. This is accomplished using formula [1]:

$$\text{Since } z = \frac{x - \mu}{\sigma}, \; P(x > 55) = P(z > \frac{55 - 45}{4})$$

$$= P(z > 2.50) = .5000 - .4938 = \underline{.0062}.$$

This correspondence of values may be seen in the following graphs for x and z:

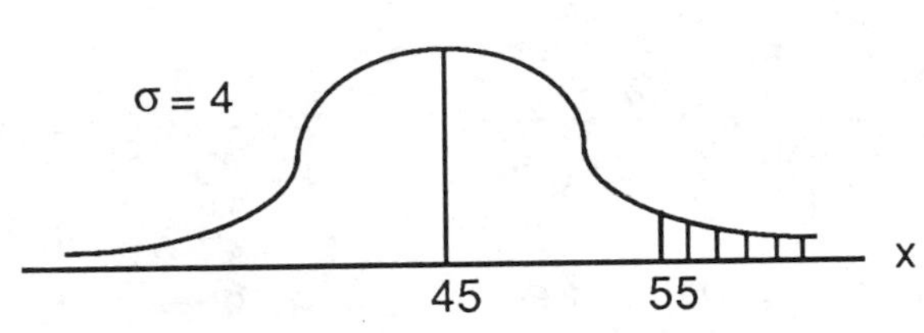

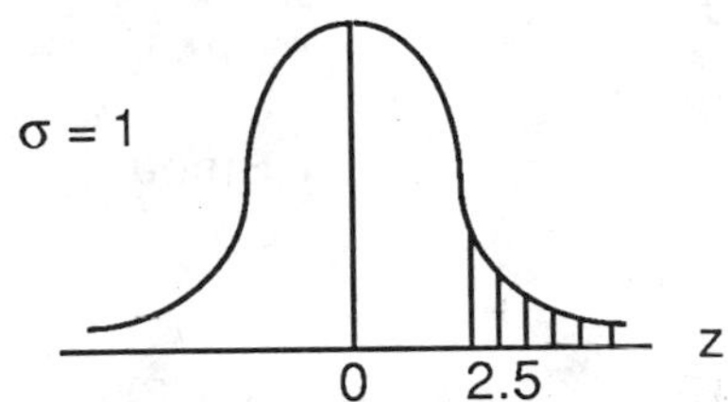

<u>Tip</u>: Notice that in this problem you are given $\sigma^2 = 16$. The formula calls for $\sigma = 4$. Do not forget to take the square root of the variance if it is the given quantity.

5. The random variable x has a binomial distribution with $n = 100$ and $p = .5$. Use the normal approximation to the binomial distribution, if possible, to find $P(x > 58)$.

<u>Solution</u>:

It is possible to use the normal distribution to approximate the binomial distribution when $np \geq 5$ and $n(1 - p) \geq 5$. These conditions are given in formula [2] of this Guide. Here, $np = 100(.5) = 50$ and $n(1 - p) = 100(.5) = 50$, so we should get a "good" approximation.

<u>Note</u>: Here we wish to determine $P(x > 58)$ for the binomial variable x. While a normal variable has no probability at a point, a discrete value does because 58 is certainly a possible value for the binomial distribution. Thus, in this problem, we do not wish to include the value of 58 and we are actually looking for $P(x \geq 57)$!

Following the steps outlined in formula [2], we must first obtain the approximating value of the normal variable by using the continuity correction factor.

$$P(x_B \leq 57) \approx P(x_N \leq 57 + 1/2) = P(x_N \leq 57.5)$$

We then convert the approximating normal variable x to z in order to use Table I:

$$\text{Since } z = \frac{(x - np)}{\sqrt{np(1 - p)}} = \frac{57.5 - 50}{\sqrt{50(.5)}} = \frac{7.5}{5} = 1.50 \text{ ,}$$

$$P(x_B \leq 57) \approx P(x_N \leq 57.5) = P(z \leq 1.50) = .5 + .4332 = \underline{.9332}.$$

Chapter 7

HAVE I LEARNED THE MATERIAL?

Problems

1. Use Table I to find each of the following probabilities for the standard normal distribution:

   (a) $P(z < -1.96)$

   (b) $P(2.46 \leq z < 3.97)$

   (c) $P(-2.14 < z \leq 0)$

   (d) $P(z > 0.75)$

   (e) $P(-2.45 \leq z \leq -1.92)$

   (f) $P(z > -3.03)$

   (g) $P(-.21 \leq z < .45)$

2. In each of the following, find the value of z, say z_0, such that

(a) $P(z > z_0) = .0694$

(b) $P(z > z_0) = .9896$

(c) $P(z \leq z_0) = .0057$

(d) $P(z < z_0) = .9406$

(e) $P(-z_0 < z < z_0) = .9250$

(f) $P(z_0 < z \leq 2.6) = .9725$

3. Light bulbs produced by the Glowgleam Light Company have a mean length of life of 35 hours with a standard deviation of 5 hours. Answer the following questions without the use of Table I.

   (a) Sketch the graph showing the distribution of the length of life of these lightbulbs.

   (b) What is the probability that a randomly selected Glowgleam light bulb will last between 30 and 35 hours?

   (c) What is the probability that a randomly selected Glowgleam lightbulb will have a length of life of more than 50 hours?

   (d) If the random variable x denotes the length of life of a randomly selected Glowgleam lightbulb, find values of a and b such that $P(a < x < b) = .95$.

4. The first assignment in an introductory computer programming class involves keypunching a short program. If past experiments indicate that 40% of all beginning students will make no keypunching errors, use the normal approximation to the binomial distribution to compute the probability that in a class of 100 students, <u>at most</u> 30 students will make no errors.

5. Inhabitants of Planet Zypq have Spqu scores that are normally distributed with a mean of 81 and a variance of 36. Find the probability that a randomly chosen inhabitant of Planet Zypq will have a Spqu score that is between 78 and 82.

6. Scores on an aptitude test for potential managers are normally distributed with a mean of 120 and a standard deviation of 30. What is the lowest score a person could make to be in the top 5% of the population of all persons taking this test?

Chapter 7

Multiple Choice Questions

1. For the standard normal variable z, $P(-1.1 < z < .85)$ equals

   (a) .6666
   (b) .3032
   (c) .3643
   (d) .9380.

2. For the standard normal variable z, the value of z, say z_0, such that $P(-z_0 < z < z_0) = .9010$ is

   (a) -.02
   (b) 1.65
   (c) 2.01
   (d) .4505.

3. If x has a normal distribution with mean of 10 and standard deviation of 4, $P(x \geq 16)$ equals

   (a) .4332
   (b) .4987
   (c) .0013
   (d) .0668.

4. If x has a binomial distribution with $n = 100$ and $p = .5$, we compute $P(x \geq 80)$ using the normal approximation to the binomial distribution by computing

   (a) $P(z \geq (81.5 - 80)/5)$
   (b) $P(z \geq (80 - 50)/5)$
   (c) $P(z \geq (79.5 - 50)/25)$
   (d) $P(z \geq (79.5 - 50)/5)$.

5. Assume that the number of 45 rpm records produced by Warmer Brothers per day follows a normal distribution with mean of 5000 and standard deviation of 100. What is the probability that 5455 or more records are produced in one day?

   (a) Approximately 1
   (b) Approximately 0
   (c) .9980
   (d) This probability cannot be determined.

6. In a normal distribution, 95.44% of the data are contained within the limits

   (a) $\mu \pm .5\sigma$
   (b) $\mu \pm \sigma$
   (c) $\mu \pm 2\sigma$
   (d) $\mu \pm 3\sigma$.

7. If x is a normal random variable with $\sigma = 5$ and the value $x = 10$ corresponds to a z-value of $z = -3.4$, the value of the mean of x, μ, is

   (a) 7
   (b) -27
   (c) -7
   (d) -29.

8. A normal distribution is symmetric about its

   (a) mean
   (b) median
   (c) mode
   (d) all of the above.

9. If x is a normally distributed random variable, then $P(20 \le x \le 30.5)$ equals

   (a) $P(20 < x \le 30.5)$
   (b) $P(20 \le x < 30.5)$
   (c) $P(20 < x < 30.5)$
   (d) all of the above.

10. The normal distribution may be used to approximate the binomial distribution in the case where

    (a) $n = 3,\ p = .5$
    (b) $n = 50,\ p = .4$
    (c) $n = 20,\ p = .2$
    (d) all of the above cases.

Chapter 7

Answers to Problems

1. (a) $.5 - .4750 = .0250$

   (b) $.5 - .4931 = .0069$

   (c) $.4838$

   (d) $.5 - .2734 = .2266$

   (e) $.4929 - .4726 = .0203$

   (f) $.5 + .4988 = .9988$

   (g) $.1736 + .0832 = .2568$

2. (a) $z_o = 1.48$

   (b) $z_o = -2.31$

   (c) $z_o = -2.53$

   (d) $z_o = 1.56$

   (e) $z_o = 1.78$

   (f) $z_o = -2$

3. (a)

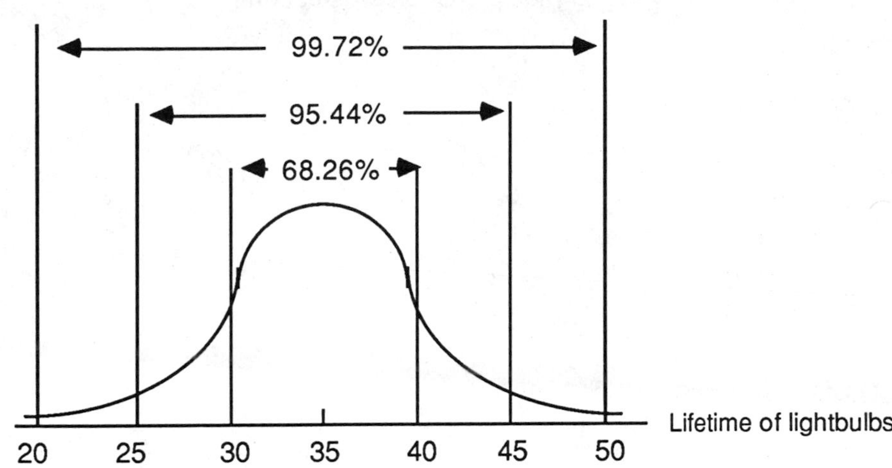

(b) .3413

(c) .0014

(d) a = 25, b = 45

4. ($\mu = 40, \sigma = 4.8890$) $P(x_B \leq 30) \approx P(x_N \leq 30.5) = P(z \leq -1.94) = .0262$

5. $P(78 < x < 82) = P(-.5 < z < .17) = .2590$

6. Lowest score = $x = (1.645)(30) + 120 = 169.35$

Chapter 7

Answers to Multiple Choice Questions

1. a
2. b
3. d
4. d
5. b
6. c
7. b
8. d
9. d
10. b

Chapter 8
SAMPLING AND SAMPLING DISTRIBUTIONS

WHAT AM I LEARNING?

Chapter Outline and Summary

The process of gathering data or of obtaining results from several performances of an experiment with chance outcomes is called *sampling*. Recall that the complete collection of data under consideration is called the *population* and a subset or portion of the population is called a *sample*. The primary objective of sampling is to select a sample that is representative of the population being studied. It is then that the conclusions of sampling theory and statistical inference are valid.

One way in which a representative sample may be obtained is by a process called *simple random sampling.* A simple random sample of size n chosen from a population of size N is a sample selected such that each possible sample of size n has the same probability of being selected. Procedures for simple random sampling can involve selecting the entire sample in one random drawing or selecting the items for the sample one at a time. Samples can also be chosen in such a way that the sampling is with or without replacement. Sampling where each member of a population may be chosen more than once is called *sampling with replacement.* If each member cannot be chosen more than once, the sampling is called *sampling without replacement.* Unless mentioned otherwise, sampling without replacement is assumed throughout the text.

After the sample values have been obtained in the simple random sample, the resulting values are summarized by one or more of the methods of descriptive statistics that we have studied in previous chapters. These characteristics of the sample that are obtained (that is, the sample mean, sample variance, and so forth) are called *sample statistics*. They are used to make inferences about the (unknown) characteristics of the population which are called *population parameters*. This chapter considers the statistical procedure of using the sample mean $\bar{x}$ to make inferences about the population mean μ.

When we consider all possible samples of size n which can be drawn from a given population and compute, for each sample, a statistic, the value of that statistic will vary from sample to sample. The *sampling distribution* of this statistic is the probability distribution for all possible values of that statistic. If, for example, the particular statistic used is the sample mean, the probability distribution for all possible values of $\bar{x}$ is called the *sampling distribution of the sample mean* or equivalently, the sampling distribution of $\bar{x}$.

We can then compute the mean, variance, standard deviation, etc. for this sampling distribution. Using the notation $E(\bar{x})$ to denote the mean of all the possible $\bar{x}$ values, it can be shown that this expected value of the sample mean is equal to the population mean μ. In other words, the center of the sampling distribution of the sample mean is the same as the center of the distribution of the population.

A measure of the variability in the sampling distribution of $\bar{x}$ is the standard deviation of $\bar{x}$. The *standard error of the mean* is another name for the standard deviation of $\bar{x}$, denoted by $\sigma_{\bar{x}}$. The exact form of the standard deviation depends on how large the sample size is relative to the size of the population. Populations are either *finite* or *infinite.* (A finite population in which sampling is done with replacement can theoretically be considered infinite.) When a population is finite with size N and the sample size n is "large" relative to the size of the population (that is, $n/N > .05$) a quantity called the *finite population correction factor* should be used to compute $\sigma_{\bar{x}}$ because it will give a more accurate estimate. In this case, formula [2] of this Guide gives the appropriate expression for $\sigma_{\bar{x}}$. When the sample size is "small" relative to the population size (that is, for very large or infinite populations such that $n/N \le .05$) the value of the finite population correction factor is so close to 1 that it does not appreciably affect the value of the standard deviation of the sample mean. In such cases, formula [3] of this Guide should be used to calculate $\sigma_{\bar{x}}$. (If a population size is not given in a problem, you may make the assumption that the population is large relative to the sample size and not use the finite population correction factor.)

In addition to knowing the mean and the standard deviation of the sampling distribution of the sample mean, there is one more piece of information that is needed to the form of the probability distribution - it's shape. Two theorems that allow us to determine the shape of the sampling distribution of $\bar{x}$ are stated below as they apply to the sampling distribution of the sample mean:

> Whenever the population being sampled has a normal probability distribution, the sampling distribution of $\bar{x}$ is a normal probability distribution for *any* sample size.
>
> In selecting simple random samples of size n from a population with mean μ and standard deviation σ, the sampling distribution of $\bar{x}$ approaches a

normal probability distribution with mean μ and standard deviation $\sigma / \sqrt{n}$ as the sample size becomes large. *(The Central Limit Theorem)*

General statistical practice is to use the "rule of thumb": $n \geq 30$ to mean a "large" sample size to satisfy the large sample size condition of the Central Limit Theorem.

Simple random samples may be selected in a variety of ways. One useful method is to select simple random samples from populations in a one-at-a-time fashion using *random numbers*. Random number tables contain the ten digits 0, 1, 2, 3, . . . , 8, 9 in groups, thus forming random numbers, whereby the digit appearing in any position in the random number table is a random selection of the possible digits with each digit having an equal chance of occurring. One such table of random numbers appears in Table 8.5 of the Anderson/Sweeney/Williams text. In order to use the random numbers in the table, enter the table at an arbitrary point and then select the required number of digits by moving systematically down a column or across a row of the table. Since the numbers selected from the table are random, this procedure guarantees that each item in the population has the same probability of being included in the sample. Thus the sample selected will be a simple random sample.

The definition given earlier for a simple random sample uses a population size N. In the case of an infinite population, this definition must be restated: A simple random sample from an infinite population is a sample selected such that each item selected comes from the same population, and each item is selected independently.

There are many ways of selecting samples from a population, and sampling methods other than simple random sampling offer alternatives that in some situations have advantages over simple random sampling. *Stratified random sampling* involves dividing the population into subgroups (strata) of similar items and then using simple random sampling within each subgroup. The best results are obtained whenever the elements within each stratum are as much alike as possible. The more alike the items in each stratum, the smaller is the size of the sample needed.

To get a *cluster sample* the population is first divided into separate groups of elements called clusters and a simple random sample of the clusters is then taken. Ideally, each cluster could be regarded as a mini-population, and cluster sampling tends to provide best results whenever the elements within the clusters are not alike. Cluster sampling generally requires a larger total sample size than either stratified or simple random sampling.

Systematic sampling may be used to eliminate the sometimes tedious and time consuming method of simple random sampling for very large populations. A list of the items in the population is required. If the items on the list are in no particular order, systematic sampling can produce a random sample by sampling every (N/n)th item on the list. The first item should be randomly chosen.

All the sampling methods thus far are *probability sampling* techniques. This means that the probability of selecting any item in the population for use in the sample is known before the sample is taken. Therefore, the amount of sampling variability can be determined. There are some cases where *nonprobability sampling* techniques may be of use. Such a method is called *convenience sampling.* Items are included in the sample primarily because they are conveniently available. Another nonprobability sampling technique is known as *judgment sampling.* In this type of sampling procedure the idea is that a person familiar with the population might be able to specify which items are most representative of the population. The quality of the sample results is dependent on the judgment of the person selecting the sample. Samples selected by nonprobability sampling may provide good results in some cases, but there is no way of measuring how representative of the population they are or how reliable they are. Thus, if these methods are used, the experimenter should be very cautious.

The following chart provides a summary of sampling techniques presented in this chapter:

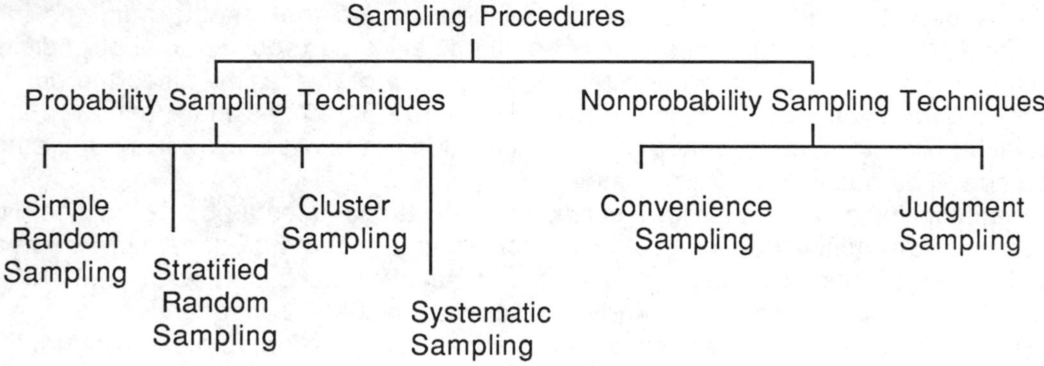

Chapter 8

WHICH FORMULA SHOULD I USE?

Formulas

When:

determining the mean of the distribution of the sample mean for samples taken from a population with mean μ

Use:

$$\text{Mean of } \bar{x} = E(\bar{x}) = \mu \qquad [1]$$

When:

determining the standard deviation of the sample mean $\bar{x}$ for a sample of size n chosen from a population of size N where the standard deviation of the population being sampled is σ

and $n/N > .05$

Use:

$$\text{Standard Deviation of } \bar{x} = \sigma_{\bar{x}} = \sqrt{\frac{N - n}{N - 1}}\,\frac{\sigma}{\sqrt{n}} \qquad [2]$$

When:

determining the standard deviation of the sample mean $\bar{x}$ for a sample of size n chosen from a population of size N where the standard deviation of the population being sampled is σ

and $n/N \leq .05$

Use:

$$\text{Standard Deviation of } \bar{x} = \sigma_{\bar{x}} = \frac{\sigma}{\sqrt{n}} \qquad [3]$$

When:

(a) finding probabilities for the sample mean $\bar{x}$ for a sample of size n chosen from a population of size N where the standard deviation of the population being sampled is σ,

(b) $n/N > .05$, and

(c) either $n \geq 30$ <u>or</u> the population is normally distributed

Use:

$$z = \frac{\bar{x} - \mu}{\sigma_{\bar{x}}} = \frac{\bar{x} - \mu}{\sqrt{\frac{N - n}{N - 1}} \frac{\sigma}{\sqrt{n}}} \qquad [4]$$

When:

(a) finding probabilities for the sample mean $\bar{x}$ for a sample of size n chosen from a population of size N where the standard deviation of the population being sampled is σ,

(b) $n/N \leq .05$, and

(c) either $n \geq 30$ <u>or</u> the population is normally distributed

Use:

$$z = \frac{\bar{x} - \mu}{\sigma_{\bar{x}}} = \frac{\bar{x} - \mu}{\frac{\sigma}{\sqrt{n}}} \qquad [5]$$

HERE'S HOW IT'S DONE!

Examples

1. The following hospitals have agreed to participate in a joint research program aimed at improving doctor-patient relationships:

Mercy Hospital	Pine Valley Hospital
General Hospital	Piedmont Hospital
Capital Hospital	Ashley Hospital

(a) Four different hospitals are to be selected from this group for participation. The nature of the research program is such that the order in which the hospitals are selected is immaterial. How many samples of size 4 are possible? List the samples.

<u>Solution</u>:

(a) Since we are told that four different hospitals are to be selected, the sampling is without replacement. (That is, is is not possible to choose the same hospital more than once.)

Also, since the order in which the hospital are selected is immaterial, a selection

Mercy, General, Ashley, Capital

is the same selection as

General, Mercy, Capital, Ashley

which is the same as

Capital, General, Ashley, Mercy, and so forth.

Thus, two samples are different only if they contain at least one different hospital.

The number of samples of size 4 could be obtained by counting the samples after you have listed them. It is a good idea to try to determine this number by a formula, if possible, to make sure you have not omitted any in your listing.

Formula [6] of Chapter 6 (page 142 of this Guide) is applicable to find the number of possible samples in this situation. Thus, we have the number of possible sample of size 4 chosen from the population of size 6 as

$$\frac{6!}{4!\,(6-4)!} = \frac{6(5)(4)(3)(2)(1)}{4(3)(2)(1)(2)(1)} = \frac{30}{2} = \underline{15}.$$

The possible samples of size 4 are

Mercy, General, Capital, Pine Valley
Mercy, General, Capital, Ashley
Mercy, General, Pine Valley, Ashley
General, Capital, Pine Valley, Piedmont
General, Capital, Piedmont, Ashley
General, Pine Valley, Piedmont, Ashley
Mercy, Capital, Pine Valley, Ashley
Mercy, Pine Valley, Piedmont, Ashley.
Mercy, General, Capital, Piedmont
Mercy, General, Pine Valley, Piedmont
Mercy, General, Piedmont, Ashley
General, Capital, Pine Valley, Ashley
Capital, Pine Valley, Piedmont, Ashley
Mercy, Capital, Pine Valley, Piedmont
Mercy, Capital, Piedmont, Ashley

(b) Using simple random sampling, what is the probability each possible sample will be selected?

Solution:

(b) For each sample to have the same probability of being selected, as the definition of simple random sampling states, we must have the probability of choosing each one of the above samples equal to 1/15.

(c) Give one procedure that would constitute simple random sampling for this problem.

Solution:

(c) A table of random numbers could be used. For this small a population, though, the most efficient procedure would be to write the names of the hospitals on identical slips of paper and place the slips in a bowl (or hat or bag). After thoroughly mixing the slips, a person would, without looking at the slips, choose one slip. The remaining slips would be again mixed, and another slip chosen. This procedure would be continued until 4 slips (hospitals) are chosen.

(d) What is the probability that Pine Valley Hospital will be one of the hospitals chosen for participation?

Solution:

(d) Looking at all the possible samples, we see that Pine Valley Hospital is included in 10 of the samples. Since the samples are equally likely, the probability that one of the chosen hospitals is Pine Valley Hospital is 10/15 = 2/3.

2. On a table are 5 identical boxes. One box contains a quarter, one contains a dime, one a nickel, one a penny, and one a Susan B. Anthony dollar. Let the variable x be the monetary value, in cents, of the coin inside the box. We have the following description of this population.

Box	Value of box in cents (x)
1	25
2	10
3	5
4	1
5	100

(a) Find the mean and variance for this population.

Solution:

(a) Using the formulas for the population mean (formula [2] on page 55 of this Guide) and variance (formula [7] on page 56 of this Guide) that were presented in Chapter 3, we have for N = 5

$$\mu = \frac{\Sigma x}{n} = \frac{25 + 10 + 5 + 1 + 100}{5} = \frac{141}{5} = \underline{28.2} \text{ cents}$$

$$\sigma^2 = \frac{\Sigma x^2 - (\Sigma x)^2 / N}{N} = \frac{10751 - (141)^2 / 5}{5} = \underline{1354.96}$$

cents squared.

(b) Two boxes are to be chosen from this population, and the amount of money in each box is considered. How many simple random samples are possible?

Solution:

(b) We are not told how the boxes are chosen, so we will assume the sampling is done without replacement and without regard to order. Again using formula [6] of Chapter 6, we have the number of simple random samples as

$$5! / (2!\,3!) = 20/2 = \underline{10}.$$

(c) List all simple random samples of size 2, and compute the sample mean for each of these samples.

Solution:

(c)

Boxes Selected in Sample	Probability of Sample	Sample Mean ($\bar{x}$)
1 and 2	1/10	(25 + 10)/2 = 17.5
1 and 3	1/10	(25 + 5)/2 = 15
1 and 4	1/10	(25 + 1)/2 = 13
1 and 5	1/10	(25 + 100)/2 = 62.5
2 and 3	1/10	(10 + 5)/2 = 7.5
2 and 4	1/10	(10 + 1)/2 = 5.5
2 and 5	1/10	(10 + 100)/2 = 55
3 and 4	1/10	(5 + 1)/2 = 3
3 and 5	1/10	(5 + 100)/2 = 52.5
4 and 5	1/10	(1 +100)/2 = 50.5

(d) Compute the mean of the sampling distribution of $\bar{x}$ using the sample means you obtained in part c). Compare your answer to the answer obtained for the population mean in part a) of this problem.

Solution:

(d) Recall that the sampling distribution of $\bar{x}$ is the probability distribution for all possible values of the sample mean. The second and third columns in the answer to part c) above give the probability distribution of $\bar{x}$. Thus, to find the mean of the sampling distribution of $\bar{x}$, we use this data and formula [3], found on page 141, of Chapter 6.

$$E(\bar{x}) = \Sigma\, \bar{x}\, f(\bar{x}) = 282/10 = \underline{28.2}\,.$$

Comparing this with the answer found for the mean of the population, μ, in part a) of this problem, we see that $E(\bar{x}) = \mu$ as is guaranteed in formula [1] of this chapter.

(e) Which formula in Chapter 6 would you use to compute, from the data in part c), the standard deviation of the sampling distribution of the sample mean?

Solution:

(e) For the same reasons mentioned with the mean above, formula [5] on page 141 of Chapter 6 would be the appropriate formula. Once this variance is computed, the standard deviation would be obtained by taking the square root of the variance.

(f) Which formula in this chapter would you use to compute the standard deviation of the distribution of the sample mean? Use the formula to find $\sigma_{\bar{x}}$.

For this problem, $N = 5$ and $n = 2$. Thus, since $n/N = .40 > .05$, formula [2] of this chapter should be used. Using that formula, we have (the value of σ is obtained from part a) of this problem)

$$\sigma_{\bar{x}} = \sqrt{\frac{N - n}{N - 1}}\ \frac{\sigma}{\sqrt{n}} = \sqrt{\frac{5 - 2}{5 - 1}}\ \frac{\sqrt{1354.96}}{\sqrt{2}} = (.8660)(26.0285) = \underline{22.54}.$$

3. Suppose samples of size 3 had been chosen from the 5 boxes in example 2. How would the values of $E(\bar{x})$ and $\sigma_{\bar{x}}$ found in example 2 change?

Solution:

Formula [1], which is used to find $E(\bar{x})$ makes no mention of sample size. Thus, we still have $E(\bar{x}) = \mu = 28.2$ for samples of size 3 chosen from this population.

Since $n/N = 3/5 = .60 > .05$, formula [2] is again the one to use to find $\sigma_{\bar{x}}$:

$$\sigma_{\bar{x}} = \sqrt{\frac{N - n}{N - 1}}\ \frac{\sigma}{\sqrt{n}} = \sqrt{\frac{5 - 3}{5 - 1}}\ \frac{\sqrt{1354.96}}{\sqrt{2}} = (.7071)(26.0285) = \underline{18.40}.$$

Notice that for samples of size 3, $\sigma_{\bar{x}}$ is smaller than for samples of size 2. Thus, the graph of the sampling distribution of $\bar{x}$ is taller and narrower for samples of size 3 than for samples of size 2. The reason for this is that with larger samples, more information is obtained about the population. Therefore, the resulting deviation of the values from the mean is less than with smaller samples.

4. For each of the following situations, give the shape of the distribution of the sample mean and the mean and variance of the distribution of the sample mean.

(a) The infinite population is of unknown shape with a mean of 16.25 and a variance of 5. A simple random sample of size 100 is chosen from this population.

Solution:

(a) Since $n = 100$, the Central Limit Theorem assures us that the shape of the distribution of the sample mean, $\bar{x}$, is approximately normal.

Formula [1] gives the mean of $\bar{x}$ as $\mu =$ 16.25.

Formula [3] gives the standard deviation of $\bar{x}$. We are asked for the variance which can be obtained by squaring the value in formula [3]. Thus, the variance of the distribution of $\bar{x}$ is $\sigma^2/n = 5/100 =$ .05.

(b) A random sample of size 64 is chosen from a binomial population of size 10,000 with mean of $\mu = 20$ and standard deviation $\sigma = 10$.

Solution:

(b) Again, since $n = 64$, the Central Limit Theorem assures us that the shape of the distribution of the sample mean, $\bar{x}$, is approximately normal even though the population is binomially distributed.

Formula [1] gives the mean of $\bar{x}$ as 20.

Since $n/N = 64/10000 < .05$, formula [3] gives the standard deviation of $\bar{x}$ as $10/8 =$ 1.25.

(c) A random sample of size 25 is chosen from a very large normal population. The population mean and variance are, respectively, 18 and 25.

Solution:

(c) Since the population is normal, we know that the distribution of the sample mean is normal. Again using formulas [1] and [3], we find the mean and standard deviation of the sample mean $\bar{x}$ to be 18 and 5/5 = 1, respectively.

(d) A population of unknown shape has a known mean of 150.68 and standard deviation of 8. The population size is 500. A simple random sample of size 100 is chosen from this population.

Solution:

(d) Even though the population is of unknown shape, the sample size is over 30 and therefore large enough for the Central Limit Theorem to apply. Thus, the sample mean has an approximately normal distribution. Formula [1] gives us the mean of the distribution of the sample mean as 150.68.

For this example, n/N = 100/500 = .20 > .05. Thus, we need to use formula [2] to find the standard deviation of the sample mean. It gives

$$\sigma_{\bar{x}} = \sqrt{\frac{N - n}{N - 1}}\,\frac{\sigma}{\sqrt{n}} = \sqrt{\frac{500 - 100}{499}}\,\frac{8}{\sqrt{100}} = .8953(.8) = \underline{.72}.$$

(e) A very large population of unknown shape has a mean of 50 and a standard deviation of 10. We need to choose a sample from this population for testing purposes. Due to the destructive nature of the testing, a small random sample, of size 5, is chosen.

Solution:

We do not know that the population is normal, and $n < 30$. Thus, neither of the theorems we have available to determine the shape of the distribution of the sample mean apply. Thus, the sampling distribution of $\bar{x}$ is of unknown shape.

Formulas [1], [2], and [3] do not require a specific shape for the population or the distribution of the sample mean. Therefore, they are still applicable. Formula [1] gives the mean of the sampling distribution of $\bar{x}$ as 50.

Since the sample size is small relative to the (large) population size, formula [3] gives $\sigma_{\bar{x}} = 10/2.2361 = \underline{4.47}$.

5. Due to problems with foam during the filling process, beer bottles are not always filled to capacity. A certain brewery advertises that their bottles contain, on the average, 12 ounces of beer. A random sample of 100 bottles off their production line is taken in order to test the mean fill of the bottles. It is known that the population standard deviation is 0.4 ounce.

(a) What are the expected value and standard deviation of $\bar{x}$?

Solution:

(a) Using formulas [1] and [3], we obtain

$$E(\bar{x}) = \underline{12} \quad \text{and} \quad \sigma_{\bar{x}} = \sigma/\sqrt{n} = .4/10 = \underline{0.04}.$$

(b) What probability distribution can be used to approximate the sampling distribution of $\bar{x}$?

Solution:

(b) The shape of the distribution of the fills of the bottles (population) is not known. However, we do not need to know this to answer the question since the sample size is large. Thus, by the Central Limit Theorem, the shape of the sampling distribution of $\bar{x}$ is approximately normal.

(c) Sketch a graph of the distribution of the sample mean fills for this problem.

Solution:

(c) Sketching a distribution for $\bar{x}$ that is approximately normal, we place the expected value (mean) of the distribution at the center. We also calculate the endpoints of the intervals $E(\bar{x}) = \mu \pm \sigma$, $\mu \pm 2\sigma$, and $\mu \pm 3\sigma$ and place these values on the graph to describe the distribution.

Note: Since $\sigma_{\bar{x}} = .04$ is very small, the graph of the sampling distribution of the sample mean will be tall and narrow.

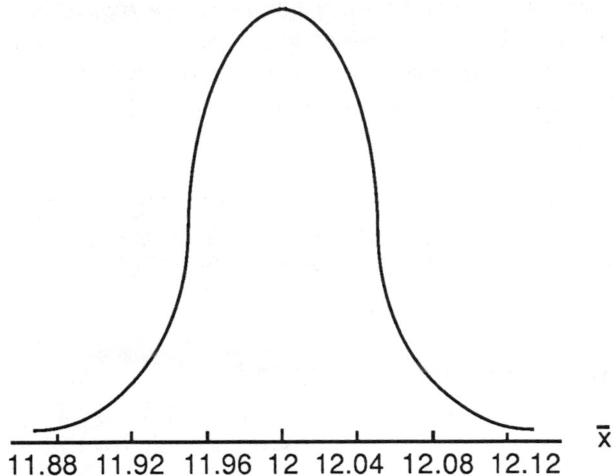

(d) Suppose the result of the random sample of 100 bottles taken in this problem was $\bar{x} = 11.9$ ounces. Do you believe the brewery's claim that their bottles contain an average of 12 ounces of beer?

Solution:

(d) Looking at the above graph, we see that the value of 11.9 is between 2 and 3 standard deviations away from the claimed mean of 12 ounces. Using the results of the last chapter, we can place the following percentages on the graph.

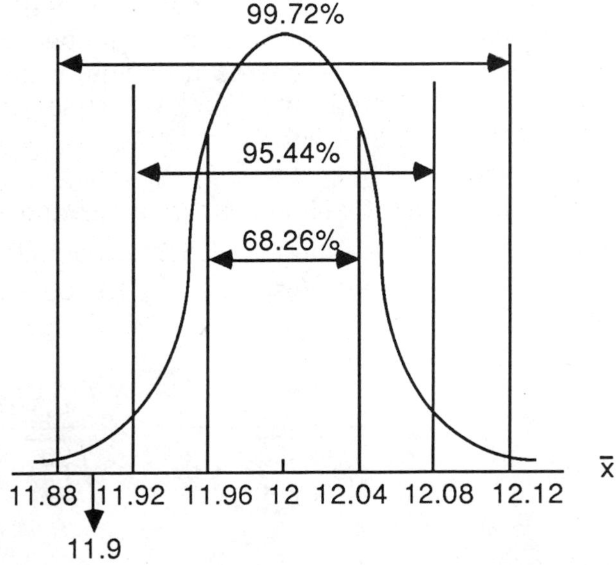

Thus, only 2.28% of the time would we expect to find a sample mean lower than 11.92 ounces when the brewer's claim that $\mu = 12$ ounces is true. This result is possible, but not very probable. Exact methods for working a problem such as this one will be covered in the next chapter.

6. The Rub-A-Dub Company manufacturers washing machines that have a mean life of 4.5 years with a standard deviation of 1.2 years. What is the probability that the mean life of a sample of 36 of these washing machines will be less than 4 years?

<u>Solution</u>:

We are given $\mu = 4.5$, $\sigma = 1.2$, and $n = 36$. We do not know the distribution of the population, but we do not need to because of the Central Limit Theorem. Since the sample size is large enough, we know that the sampling distribution of $\bar{x}$ is approximately normal. Since we are not given a population size, we assume it is large relative to the sample size and use formula [5] to find the probability.

$$\text{Since} \quad z = \frac{\bar{x} - \mu}{\sigma_{\bar{x}}} = \frac{\bar{x} - \mu}{\frac{\sigma}{\sqrt{n}}} = \frac{4 - 4.5}{\frac{1.2}{6}} = \frac{-.5}{.2} = -2.5,$$

$P(\bar{x} < 4) = P(z < -2.5) = .5 - .4938 = \underline{.0062}$.

7. The owner of a small business is examining his records and calculating the number of days between billing and payment of the charge accounts on his books. He knows that the mean and standard deviation of this normally distributed population of 100 charge accounts are 18 days and 4 days, respectively. If he takes a simple random sample of 10 of these charge accounts, what is the probability that the mean time between billing and payment for the sample will be less than 16 days?

<u>Solution</u>:

For this problem, $n = 10$, $N = 100$, $\mu = 18$, and $\sigma^2 = 4$. We are asked to find $P(\bar{x} < 16)$. Since the population is normally distributed, the sampling distribution of $\bar{x}$ is normal. Also, $n/N = 10/100 = .10 > .05$. Hence, we use formula [4] to find $P(\bar{x} < 16)$.

$$z = \frac{\bar{x} - \mu}{\sigma_{\bar{x}}} = \frac{\bar{x} - \mu}{\sqrt{\frac{N - n}{N - 1}}\ \frac{\sigma}{\sqrt{n}}} = \frac{16 - 18}{\sqrt{\frac{90}{99}}\ \frac{2}{\sqrt{10}}} = \frac{-2}{.603} = -3.32\,.$$

Thus, $P(\bar{x} < 16) = P(z < -3.32) = .5 - .5 = \underline{0}$.

Note: The answer of zero for this probability does not mean that the owner will not have anyone paying less than 16 days after being billed. The probability above was calculated for the distribution of mean time between billing and paying. Also, the answer of zero is actually interpreted as a value that is so small that it rounds off to zero when using four-decimal place accuracy from Table I.

8. Plastic bags used for packaging produce are manufactured in such a way that the breaking strength of the bags are normally distributed with a mean of 5 pounds per square inch and a standard deviation of 2 pounds per square inch. The results of a recent survey stated that the standard error of the mean was calculated to be 0.5.

(a) How large a sample was used to obtain the results of the survey?

Solution:

(a) Recall that the standard error of the mean is $\sigma_{\bar{x}}$. Thus, we are given that $\sigma_{\bar{x}} = .5$. We also know from the statement of the problem that $\mu = 5$ and $\sigma = 2$. Assuming that the population size is very large compared to the sample size, we use formula [3] to obtain $.5 = 2/\sqrt{n}$ or $\sqrt{n} = 2/.5 = 4$.

Thus, a sample size of $n = \underline{16}$ was used.

(b) For samples of size 16 chosen from this population, what is the probability that the mean breaking strength of the bags in the sample will be between 6 and 8.5 pounds per square inch ?

Solution:

(b) Even though the sample size is small, we know that the sampling distribution of the sample mean is normal because the population is normally distributed. Thus, using formula [5] to convert the sample mean values of 6 and 8.5 to z, we have

$$P(6 < x < 8.5) = P(\frac{6-5}{.5} < z < \frac{8.5-5}{.5}) = P(2 < z < 7) =$$

$$.5 - .4772 = \underline{.0228.}$$

9. Show how to use Table 6 of Appendix B of the Anderson/Sweeney/Williams text to select a simple random sample of size 15 from a population of size 800. Assume the population has been numbered 1 - 800.

Solution:

The starting point we choose in the table is arbitrary. The direction we proceed (horizontally or vertically) is also arbitrary. Therefore, let us just choose to begin with the fifth row of Table 6 and proceed horizontally. The fifth and sixth rows of the table are reproduced below:

55363	07449	34835	15290	76616	67191	12777	21861	68689	03263
69393	92785	49902	58447	42048	30378	87618	26933	40640	16281

Let us choose to begin with the second number in row 5 (07449). Since the population is numbered from 1 - 800, we need only three digits of each of the above numerals. Any three could be chosen, but let us just say we will pick the first 3 digits. Also, any values obtained from this table greater than 800 will be discarded since they do not apply to our population. Proceeding horizontally, we obtain the following numbers to choose from the population for our simple random sample of size 15:

74, 348, 152, 766, 671, 127, 218, 686, 32, 693, 499, 584, 420, 303, 269.

10. A manufacturer of whistles sends every hundredth whistle it manufacturers to quality control for testing. What type of sampling is being used here?

Solution:

This is systematic, not simple random, sampling. One problem that may arise with this type of sampling procedure is that the machine that manufacturers the whistles may have a cyclic defect that causes trouble on every hundredth whistle (in which case many defective items would be sampled) or on every thirty-fifth whistle (in which case very few, if any, defective whistles would be found).

Chapter 8

HAVE I LEARNED THE MATERIAL?

Problems

1. For each of the following give
   1) the shape of the sampling distribution of $\bar{x}$,
   2) the standard deviation of the distribution of $\bar{x}$,
   3) the expected value of the distribution of $\bar{x}$.

   (a) A simple random sample of size 49 is chosen from a binomial population whose mean is 10 and whose standard deviation is 7.

   (b) A normal population has a mean of 3.3 and a standard deviation of 8. A random sample of size 16 is chosen from this population.

   (c) A simple random sample of size 100 is chosen from a large population of unknown shape. The mean and the variance of the population are, respectively, 5 and 9.

(d) A random sample of size 64 is chosen from a population that is symmetrical, but not normal in shape. There are 400 items in this population. The mean of the population is known to be 35 and the population standard deviation is known to be 10.

(e) A simple random sample of size 25 is chosen from a population whose shape is not normal. The population is of size 1000 with mean of 8.2 and variance of 100.

2. Is the following a sampling procedure that would yield a simple random sample? Explain why not if a simple random sample is not obtained.

   A statistical society is interested in the number of technical papers written by all college instructors with the rank of assistant professor or higher in the last 4 years. It sends a questionnaire to all members of the society, and bases its estimate on the replies received.

3. The daily wages of workers in a particular industry are normally distributed with a mean of \$97 and a standard deviation of \$13.20. If a random sample of size 36 is taken, what is the probability that the mean daily wage of the workers in the sample will be less than \$92?

4. A population consists of four numbers: 2, 4, 5, and 7.

   (a) List all possible samples of size 2 that can be taken from this population when it is sampled one-at-a-time with replacement, taking the order of selection into consideration.

   (b) List all possible samples of size 2 that can be taken from this population when it the entire sample is selected in one random drawing.

5. For each situation below, answer the following two questions:

   (1) What is the name of the sampling procedure that is being used?
   (2) Is the procedure a technique of probability or nonprobability sampling?

(a) We take a random sample of 40 of the 4000 female students and a random sample of 60 of the 6000 male students at a certain university and measure the height of each student in order to determine the average height of the 10,000 students attending the university.

(b) An investor, trying to decide on which stock broker to use, calls 5 of his friends who have been successful in stock investments for recommendations of brokers.

(c) A numbered list contains 8500 names and telephone numbers. You use a random number table to obtain a sample of 100 names from this list.

(d) We wish to determine the percentage of all registered voters who are Republicans in cities with populations under 10,000 in the state of South Carolina. We decide to take a random sample of 20 of these cities.

(e) To determine if their product meets weight specifications, a bakery measures the weight of every 75th loaf of bread coming out of the ovens. The first loaf of bread was randomly selected from the first group of 75 loaves.

6. The following data show the number of cats living in a population of 5 households:

Household	Number of Cats in Residence
A	2
B	1
C	4
D	1
E	0

(a) Compute the population mean μ and the population variance σ^2.

(b) If a simple random sample of four households is used to estimate the mean number of cats in residence per household, show the sampling distribution of the sample mean.

(c) What is the expected value of $\bar{x}$?

(d) What is the standard deviation of $\bar{x}$?

7. The population of the length of time (in minutes) between arrivals of buses at a certain metropolitan bus station is normally distributed and is estimate to have mean $\mu = 5$ and variance $\sigma^2 = 16$. A random sample of size 36 is chosen from this population.

(a) What is the probability that the length of time between arrivals of buses will be 9 minutes or more?

(b) What is the probability that the mean length of time between arrivals of buses will be between 2 and 8 minutes?

8. Consider all possible samples of size 2 that can be chosen from the population {3, 6, 15}. The sampling procedure is to choose the elements of the sample one-at-a-time without replacement but with regard to order of the elements.

(a) List these samples.

(b) Using simple random sampling, what is the probability of each possible sample being selected?

(c) Give the sampling distribution of the sample mean in table form and graphical form. Would you expect to be able to use a normal probability distribution to describe the sampling distribution of $\bar{x}$ in this problem?

9. The mean and standard deviation for the weight of a standard bag of potato chips are $\mu = 7$ ounces and $\sigma = 2$ ounces, respectively. Let the random variable x denote the weight of a randomly selected bag of potato chips chosen from this population.

(a) Is x discrete or continuous?

(b) Assuming the population of weights of these bags is normally distributed, draw a graph for the distribution of x.

(c) Draw a graph for the sampling distribution of $\bar{x}$, the mean weight of samples of size 4 chosen from this population.

10. Mrs. Brann has 30 cats. She wishes to take 8 of them with her to her camp in Bay St. Louis, Mississippi. She cannot decide which ones to take with her, so she decides to select a simple random sample from the population of all her cats. Assume the cats are numbered 1 through 30. Use the fourth column from the left of Table 6, beginning with the third number in this column, to obtain a simple random sample for Mrs. Brann. (Use the last two digits of each numeral in this column for your selection.)

Chapter 8

Multiple Choice Questions

1. Given a sample of size $n = 100$ chosen from an infinitely large population for which $\mu = 15$, and $\sigma^2 = 4$, the probability that the sample mean will be less than 15.5 is

   (a) .4938
   (b) .0987
   (c) .9938
   (d) not able to be computed since we do not know that the population is normally distributed.

2. A sample of 100 data values is chosen from a population of size 5000 with mean equal to 60 and standard deviation equal to 121. The mean of the sampling distribution of the sample mean equals

   (a) 100
   (b) 12.1
   (c) 60
   (d) none of these.

3. A random sample of size 64 is chosen from a population of size 1000 whose mean is 8 and whose variance is 16. The standard deviation of the sampling distribution of the sample mean is

   (a) .4840
   (b) .4685
   (c) 1.9359
   (d) .5000.

4. Using simple random sampling, the probability each possible sample will be selected when choosing samples of size 2 from a population of size 6 is

   (a) 4/9
   (b) 1/15
   (c) 1/3
   (d) none of these.

5. The standard error of the mean

   (a) decreases as the sample size increases
   (b) is smaller than the standard deviation of the population
   (c) is a measure of the variability of the sampling distribution of the sample mean
   (d) all of the above.

6. The State Highway Department wishes to sample the listings of people in the state with driver's licenses in such a way that will give each listing an equal probability of being selected. These listings are on pages of a large list and there are not an equal number of listings on each page. A procedure is suggested whereby 10 pages are selected at random and the same percentage of listings from each page is chosen by simple random sampling. This suggested procedure is an example of

   (a) stratified sampling
   (b) cluster sampling
   (c) systematic sampling
   (d) convenience sampling.

7. For samples of size $n = 20$, the sampling distribution of the sample mean will be normally distributed

   (a) whenever the population is symmetrical
   (b) regardless of the distribution of the population
   (c) if the population is normally distributed
   (d) whenever the population has a binomial distribution.

8. A simple random sample can be selected

   (a) in any way the experimenter desires
   (b) by taking every 15th item from the population
   (c) by making sure each possible sample has the same probability of being selected
   (d) by asking an expert to decide which population items should be included in the sample.

9. A random sample of size 25 is chosen from a very large population whose mean is 5 and whose standard deviation is 100. The standard error of the mean

   (a) equals 20
   (b) equals 5
   (c) equals 1
   (d) does not exist for this problem.

10. A simple random sample of size 4 is chosen from a normal population whose mean and variance are $\mu = 52$ and $\sigma = 10$. The probability that the sample mean be within one population standard deviation of the population mean is

   (a) .6826
   (b) .9544
   (c) .9972
   (d) none of these.

Chapter 8

Answers to Problems

1. (a) 1) shape is approximately normal 2) $\sigma_{\bar{x}} = 1$ 3) $E(\bar{x}) = 10$

   (b) 1) shape is normal 2) $\sigma_{\bar{x}} = 2$ 3) $E(\bar{x}) = 3.3$

   (c) 1) shape is approximately normal 2) $\sigma_{\bar{x}} = 0.3$ 3) $E(\bar{x}) = 5$

   (d) 1) shape is approximately normal 2) $\sigma_{\bar{x}} = 1.15$ 3) $E(\bar{x}) = 35$

   (e) 1) shape is unknown 2) $\sigma_{\bar{x}} = 2$ 3) $E(\bar{x}) = 8.2$

2. This is not an example of simple random sampling. In the first place, not all college professors with the rank of assistant professor or higher would be members of the society. Thus a large part of the population would be omitted. Secondly, those who have written no papers are less likely to respond to the questionnaire.

3. $P(\bar{x} < 92) = P(z < -2.27) = .5 - .4884 = \underline{.0116}$.

4. (a) (2,4), (2,5), (2,7), (4,5), (4,7), (5,7), (4,2), (5,2), (7,2), (5,4), (7,4), (7,5), (2,2), (4,4), (5,5), and (7,7)

   (b) (2,4), (2,5), (2,7), (4,5), (4,7), (5,7)

5. (a) (1) stratified sampling
   (2) probability sampling

   (b) (1) judgment sampling
   (2) nonprobability sampling

   (c) (1) simple random sampling
   (2) probability sampling

   (d) (1) cluster sampling
   (2) probability sampling

   (e) (1) systematic sampling
   (2) probability sampling

6. (a) $\mu = 8/5 = \underline{1.6}$ and $\sigma^2 = (22 - 64/5)/5 = \underline{1.84}$.

(b) There are 5 possible samples. The sampling distribution of the sample mean is obtained by first filling in the following table:

Households in Sample	Probability of Sample	Sample Mean
A, B, C, D	1/5	8/4 = 2
A, B, C, E	1/5	7/4 = 1.75
A, B, D, E	1/5	4/4 = 1
A, C, D, E	1/5	7/4 = 1.75
B, C, D, E	1/5	6/4 = 1.5

Thus , the probability distribution of the sample mean is:

Sample Mean $\bar{x}$	$f(\bar{x})$
1	1/5
1.5	1/5
1.75	2/5
2	1/5.

(c) $E(\bar{x}) = (1)(1/5) + 1.5(1/5) + 1.75(2/5) + 2(1/5) = \underline{1.6}$ or $E(\bar{x}) = \mu = \underline{1.6}$.

(d) $\sigma_{\bar{x}} = \underline{.339}$ using formula [2].

7. (a) Let the random variable x be the length of time between arrivals. Then x is given to have a normal distribution with $\mu = 5$ and $\sigma^2 = 16$. Here we are asked for $P(x \geq 9)$. Using formula [1] of Chapter 7, we have

$$P(x \geq 9) = P[z \geq (9-5)/4] = P(z \geq 1) = \underline{.1587}.$$

(b) Here we are asked for $P(2 \leq \bar{x} \leq 8)$. Since the population is normal, $\bar{x}$ has a normal distribution with mean of 5 and standard deviation of $4/6 = 2/3$. Thus,

$$P(2 \leq \bar{x} \leq 8) = P(-4.5 \leq z \leq 4.5) = .5 + .5 = \underline{1}.$$

8. (a) The samples are (3, 6), (6, 3), (3, 15), (15, 3), (6, 15), (15, 6).

   (b) 1/6

   (c) To determine the mean $\bar{x}$ of each of the samples, use the formula $\bar{x} = (\Sigma x)/n$.

Sample	(3, 6)	(6,3)	(3, 15)	(15, 3)	(6, 15)	(15, 6)
Mean of Sample	4.5	4.5	9	9	10.5	10.5

The tabular and graphical forms of the probability (sampling) distribution of $\bar{x}$ are:

$\bar{x}$	$f(\bar{x})$
4.5	1/3
9	1/3
10.5	1/3

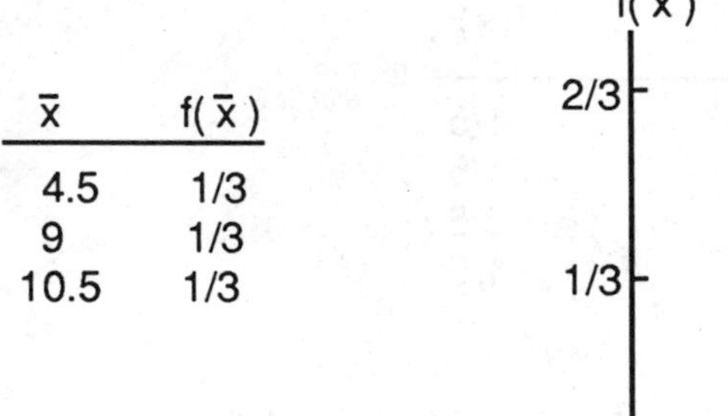

No, the normal distribution would not be appropriate to describe this graph for the sample mean, as you can see from the graph. (The Central Limit Theorem does not apply because of the small sample size, and the population is certainly not normally distributed.)

9. (a) continuous

   (b) and (c)

Note that the standard deviation of the distribution of the weights x of the bags, σ, equals 2, while the standard deviation of the mean weights of the bags, $\bar{x}$, is $\sigma_{\bar{x}} = 1$.

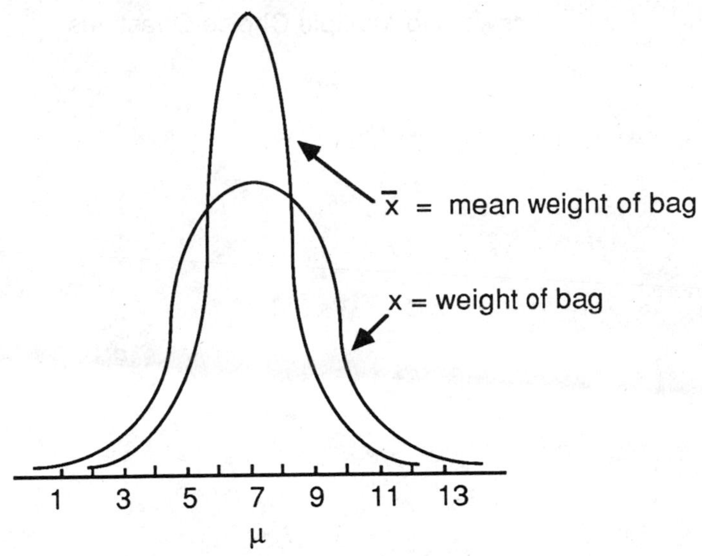

10. Mrs. Brann should take the cats numbered

11, 22, 15, 1, 28, 25, 16, and 24.

Chapter 8

Answers to Multiple Choice Questions

1. c
2. c
3. a
4. b
5. d
6. b
7. c
8. c
9. a
10. b

Chapter 9

INFERENCES ABOUT A POPULATION MEAN

WHAT AM I LEARNING?

Chapter Outline and Summary

In Chapter 1 we learned that the study of statistics is divided into two main areas: descriptive statistics and statistical inference. Statistical inference is also divided into two main areas: *estimation* and *tests of hypotheses.* In the statistical process of *estimation*, we choose a sample statistic satisfying certain requirements and use knowledge of the sampling distribution of the statistic to establish the degree of accuracy of the estimate. *Hypothesis testing* involves the formulation of a hypothesis about the population parameter of interest and a decision is made to accept or reject the hypothesis on the basis of a statistical test involving summary data about the appropriate sample statistic. The accuracy of the conclusion is again dependent upon knowledge of the sampling distribution of the sample statistic.

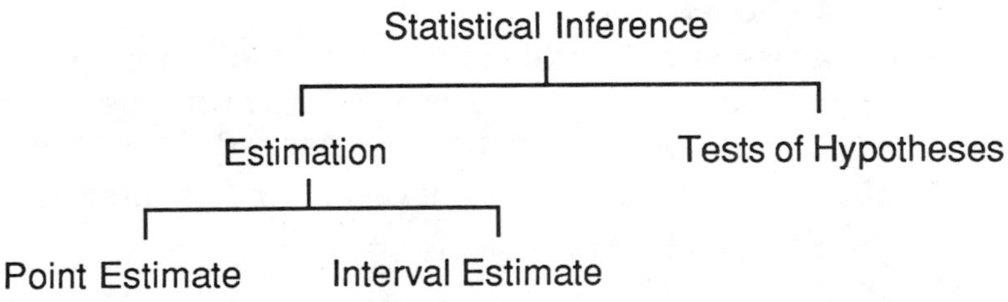

Estimation may be made by a point estimate or an interval estimate. A *point estimate* is a single value of the sample statistic used to estimate the population parameter of interest. The point estimate of the population mean μ is the sample mean $\bar{x}$. Recall that the difference between the sample mean and the population mean is called the *sampling error.* Using the notation $z_{\alpha/2}$ to represent the z value that has an area of $\alpha/2$ in the upper tail of the standard normal probability distribution, the term $e = z_{\alpha/2}(\sigma/\sqrt{n})$ denotes the bound, or maximum value, for the sampling error in using the sample mean as the point estimate of the population mean μ.

An *interval estimate* is a range of values within which the population parameter is estimated to lie. An interval estimate incorporates the degree of accuracy in the formula for the estimate. The quantity $1 - \alpha$ is called the *confidence coefficient* for an interval estimate, and we have a probability of $1 - \alpha$ of selecting a random sample that will produce an interval containing the population parameter of interest. The interval is then called a $(1 - \alpha)100\%$ *confidence interval..* A $(1 - \alpha)100\%$ confidence interval for the population mean μ is given by $\bar{x} \pm z_{\alpha/2}(\sigma/\sqrt{n})$.

When expressed as a percentage, the confidence coefficient is usually referred to as the *confidence level.* Using the table of areas for the standard normal distribution (Table I), the z values corresponding to the confidence levels can be found. Some commonly used (standard) confidence levels and the corresponding z values are

Confidence Level	Corresponding $z_{\alpha/2}$ Value
90% confidence	$z_{.05} = 1.645$
95% confidence	$z_{.025} = 1.96$
98% confidence	$z_{.01} = 2.33$
99% confidence	$z_{.005} = 2.58$

Note that as the confidence level increases, the corresponding z value also increases. Thus, the wider the confidence interval is, the more confident we are that the given interval contains the unknown parameter.

One question that arises in statistical inference is "How large a random sample is needed to achieve a desired degree of precision?" Knowing the maximum sampling error, e, that the user is willing to tolerate, the desired confidence level, and an approximate value of the population standard deviation σ, the formula for the bound on the sampling error can be solved for the sample size, n, giving $n = (z_{\alpha/2})^2 \sigma^2/e^2$. To ensure that the bounds on the sampling error are maintained, the value of n obtained from this formula is rounded up to the next highest integer.

In the area of hypothesis testing, we usually begin with a designated or hypothesized value for a population parameter. The statement involving an equality of this population parameter to the hypothesized value is called the *null hypothesis,* denoted by H_o. The direct opposite to this hypothesis, which does not overlap the value(s) specified in the null hypothesis, is called the *alternative hypothesis* and is denoted by H_1. Using μ_o as the hypothesized value for the population parameter mean μ, alternative hypotheses for tests involving the mean of one population may be one of three forms: $\mu < \mu_o$, $\mu > \mu_o$, or $\mu \neq \mu_o$. The first two forms ($\mu < \mu_o$, $\mu > \mu_o$) result in what are called *one-tail tests* of hypotheses. The form $\mu \neq \mu_o$ results in a *two-tail test* of hypothesis. These terms refer to whether we are concerned about *any* differences between the value of the sample statistic and the hypothesized value of the population parameter (two-tail tests) or only differences in a particular direction (one-tail tests). After performing the procedure of hypothesis testing, we arrive at a conclusion of accepting the null hypothesis or rejecting it.

Because hypothesis testing is based on sampling procedures, there is always the chance that an error will be made in the decision at which we arrive. The following figure summarizes the conditions under which error can be made in a hypothesis test. It also shows the situations where the hypothesis testing procedure leads to correct decisions.

		True Situation in the Popualtion	
		H_o True	H_o False
Conclusion	Accept H_o	Correct Decision	Type II Error
	Reject H_o	Type I Error	Correct Decision

We denote the probability of making a Type I error by the symbol α . Thus,

$$\alpha = P\text{ (reject } H_o \text{ when } H_o \text{ is actually true).}$$

The probability of making a Type II error is denoted by the symbol . Therefore,

$$\beta = P\text{ (accept } H_o \text{ when } H_o \text{ is actually false).}$$

The actual hypothesis testing procedure, as applied to the mean of one population, consists of the following six steps:

Step 1: State, in symbolic form, the null hypothesis. In this chapter, we will have H_o: $\mu = \mu_o$.

Step 2: State, in symbolic from, the alternative to the null hypothesis. Here, we will have $H_1: \mu > \mu_o$ or $H_1: \mu < \mu_o$ or $H_1: \mu \neq \mu_o$. The exact form is determined by the statement of the problem.

Step 3: Determine the test statistic you will use decide whether or not to reject the null hypothesis. In this chapter, you will use formula [5] or formula [7] of this Guide to determine the value of the test statistic. Which formula is used is determined by the conditions stated in the problem.

Step 4: Determine the decision rule that provides the appropriate level of significance. The probability of a Type I error, α, is called the *level of significance* for the test. The designer of the test must specify this allowable probability of making the error of falsely rejecting the null hypothesis. The *acceptance region* for the test is the region of numerical values of the test statistic for which the null hypothesis will be accepted or believed. The *rejection region* for the test is the region of numerical values of the test statistic for which the null hypothesis will be rejected. The rejection region is chosen so that the probability of a Type I error, α, is equal to the area of the rejection region. The value(s) of the test statistic that separate the acceptance region from the rejection region is called the *critical value(s)* for the test. For a one-tail test there is one critical value and the area of the rejection region would be contained in one tail of the distribution of the test statistic. In a two-tail test there are two critical values since one-half of the total area of the rejection region is in the upper tail and the other half is in the lower tail.

Step 5: Obtain the results of the experiment and use this sample information to calculate the value of the test statistic. The numerical value of the test statistic is determined by substituting the summary data obtained from the sample in either formula [5] or formula [7], whichever one was chosen in Step 3.

Step 6: Give the conclusion of the test of hypothesis.

(a) If the calculated value of the test statistic falls in the rejection region, we "reject the null hypothesis" and conclude that the alternative hypothesis is true. The probability of making an error in this decision is α.

(b) If the calculated numerical value of the test statistic falls in the acceptance region, we are lead to believe the null hypothesis is true and generally say "accept the null hypothesis". In this case, we are very careful *not* to say that we have proven the null hypothesis is true. By saying "accept H_o" we are simply indicating that we do not have sufficient evidence to reject H_0. Also, the probability of making an error in this decision is β, an unknown quantity until its value is calculated. For this reason, some people prefer to say "H_0 is not rejected" rather than "accept H_0".

Another criterion that can be used to establish a decision rule for a hypothesis test (Step 4) is called a *p value.* The p value is the probability, when the null hypothesis is true, of obtaining a difference between a sample mean $\bar{x}$ and a hypothesized value of the population mean μ that is larger than the difference actually observed. The p value criterion for hypothesis testing is

Accept H_0 if p value is greater than or equal to α

Reject H_0 if p value is less than α.

The p value and the test statistic will always provide the same hypothesis testing conclusion at the specified level of significance.

In many realistic situations, the population variance σ^2 is not known. In the *large-6 sample case* where $n \geq 30$, a good estimate of σ^2 is provided by the sample variance s^2. In this case, we replace σ by s in the formulas for z when determining confidence intervals and testing hypotheses (formulas [1] and [5] of this Guide). If the sample data, rather than the summary statistics $\bar{x}$ and s are given, we use the formula presented in Chapter 3 (repeated in this chapter as formula [2]) to find the sample mean and sample standard deviation.

In the *small-sample case* where $n < 30$, s^2 and σ^2 can differ appreciably and the replacement of σ by s is no longer valid. When the sample is drawn from a normally distributed population, the statistic $(\bar{x} - \mu) / (s/\sqrt{n})$ has what is called a *t distribution* or *Student t distribution.* The t distribution, like z, is symmetric about a mean of zero. However, the variance of t is more than that of z because t involves two variable quantities, $\bar{x}$ and s. In fact, the variance of the t distribution depends on the sample size, becoming closer to the z distribution as the sample size, n, approaches 30. Each t distribution has an associated number of *degrees of freedom* that is related to the size of the sample. For the formulas involving the t distribution in this chapter, the number of degrees of freedom of the t statistic is $n - 1$.

The t distribution is appropriate to use in *any* statistical inference concerning population means whenever the population standard deviation σ is unknown and the population is normally distributed. However, due to the fact that for samples of size 30 or more, t and z are almost identical, we usually use the z formulas with σ estimated by s to develop confidence intervals and test hypotheses. By doing this, we do not need the required assumption of a normally distributed population for the t distribution. In the small-sample case, however, we must use t.

Table 2 of Appendix B of the Anderson/Sweeney/Williams text is a table of values of the t distribution that correspond to certain selected areas in the right hand tail of the t distribution. With this table giving t values rather than areas, as did Table 1, p values are slightly more difficult to determine exactly. Consequently, p values are usually interpolated or expressed in the form of an inequality when not exactly appearing in Table 2.

WHICH FORMULA SHOULD I USE?

Formulas

When:

a) determining a $(1-\alpha)100\%$ confidence interval for a population mean μ
b) the population standard deviation σ is known <u>or</u> $s \approx \sigma$ $(n \geq 30)$
c) the population is normal <u>or</u> the Central Limit Theorem applies $(n \geq 30)$

Use:

$$\bar{x} \pm z_{\alpha/2} \frac{\sigma}{\sqrt{n}} \qquad [1]$$

When:

determining the mean $\bar{x}$ and variance s^2 of a sample of size n

Use:

$$\bar{x} = \frac{\Sigma x}{n} \quad \text{and} \quad s^2 = \frac{\Sigma x^2 - (\Sigma x)^2/n}{n-1} \qquad [2]$$

When:

determining a bound e on the value of the sampling error in using the sample mean $\bar{x}$ as a point estimate of a population mean μ

Use:

$$e = z_{\alpha/2} \frac{\sigma}{\sqrt{n}} \qquad [3]$$

When:

Finding the sample size n for interval estimation of a population mean with confidence of $(1-\alpha)100\%$ for a given bound e on the value of the sampling error

Use:

$$n = \frac{(z_{\alpha/2})^2 \sigma^2}{e^2} \qquad [4]$$

When:

a) determining the value of the test statistic in a test of hypothesis about a population mean μ
b) the population standard deviation σ is known <u>or</u> $s \approx \sigma$ $(n \geq 30)$
c) the population is normal <u>or</u> the Central Limit Theorem applies $(n \geq 30)$

Use:

$$z = \frac{\bar{x} - \mu}{\frac{\sigma}{\sqrt{n}}} \qquad [5]$$

When:

a) determining a $(1-\alpha)100\%$ confidence interval for a population mean μ
b) the population standard deviation σ is unknown
c) the population is normal

Use:

$$\bar{x} \pm t_{\alpha/2} \frac{s}{\sqrt{n}} \qquad [6]$$

where the t distribution has $n - 1$ degrees of freedom

When:

a) determining the value of the test statistic in a test of hypothesis about a population mean μ
b) the population standard deviation σ is unknown
c) the population is normal

Use:

$$t = \frac{\bar{x} - \mu}{\frac{s}{\sqrt{n}}} \qquad [7]$$

where the t distribution has $n - 1$ degrees of freedom

HERE'S HOW IT'S DONE!

Examples

1. Verify the following z values used in confidence intervals:

(a) 90% confidence: $z_{\alpha/2} = 1.645$

Solution:

(a) The confidence is 90% = $(1 - \alpha)100\%$. Thus, the confidence coefficient for this problem is $1 - \alpha = .90$. Solving for α, we have $\alpha = .10$ and thus, $\alpha/2 = .05$. Recall that $z_{\alpha/2}$ is, by definition, the point of the standard normal distribution that has $\alpha/2$ of the area to the right of that point. Thus,

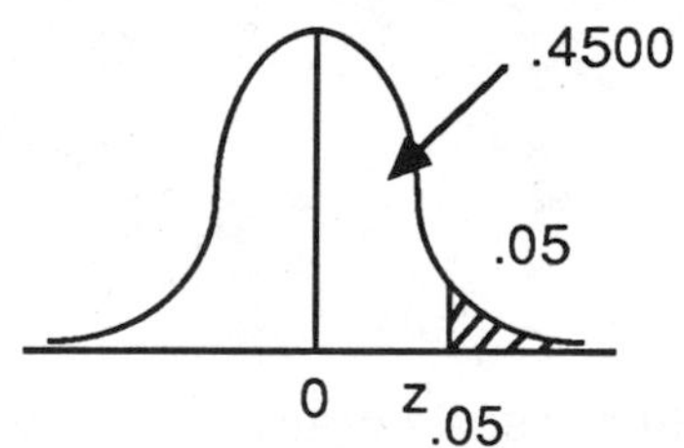

Looking in Table I for the area .4500, we find the z value corresponding to that point is midway between 1.64 and 1.65. Thus, $z_{\alpha/2} = z_{.05} = \underline{1.645}$.

(b) 98% confidence: $z_{\alpha/2} = 2.33$

Solution:

(b) The confidence is 98% = $(1 - \alpha)100\%$. Thus, the confidence coefficient for this problem is $1 - \alpha = .98$. Solving for α, we have $\alpha = .02$ and thus, $\alpha/2 = .01$.

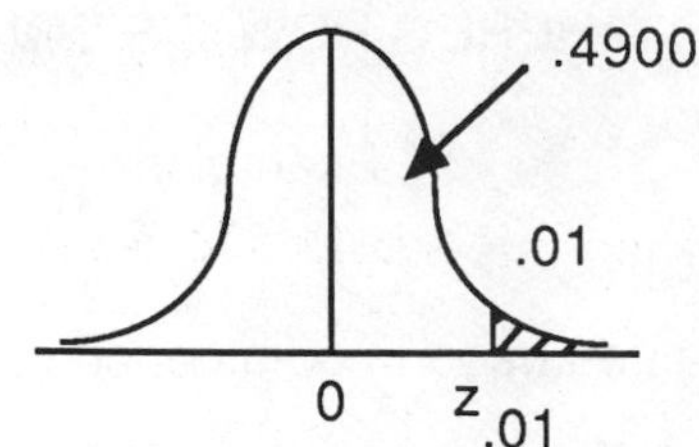

Looking in Table I for the area .4900, we see that there are values of .4898 and .4901. Without interpolating, we choose the closer value and obtain $z_{.01}$ = 2.33.

Hint: These z values for the standard confidences are used many times throughout the text. It would be helpful if you wrote them down somewhere for easy reference.

Standard z values:

$z_{.10} = 1.28$
$z_{.05} = 1.645$
$z_{.025} = 1.96$
$z_{.01} = 2.33$
$z_{.005} = 2.58$

2. If 36 measurements of the specific gravity of aluminum had a mean of 2.705 and a standard deviation of .028, estimate the mean specific gravity of the population of aluminum from which the sample was drawn with a 95% confidence interval.

Solution:
We are given the following sample information:

$n = 36 \qquad \bar{x} = 2.705 \qquad s = .028.$

The desired confidence is $1 - \alpha = .95$. Formula [1] is the appropriate formula for this problem because conditions b) and c) are satisfied since $n \geq 30$. Thus, the 95% confidence interval for the population mean μ is

$$\bar{x} \pm z_{\alpha/2}\frac{\sigma}{\sqrt{n}} = 2.705 \pm 1.96\frac{(.028)}{6} = 2.705 \pm .009$$

or a confidence interval of 2.696 to 2.714.

Note: Confidence intervals may be written as is done above, that is, 2.696 to 2.714 or in the form (2.696, 2.714).

3. A simple random sample of size 100 yielded a sample mean of $\bar{x}$ = 10.82 and a sample standard deviation of s = 81.

(a) Find a 99% confidence interval for the mean of the population from which this sample was chosen.

Solution:

(a) For the confidence coefficient .99 = 1 - α, $\alpha/2$ = .005. The large sample allows us to use formula [1], approximating σ with s. Thus, we have the interval

$$\bar{x} \pm z_{\alpha/2} \frac{s}{\sqrt{n}} = 10.82 \pm 2.58 \frac{(9)}{10} = 10.82 \pm 2.32$$

Therefore, we are 99% confident that the interval 8.50 to 13.14 contains the population mean μ.

(b) Interpret what is meant by the statement " We are 99% confident that the interval 8.50 to 13.14 contains the population mean μ".

Solution:

(b) It is not correct to make the statement: "The probability that μ is in the interval 8.50 to 13.14 is .99". Recall that μ is a population parameter, a constant, and therefore does not have a sampling distribution. The probability that μ is in the interval (8.50, 13.14) is either 0 or 1, depending whether or not μ is in the interval. The correct way to interpret a confidence interval is the following:

"If many such intervals were constructed using the same sample size in a similar manner, 99% of those intervals would contain μ; 1% of those intervals would not contain μ."

4. In order to determine the mean time, μ, it takes for the population of auto mechanics to rotate the tires of a car, an experimenter times a random sample of 36 mechanics. The sample standard deviation was 12.45 minutes. What can the experimenter say with a probability of .95 about the bound on the value of the sampling error if the sample mean of $\bar{x}$ = 15.8 minutes is used as a point estimate of μ?

Solution:

Using formula [3] with s approximating σ, we have for $1 - \alpha = .95$,

$$e = z_{\alpha/2} \frac{\sigma}{\sqrt{n}} = \frac{(1.96)(12.45)}{6} = \underline{4.07} \text{ minutes}$$

5. In order to bid competitively for the lumbering rights for a certain tract of land, a company needs to know the mean diameter of the trees on the tract to within 1.5 inches. If the company can assume that the standard deviation of the mean diameter of all the trees on the tract is 8 inches, how large a sample of trees on this tract should be taken for the company to be 90% confident of their answer?

Solution:

We are given the following information:

$e = 1.5 \qquad \sigma = 8 \qquad 1 - \alpha = .90$

To find the required sample size, we need to compute n using formula [4]:

$$n = \frac{(z_{\alpha/2})^2 \sigma^2}{e^2} = \frac{(1.645)^2 (8)^2}{2.25} = 76.97.$$

It makes no sense to talk about sampling a part of an item in a population (in this case, a tree). Thus, sample size must always be an whole number value.

In order to not exceed the given bound in the problem, the value in formula [4] must always be rounded to the next highest integer (that is, rounded up).

Thus, the company should select a sample of 77 trees.

6. In testing the hypothesis H_0: $\mu = 18$ against the alternative H_1: $\mu < 18$, a decision rule is formulated as: "Accept H_0 if $\bar{x} \geq 16.5$; Reject H_0 if $\bar{x} < 16.5$." It is known that $\sigma = 15$ for the population under investigation, and a sample of size $n = 100$ is randomly chosen from this population.

(a) Find the probability of a Type I error for this test of hypothesis.

Solution:

(a) Being given the decision rule in terms of the sample mean, we are able to use the definition of a Type I error to find its value.

P(Type I error) = α = P(falsely rejecting H_0) = P(rejecting H_0 when H_0 is true) = P($\bar{x} < 16.5$ when $\mu = 18$). Now, since we have a large sample and σ is known, we know that $\bar{x}$ has approximately a normal distribution. Thus, we may convert to the corresponding z value to find this probability.

$$\alpha = P(\bar{x} < 16.5 \text{ when } \mu = 18) = P[z < (16.5 - 18) / (15/10)]$$

$$= P(z < -1) = .5 - .3413 = \underline{.1587}.$$

(b) Find the probability of a Type II error if the value of the population mean is 14.55.

Solution:

(b) P(Type II error) = β = P(falsely accepting H_0) = P(accepting H_0 when H_0 is false) = P($\bar{x} \geq 16.5$ when μ = 14.55). For the same reasons as above, we find the corresponding z value to find the required probability. Thus,

$$\beta = P(\bar{x} \geq 16.5 \text{ when } \mu = 14.55) = P[z \geq (16.5 - 14.55) / (15/10)]$$

$$= P(z \geq 1.30) = .5 - .4032 = \underline{.0968}.$$

(c) Draw a graph showing α and β for this problem.

Solution:

(c) The graph is drawn directly from the definitions of α and β. Recall that

$$\alpha = P(\bar{x} < 16.5 \text{ when } \mu = 18) \quad \text{and} \quad \beta = P(\bar{x} \geq 16.5 \text{ when } \mu = 14.55).$$

Notice that there are actually two normal curves involved since the population mean is not the same in the two hypotheses H_0 and H_1. In fact, as you have probably noticed, the value the probability of a Type II error depends on the value of the alternative hypothesis. Thus, there are many different values of β to consider for each particular test of hypothesis problem since we do not know the true value of the population mean if the null hypothesis is false. In this problem, we are given one of the possible alternative mean values with which to work, namely μ = 14.55.

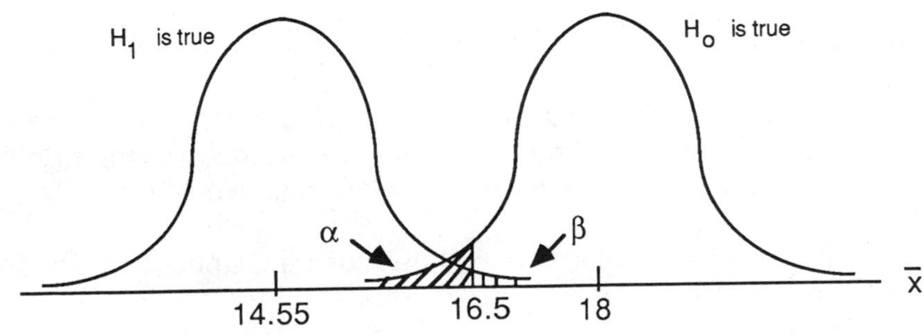

7. For each of the following situations,

(1) state the null and alternative hypotheses to be used in testing the claim.
(2) tell in which tail(s) of the distribution of the test statistic the rejection region would be located.

(a) Eat Slim Weight Program brochures advertise a mean weight loss of 5 pound per week

Solution:

(a) No one going through a diet program will be upset if they lose more weight than expected. Thus, the claim of "5 pounds per week" actually means "5 pounds or more per week". The alternative to this claim is "less than 5 pounds per week". Thus, we have

H_0: $\mu = 5$ and H_1: $\mu < 5$.

Recall that the rejection region is the region of values of the statistic where the null hypothesis is rejected. Sample results near the mean of 5 or more than 5 would be supportive of the null hypothesis. Thus, we would reject the null hypothesis for value of the sample mean significantly less than the hypothesized mean. Therefore,

The rejection region is in the lower tail of the distribution of the test statistic.

(b) The mean snowfall at Lake Tasmin during the month of January is 18.6 inches.

Solution:

(b) Here we have no indication as to who is making the claim or why. Possibly it is used in an advertisement for skiing in which case 18.6 inches of snow or more would be the interpretation. Possibly it is used by a snow plow operator who would be glad that there was not more snow than an average of 18.6 inches. Since we do not know, we would consider both possibilities and formulate

H_0: $\mu = 18.6$ and H_1: $\mu \neq 18.6$.

Values on either side of the mean 18.6 would tend to be supportive of the null hypothesis. Only when the sample results are significantly far away from the value of 18.6, in either direction, would the null be rejected. Thus,

The rejection region is in both tails of the distribution of the test statistic.

8. A random sample of 100 recorded deaths in the United States during the past year showed a mean life span of 71.8 years, with a standard deviation of 8.9 years. Does this sample data seem to indicate that the mean life span in the United States today is greater than 70 years at the .05 level of significance?

Solution:
To answer this question, we perform the six steps of any test of hypothesis problem.

Step 1: State, in symbolic form, the null hypothesis.

H_0: $\mu = 70$ (The mean life span in the U.S. today equals 70 years.)

Tip: The null hypothesis must be an equality. The numerical value which the mean equals in the null hypothesis will usually be mentioned in the question you are asked. Do not confuse it with the value of the sample mean stated in the problem. Also, the null hypothesis must be stated for a population parameter. You would never test sample means since they are known and do not need to be estimated.

Step 2: State, in symbolic from, the alternative to the null hypothesis.

H_1: $\mu > 70$ (The mean life span in the U.S. today is greater than 70 years.)

Tip: The alternative hypothesis must involve one of the following symbols: ">, <, or ≠" . The null hypothesis and alternative hypothesis can never overlap, and together they must include all possible values of the population parameter μ. Watch the problem for key words - here the word "greater" is in the question you are asked in the problem.

Step 3: Determine the test statistic you will use decide whether or not to reject the null hypothesis.

For this problem, the sample size is large (n = 100). Thus, the Central Limit Theorem applies and we use the test statistic given in formula [5], approximating σ with s:

$$z = \frac{\bar{x} - \mu}{\frac{\sigma}{\sqrt{n}}}$$

Step 4: Determine the decision rule that provides the appropriate level of significance.

We are given a level of significance $= \alpha = .05$. Since the alternative hypothesis is $\mu > 70$, the rejection region goes in the upper tail of the distribution of the test statistic. Hence, we have the following decision rule:

Accept H_0 if $z \leq 1.645$
Reject H_0 if $z > 1.645$ (that is, "otherwise").

Note: The decision rule can be written out as above or shown on a graph:

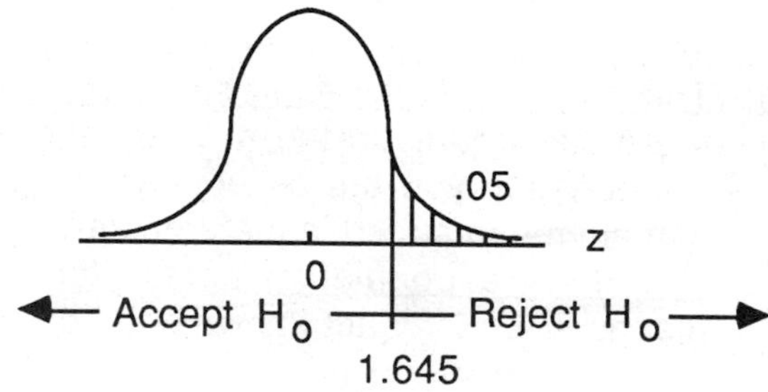

Step 5: Obtain the results of the experiment and use this sample information to calculate the value of the test statistic.

We are given in the problem that $\bar{x} = 71.8$ and $s = 8.9$ for $n = 100$.

Using this information in formula [5], that is, the formula decided on in step3 of this procedure, we have:

$$z = \frac{\bar{x} - \mu}{\frac{\sigma}{\sqrt{n}}} = \frac{71.8 - 70}{\frac{8.9}{10}} = \underline{2.02}$$

Note: The null hypothesis value of 70 is what is used in this formula for μ since we are using α for the decision rule. Recall that a Type I error is made when the null hypothesis is rejected if it is actually true.

Step 6: Give the conclusion of the test of hypothesis.

We see that the value of 2.02 falls in the rejection region determined in step 4. Thus, the conclusion we arrive at is

"Reject H_0". The sample evidence indicates that the mean life span in the U. S. today is greater than 70 years. The answer to the question posed in the problem is therefore "yes".

(b) What is the p value for this problem?

Solution:

(b) The p value, by definition, is the probability, when the null hypothesis is true, of obtaining a difference between a sample mean $\bar{x}$ and a hypothesized value of the population mean μ that is larger than the difference actually observed.

For calculation purposes, the p value will be the area to the right of the value of the test statistic found in step 5 of the hypothesis test procedure when that value is positive for a one-tail test of hypothesis. For a one-tail test of hypothesis when the value of the test statistic found in step 5 is negative, the p value will be the area to the left of that number. For a two-tail test of hypothesis, follow the procedure for a one-tail test and double the resulting area.

In this problem, we have a one-tail test of hypothesis with a z value of 2.02.

Thus, the p value $= P(z > 2.02) = .5 - .4783 = .0217$.

Graphically, the p value is shown as

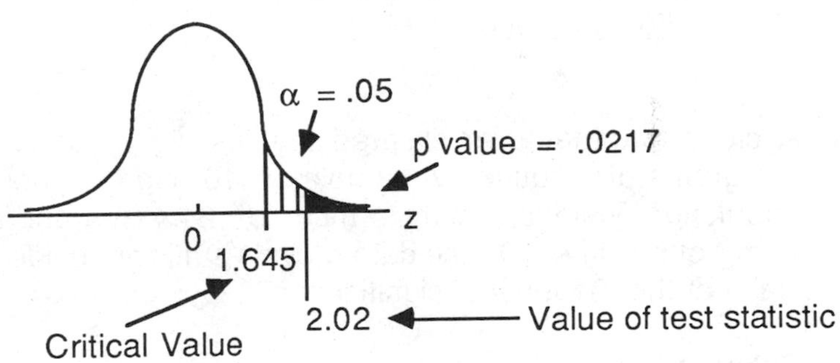

Note:

If we had been using the p value criterion for hypothesis testing, we would have reached the same conclusion since we reject the null hypothesis whenever the p value is less than α.

9. Find a 90% confidence interval for the mean of the normal population from which the following sample data were obtained: 4, 2, 0, 1, 3

Solution:

To obtain the confidence interval, we need to know the mean and standard deviation of the sample {4, 2, 0, 1, 3}. These are found using formula [2]:

$$\bar{x} = \frac{\Sigma x}{n} = \frac{10}{2} = 5 \quad \text{and}$$

$$s^2 = \frac{\Sigma x^2 - (\Sigma x)^2/n}{n - 1} = \frac{30 - 100/5}{4} = 2.5$$

Since we are given the population is normal and is unknown, with n = 5, we use formula [6] to find the required interval. Since $1 - \alpha = .90$, $\alpha/2 = .05$. Looking in the t table (Table 2) under the column .05 in the row for n - 1 = 4 degrees of freedom, we obtain the value $t_{.05} = 2.132$. Formula [6] then gives

$$\bar{x} \pm t_{\alpha/2} \frac{s}{\sqrt{n}} = 2 \pm 2.132 \frac{(\sqrt{2.5})}{\sqrt{5}} = 2 \pm 1.51$$

Thus, we are 90% confident that the population mean μ is between the values of .50 and 3.50.

10. A cigar manufacturer claimed that its cigars contained less than a mean of 25 milligrams of nicotine. A sample of 16 cigars, chosen from a normally distributed population, yielded a sample mean of 24.4 mg and a sample standard deviation of 2 mg of nicotine. Do the data provide sufficient evidence to refute the manufacturer's claim at the .01 level of significance?

Solution:

Again following the six steps of the hypothesis testing procedure, we are testing the claim:

H_0: $\mu = 25$ (The cigars contain 25 or more mg of nicotine.)

H_1: $\mu < 25$ (The manufacturer's claim that the cigars contain less than 25 mg of nicotine.)

Since $n = 16$ and the population is normal with unknown standard deviation, σ, we use formula [7].

The decision rule, with $\alpha = .01$, is

Accept H_o if $t \geq -2.602$
Reject H_o if $t < -2.602$.

Substituting in formula [7], we have

$$t = \frac{\overline{x} - \mu}{\frac{s}{\sqrt{n}}} = \frac{24.4 - 25}{\frac{2}{4}} = \underline{-1.20}$$

Thus, our decision is to "accept H_o".

<u>Note</u>:

It is <u>very important</u> to remember two things when saying "accept H_o":

1. "Accepting H_o" simply indicates that we do not have sufficient evidence to claim that the alternative hypothesis is true.

2. We cannot conclude that we have *proven* that $\mu = 25$. There is still a chance that an error has been made. In this case, the error would be falsely accepting a null hypothesis that is not true. Therefore, there is a probability β of making a mistake in this decision of accepting H_o. β has not been calculated for this problem - it may be quite large. Thus, many statisticians prefer saying "do not reject H_o" rather than "accept H_o" until they determine value(s) for β.

Chapter 9

HAVE I LEARNED THE MATERIAL?

Problems

1. A simple random sample chosen from a normal population yielded the data values

   4, 4, 3, 3, 1, 2, and 5.

   (a) Develop a 98% confidence interval for the mean of this population.

   (b) Interpret what is meant by "98% confidence" for this problem.

2. Joe Small wishes to estimate the height of adults in his hometown. A random sample of 100 adults in this town gave a sample mean height of 5'8" with a sample standard deviation of 3'.

   (a) Provide a point estimate of the population mean height.

   (b) What can Joe say with probability .95 about a bound on the value of the sampling error using the above estimate for the population mean height?

3. (a) Verify $z_{\alpha/2} = 1.28$ if $1 - \alpha = .90$.

(b) Find $z_{\alpha/2}$ for $1 - \alpha = .9556$.

4. A machine is designed to fill cereal boxes with a net weight of 16 ounces. It is important that the machine operate accurately: If it fills too much, the company wastes excess cereal; if it underfills the boxes, the consumer will not be satisfied. The company has instituted a new quality control program to monitor the amount of fill for its cereal boxes. Every day, a random sample of 100 boxes is selected for the production line, and the amounts of fill are measured.

(a) Suppose the results of one day's inspection gave the following: $\bar{x} = 15.98$ oz and $s = 0.21$ oz. Construct a 98% confidence interval for the mean amount of fill for the population of cereal boxes.

(b) The quality control manager decides that if there is evidence (at the .05 level of significance) that the mean amount of fill differs from 16 ounces, the machine should be reset. Using the above sample results ($\bar{x} = 15.98$ oz and $s = 0.21$ oz), should the machine be reset?

(c) Is it possible that an error was made in the above decision? If so, which type of error?

(d) Calculate the p value for the test of hypothesis problem.

5. State the null and alternative hypotheses that would be used in testing each of the following claims. Tell in which tail(s) of the sampling distribution of the test statistic the rejection region would be located.

(a) The average rib-eye steak at the Longhorn Steak House is at least 340 grams in weight. (You are a customer eating there.)

(b) No more than a mean of $40 is contributed by the faculty of the local high school to the annual loyalty fund.

(c) The mean number of children per family in Pawpawn is 2.45.

6. In testing H_0: μ = 15 against the alternative hypothesis H_1: μ < 15, it was decided to randomly sample the population, for which σ = 14, with a sample of size 49. It is decided that the null hypothesis will be rejected when the mean of the sample is less than 10.

(a) Find P(Type I error) for this test of hypothesis.

(b) Find P(Type II error) for this test of hypothesis for the value $\mu = 12$.

(c) Draw a graph showing α and β.

7. If a company wants to check an "improved" process for making bearings, how large a sample would be needed to be able to assert with a probability of .98 that the sample mean diameter is within .002 cm of the true mean diameter? Assume it is known from past experience that $\sigma = .016$ cm.

8. Assume the following are to be used with the t distribution in the process of estimating a population mean μ. Find each of the following for the specified sample size.

   (a) $t_{.025}$ for n = 26

   (b) $t_{.05}$ for n = 18

   (c) $t_{.95}$ for n = 6

   (d) $t_{.90}$ for n = 11

   (e) $t_{.90}$ for n = 30

   (f) $P(t < 2.069)$ for n = 24

   (g) $P(t > 2.467)$ for n = 29

   (h) $P(t \leq 3.35)$ for n = 10

9. A random sample of 12 female students in a certain dormitory showed an average weekly expenditure of \$8 per week for snack foods, with a standard deviation of \$1.75.

   (a) Construct a 90% confidence interval for the average amount spent on snack foods by all female students living in the dormitory, assuming these expenditures to be approximately normally distributed.

(b) Suppose it is desired to obtain a narrower confidence interval that the one obtained in part a). Name two ways this might be accomplished.

10. A manufacturer of electric hair dryers claims that his product possesses a mean defect-free life of at least 3 years. Six purchasers of these hair dryers stated that the defect-free life of their hair dryers were 1, 2, 1.5, 4, 3.2, and 3 years, respectively. Do these data support the manufacturer's claim? Test using $\alpha = .05$.

Chapter 9

Multiple Choice Questions

1. How does the t distribution compare with the standard normal distribution?

   (a) They both have the same mean, but the standard deviation of t is smaller.
   (b) They are identical.
   (c) They both have the same variance, but their means are different.
   (d) They both have the same mean, but the variance of the t distribution is larger.

2. What can be said about the relationship between α and β, the possible errors in a hypothesis testing problem?

   (a) $\alpha + \beta = 1$.
   (b) $\alpha = \beta$.
   (c) As β increases, α decreases for a fixed sample size.
   (d) As β increases, α increases for a fixed sample size.

3. Below is a graph showing the t distribution for sample sizes n = 34, n = 3, and n = 15 (these sample sizes are not arranged in any particular order). The arrow is pointing to the graph for

   (a) n = 34
   (b) n = 3
   (c) n = 15
   (d) none of these - the graph is actually showing the standard normal distribution.

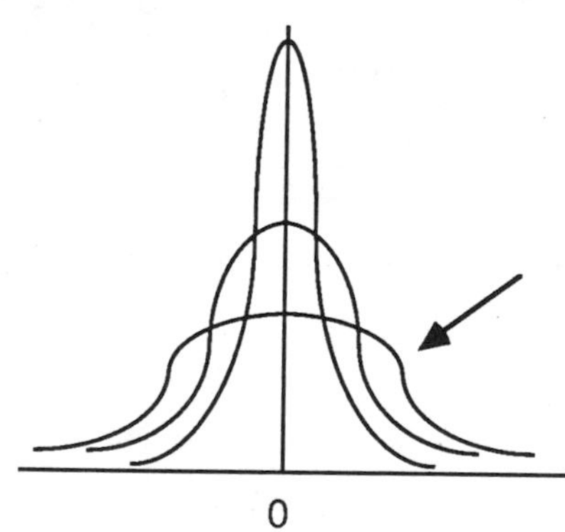

4. After taking a sample and computing $\bar{x}$, a statistician says "I am 98% confident that μ is between 106 and 122". What does he really mean?

   (a) The probability that $106 \leq \mu \leq 122$ equals 98%.
   (b) The probability is .98 that $\mu = 114$, the midpoint of the interval.
   (c) 98% of all the intervals calculated from samples of the same size, using the same procedure, will contain μ.
   (d) all of the above.

5. If we say that $\alpha = .10$ for a particular hypothesis test, then we are saying that

   (a) The probability of a Type II error is .10.
   (b) 10% is the risk we are taking of rejecting a null hypothesis that is actually true.
   (c) 10% is the risk we are taking of accepting a null hypothesis that is actually false.
   (d) The finite population correction factor should have been used to compute the value of the test statistic.

6. $P(-2.064 \leq t \leq 2.064)$, where t has the t distribution with 24 degrees of freedom, equals

   (a) .025
   (b) .05
   (c) .95
   (d) .975.

7. A random sample of 100 of the waitresses in Greenville revealed that the mean of their daily tips is $15 with a standard deviation of $5. A 95% confidence interval for the mean tips of all waitresses in Greenville is given by

   (a) $15 \pm 1.645(.5)$
   (b) $15 \pm 1.96(.5)$
   (c) $10 \pm 2.56(.33)$
   (d) $15 \pm .95(5)$.

8. A large sample test of hypothesis is to be used to test H_0: $\mu = 50.4$ against the alternative H_1: $\mu > 50.4$. For a level of significance of .10, the rejection region for this test is

   (a) $z \leq -1.28$
   (b) either $z < -1.28$ or $z > 1.28$
   (c) $z > 1.28$
   (d) none of these.

9. A vice-president in charge of sales for a large corporation claims that a new training program is needed for salesmen since they are averaging no more than 11 sales per week. What null and alternative hypotheses should be used to test his claim?

   (a) H_0: $\mu = 11$
   H_1: $\mu > 11$

   (b) H_0: $\mu = 11$
   H_1: $\mu \neq 11$

   (c) H_0: $\mu = 11$
   H_1: $\mu < 11$

   (d) none of these.

10. For a two-tailed test of hypothesis involving a sample of size 12 chosen from a normal population with an unknown variance , the probability of a Type I error is set at 0.05. The value of the test statistic, calculated from the sample results, is found to be 1.43. The p-value for this test of hypothesis problem is

    (a) $2P(t > 1.43)$
    (b) $P(t > 1.43)$
    (c) 1.96
    (d) 0.10.

Chapter 9

Answers to Problems

1. (a) $\Sigma x = 22$, $\Sigma x^2 = 80$, $n = 7$ giving $\bar{x} = 3.14$ and $s^2 = 1.81$; $t_{.01} = 3.143$

   We are 98% confident that μ is in the interval <u>1.54 to 4.74</u>.

   (b) Of all such intervals constructed in this manner, 98% of them will contain the value of μ; 2% of them will not contain the value of μ.

2. (a) 5' 8"

   (b) e = .588"

3. (a) $z_{\alpha} = z_{.10}$ = <u>1.28</u> since

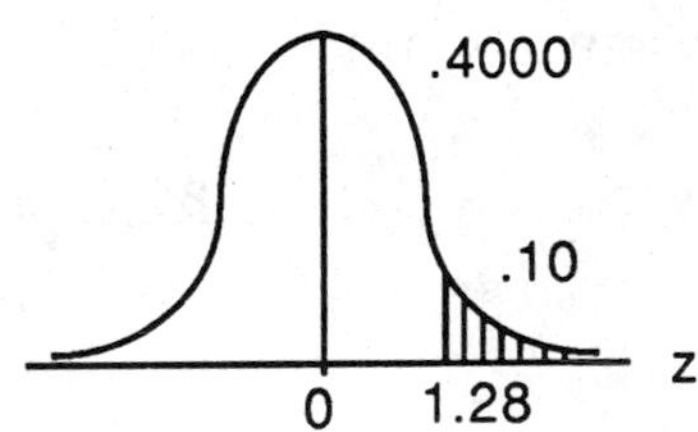

   (b) $z_{\alpha/2} = z_{.0222}$ = <u>2.01</u> since

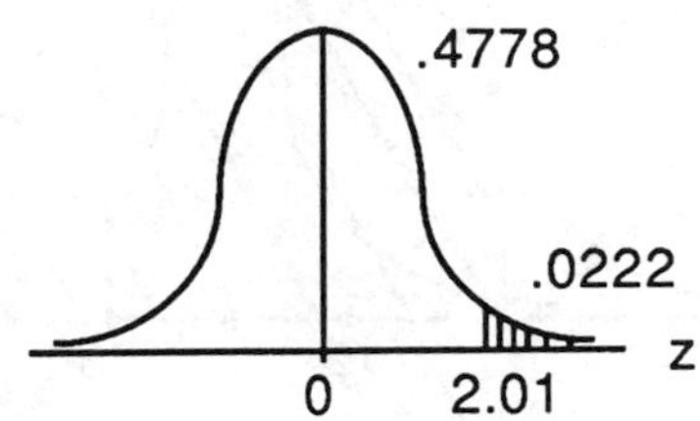

4. (a) $15.98 \pm 2.33(.21/10)$ = <u>15.93 to 16.03</u>

   (b) H_0: $\mu = 16$ and H_1: $\mu \neq 16$; Use formula [5];

   The decision rule is: Accept H_0 if $-1.96 \leq z \leq 1.96$; Reject H_0 otherwise.

   $z = (15.98 - 16)/.021$ = <u>-.95</u>

   Conclusion: H_0 cannot be rejected. <u>No</u>, the machine does not need resetting.

(c) Yes, Type II error.

(d) p value = $2P(z < -.95) = 2(.1711) = \underline{.3422}$

5. (a) H_0: $\mu = 340$ (or H_0: $\mu \geq 340$)
H_1: $\mu < 340$ Rejection region is in lower tail.

(b) H_0: $\mu = 40$ (or H_0: $\mu \leq 40$)
H_1: $\mu > 40$ Rejection region is in upper tail.

(c) H_0: $\mu = 2.45$
H_1: $\mu \neq 2.45$ Rejection region is in both tails.

6. (a) $\alpha = P(\bar{x} < 10 \text{ when } \mu = 15) = \underline{.0062}$.

(b) $\beta = P(\bar{x} \geq 10 \text{ when } \mu = 12) = \underline{.8413}$.

(c)

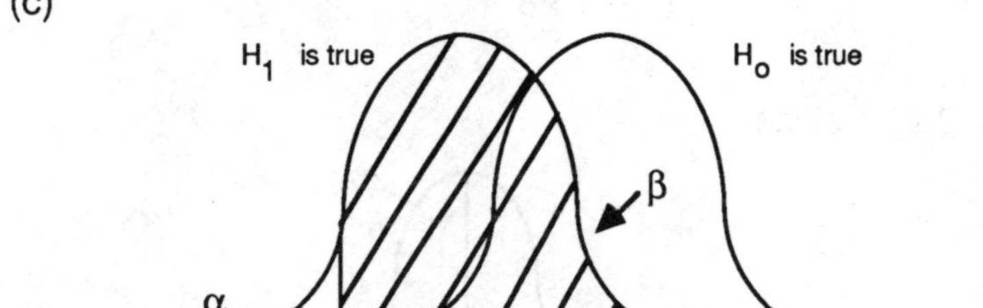

7. $n = (2.33)^2(.016)^2 / (.002)^2 = \underline{348}$

8. (a) 2.060
(b) 1.740
(c) -2.015
(d) -1.372
(e) -1.311
(f) 0.975
(g) 0.01
(h) 0.995

9. (a) $8 \pm 1.796\,(1.75/\sqrt{12}) = \underline{\$7.09 \text{ to } \$8.91}$

(b) Increase the sample size; decrease the confidence coefficient.

10. H_0: $\mu \geq 3$ and H_1: $\mu < 3$; Use formula [7];

The decision rule is: Accept H_0 if $t \geq -2.015$; Reject H_0 if $t < -2.015$

$t = (2.45 - 3) / (1.14/\sqrt{6}) = \underline{-1.183}$

Conclusion: H_0 cannot be rejected.

Chapter 9

Answers to Multiple Choice Questions

1. d
2. c
3. b
4. c
5. b
6. c
7. b
8. c
9. a
10. a

Chapter 10
INFERENCES ABOUT A POPULATION PROPORTION

WHAT AM I LEARNING?

Chapter Outline and Summary

We have divided inferential statistics into two main areas: estimation and hypothesis testing. In Chapter 9 we studied these basic areas as applied to population means. This chapter extends our coverage of statistical estimation and hypothesis testing to population proportions. To do this, we need to identify the sampling distribution for the sample statistic used to estimate p, the *population proportion.*

The *sample proportion* (also called percentage), denoted by $\bar{p}$, is computed using the formula $\bar{p} = x/n$ where x is the number of items in the sample with the characteristic of interest in the problem, and n is the size of the simple random sample chosen from the population. The sample proportion $\bar{p}$ is the *point estimate* of the population proportion p.

The sample proportion $\bar{p}$, like the sample mean $\bar{x}$, will have different values for different random samples chosen from the same population. Thus, there is an associated probability distribution of all possible values of the sample proportion called the *sampling distribution of* $\bar{p}$. The *expected value* of this distribution (that is, the mean of the sampling distribution of $\bar{p}$) is the population proportion p. A measure of the variance of this sampling distribution is the *standard deviation* of $\bar{p}$. The standard deviation of $\bar{p}$ is denoted by $\sigma_{\bar{p}}$, and $\sigma_{\bar{p}} = \sqrt{p(1 - p)/n}$. The standard deviation of $\bar{p}$ is called the *standard error of the proportion.*

In Chapter 8 we saw the Central Limit Theorem was very useful in enabling us to approximate the sampling distribution of $\bar{x}$ by a normal probability distribution whenever the sample size n is large. The Central Limit Theorem as it relates to the sample proportion $\bar{p}$ is

> In selecting simple random samples of size n from a population with porportion p, the probability distribution of the sample proportion $\bar{p}$ approaches a normal distribution with mean p and standard deviation $\sqrt{p(1-p)/n}$ as the sample size becomes large.

Thus, we can also use a normal probability distribution to approximate the sampling distribution of $\bar{p}$ provided the sample size is large. The condition for *large samples* with means is $n \geq 30$. With proportions, the sample size is considered large whenever $np \geq 5$ and $n(1 - p) \geq 5$. Note that the population proportion p is equivalent to the probability of success for a binomial experiment. Thus, it is natural that the condition for large samples here be equivalent to the condition under which the binomial distribution can be approximated by the normal distribution.

Large sample confidence intervals and tests of hypotheses of means and proportions are quite similar since both use the normal distribution for the approximating sampling distribution. The formulas will change in appearance because of the difference in sample statistics used, but the basic ideas behind estimation and hypothesis testing remain the same.

A $(1 - \alpha)100\%$ confidence interval for the population proportion is given by the formula $\bar{p} \pm z_{\alpha/2} \sqrt{\bar{p}(1-\bar{p})/n}$. In this formula the standard deviation of $\bar{p}$ has the value p replaced by $\bar{p}$ since the value of p is what we are trying to estimate and is therefore unknown. The notation $z_{\alpha/2}$ and the z values for the standard confidence levels are the same as in Chapter 8.

Also, as in Chapter 8, we can use the specified maximum sampling error, e, that the user is willing to tolerate, the desired confidence level, and an estimate of the population proportion p to develop an expression for the size of the simple random sample needed to estimate p with a reasonable degree of precision. We thus have the formula for the sample size $n = (z_{\alpha/2})^2\, p\,(1-p)/\, e^2$. If we have no preliminary idea of the population proportion p, we use the value that yields a maximum sample size, $p = .50$. As usual, the value of n obtained from this formula is rounded up to ensure that the bounds on the sampling error are maintained.

To perform tests of hypotheses about a population proportion p, follow the logic outlined in the six steps of a hypothesis test give in Chapter 8. These are:

The six steps of any hypothesis testing procedure:

- Step 1: State, in symbolic form, the null hypothesis.
- Step 2: State, in symbolic from, the alternative to the null hypothesis.
- Step 3: Determine the test statistic you will use decide whether or not to reject the null hypothesis.

Step 4: Determine the decision rule that provides the appropriate level of significance.
Step 5: Obtain the results of the experiment and use this sample information to calculate the value of the test statistic.
Step 6: Give the conclusion of the test of hypothesis.

WHICH FORMULA SHOULD I USE?

Formulas

When:

finding the sample proportion $\bar{p}$ where x is the number of items in the sample with the characteristic of interest and n is the size of the simple random sample

Use:

$$\bar{p} = x/n \qquad [1]$$

When:

determining the expected value (mean) of the sampling distribution of $\bar{p}$ and p is the population proportion

Use:

$$E(\bar{p}) = p \qquad [2]$$

When:

calculating the standard deviation of $\bar{p}$ with p equal to the population proportion

Use:

$$\sigma_{\bar{p}} = \sqrt{\frac{p(1-p)}{n}} \qquad [3]$$

When:

a) testing the null hypothesis H_0: $p = p_0$ where p is the population proportion

b) both $np \geq 5$ and $n(1 - p) \geq 5$

Use:

$$z = \frac{\bar{p} - p}{\sqrt{\frac{p(1-p)}{n}}} \qquad [4]$$

When:

a) developing a $(1 - \alpha)100\%$ confidence interval for the population proportion p
b) both $np \geq 5$ and $n(1 - p) \geq 5$

Use:

$$\bar{p} \pm z_{\alpha/2} \sqrt{\frac{\bar{p}(1 - \bar{p})}{n}} \qquad [5]$$

When:

determining the sample size n to be used in the estimation of a population proportion p for a maximum sampling error e

Use:

$$n = \frac{z_{\alpha/2}^{2}\ p(1 - p)}{e^{2}} \qquad [6]$$

HERE'S HOW IT'S DONE!

Examples

1. An editor checked a random sample of 8 pages of a large manuscript for typographical errors to determine whether or not the entire manuscript needed to be checked for mistakes. The results of her sample were

Page of Manuscript	1	2	3	4	5	6	7	8
Number of Errors	0	2	0	1	0	2	0	1

Develop a point estimate for the proportion of all pages of this manuscript that contain at least one typographical error.

Solution:

The characteristic of interest for the population in this problem is having at least one mistake on a page. Looking at the sample data, we find the number of pages with at least one typographical mistake is $x = 4$. The sample size is $n = 8$. Thus, using formula [1], we determine $\bar{p} = x/n = 4/8 = \underline{.50}$.

2. Comfy Shoe Company believes that the percentage of defective shoes (that is, shoes that are not first quality) produced by its plant located in Anderson is $p = .20$.

(a) If a random sample of 100 shoes is selected from the production of this plant, describe the sampling distribution of $\bar{p}$, where $\bar{p}$ is the proportion of defective shoes in the sample.

Solution:

(a) From formula [2], we know the mean of the sampling distribution of $\bar{p}$ is p, the proportion of defective shoes for the population. Thus, $E(\bar{p}) = \underline{.20}$.

Using formula [3], the standard deviation of the distribution of $\bar{p}$ is

$$\sigma_{\bar{p}} = \sqrt{\frac{p\,(1 - p)}{n}} = \sqrt{\frac{(.2)(.8)}{100}} = \underline{.04}\ .$$

(b) Draw a graph showing the sampling distribution of $\bar{p}$.

Solution:

(b) For the sample size $n = 100$, we have $np = 100(.2) = 20$ and $n(1 - p) = 100(.8) = 80$. The large sample conditions are therefore satisfied since both of these quantities are greater than 5. Thus, the sampling distribution can be approximated by a normal probability distribution. Using the mean of .2 and standard deviation of .04 , we have the graph of the sampling distribution of $\bar{p}$ as

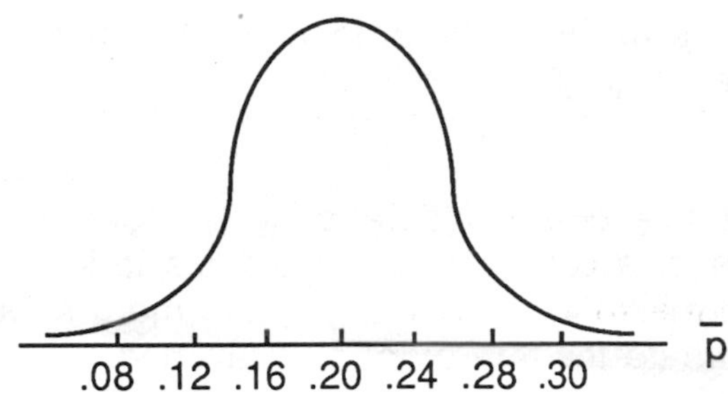

(c) Determine the probability that a random sample of 100 Comfy shoes will have a proportion of defective shoes that is between .15 and .25.

Solution:

(c) We are asked to find $P(.15 < \bar{p} < .25)$. This probability can be computed using the mean and standard distribution of the sampling distribution of $\bar{p}$ and formula [4].

Since $z = \dfrac{\bar{p} - p}{\sqrt{\dfrac{p(1-p)}{n}}}$, $P(.15 < \bar{p} < .25) =$

$$P\left(\frac{.15 - .2}{.04} < z < \frac{.25 - .2}{.04}\right) = P(-1.25 < z < 1.25)$$

$$= 2(.3944) = \underline{.7888}.$$

3. Each year the IRS conducts a study of the acccuracy of tax returns for the purpose of possible simplification (or other revision) of forms for future years. Suppose that in this year's study, a random sample of 500 tax returns showed that 90% contained at least one error. Construct a 99% confidence interval for the proportion of all tax returns which contain at least one error.

Solution:

We are given the information $n = 500$, $\bar{p} = .90$, and $1 - \alpha = .99$. Thus, substituting in formula [5] with $\alpha/2 = .005$, we have

$$\bar{p} \pm z_{\alpha/2} \sqrt{\frac{\bar{p}(1-\bar{p})}{n}} = .90 \pm 2.58 \sqrt{\frac{(.9)(.1)}{500}} = .9 \pm .0346$$

Thus, we estimate the proportion of all tax returns with errors to be between .8654 and .9346.

4. Before a bill to increase federal price supports for rural farmers comes before the U.S. Congress, a congressman would like to know how nonfarmers feel about the issue. Approximately how many nonfarmers should the congressman survey in order to estimate the true proportion favoring this bill to within .05 with probability equal to .99?

Solution:

The confidence level is $.99 = 1 - \alpha$ giving $\alpha/2 = .005$. The maximum sampling error that the congressman is willing to tolerate is .05. Since we are not told a planning value for the population proportion p, we use the value $p = .5$ to obtain the largest possible sample size to guarantee that the required precision will be obtained. Thus, we have, using formula [6],

$$n = \frac{z^2_{\alpha/2}\, p(1-p)}{e^2} = \frac{(2.58)^2\,(.5)(.5)}{(.05)^2} = 665.64 .$$

The sample size must be a whole number, so we round up the value of 665.64 to obtain a sample size of 666.

5. A builder claims that heat pumps are installed fewer than 70% of all homes being constructed today in the city of Pineville. Would you agree with this claim if a random survey of 20 new homes in this city shows that 12 out of 20 had heat pumps installed? Use a level of significance of .10, and use the p value criterion for testing this claim.

Solution:

Letting p be the proportion of the population of new homes in Pineville that have a heat pump installed, we again follow the six steps in the hypothesis testing procedure.

Steps 1 and 2: The hypotheses are H_0: $p = .7$ versus H_1: $p < .7$

Step 3: For $n = 20$ and $p = .7$, $np = 20(.7) = 14$ and $n(1-p) = 20(.3) = 6$.

Since both of these values are greater than 5, it is appropriate to use the z statistic of formula [4].

Step 4: The decision rule is: If $\alpha < $ p value, H_0 is accepted

If $\alpha > $ p value, H_0 is rejected.

Step 5: Substituting in formula [4], we have

$$z = \frac{\bar{p} - p}{\sqrt{\frac{p(1-p)}{n}}} = \frac{12/20 - .7}{\sqrt{\frac{(.7)(.3)}{20}}} = \frac{-.1}{.1025} = \underline{-.976}.$$

Step 6: Rounding the value of z to two decimal places and using Table 1, we find the p value for this problem is $P(z < -.98) = .5 - .3365 = .1635$.

Since $\alpha = .10 < $ p value $= .1635$, H_0 is not rejected. <u>No</u>, there is insufficient evidence at the .10 level of significance to believe the builder's claim.

HAVE I LEARNED THE MATERIAL?

Problems

1. Dr. Sneeze believes that approximately 20% of his patients have serious common colds during the month of December. If he wishes to estimate the true percentage to within 5%, how large a random sample of his patients should he take? Assume that he wishes to be 95% confident of his answer.

2. A commonly prescribed drug on the market for relieving nervous tension is believed to be only 60% effective. Experimental results with a new drug administered to a random sample of 100 adults who were suffering from nervous tension showed that 70 received relief.

   (a) Is this sufficient evidence, at the .05 level of significance, to conclude that the percentage of people who received relief from the new drug is more than 60%?

   (b) What is the p value for this test of hypothesis?

3. In an effort to determine community feelings toward expanding cable TV service in a certain town, Cable USA takes a random sample of 20 homes in that town. The questions they asked are the following:

   Question 1: Do you presently have cable TV in your home?

   Question 2: Would you like to see the cable TV service in this town expanded?

   Question 3: Would you be willing to pay an extra $2 per month for expanded cable TV service?

   The responses for the 20 homes that were surveyed are as follows:

Question 1	Question 2	Question 3
Yes	No	No
Yes	Yes	No
Yes	Yes	Yes
No	Yes	No
Yes	No	No
Yes	Yes	Yes
No	Yes	No
Yes	Yes	Yes
Yes	No	No
No	No	No
Yes	Yes	Yes
No	Yes	No
Yes	No	No
Yes	Yes	Yes
Yes	No	No
No	No	No
Yes	Yes	Yes
Yes	Yes	No
Yes	No	No
Yes	No	Yes

   Develop a point estimate for the proportion of homes in this town who have Cable USA service, would like to see it expanded, and would pay an extra $2 per month for that expanded service.

4. A national retail chain wishes to estimate p, the proportion of charge customers who are more than one month behind in their payments. If they wish to be 95% confident that their estimate is within .04 of the true value of p, how many accounts should be sampled?

5. Private I. M. Doubtful, one of General Custer's soldiers, took a random sample of 50 men in his regiment. Thirty of them felt that they had the Indians outnumbered. Find a 95% confidence interval for the true proportion of General Custer's men who felt that way.

Chapter 10

Multiple Choice Questions

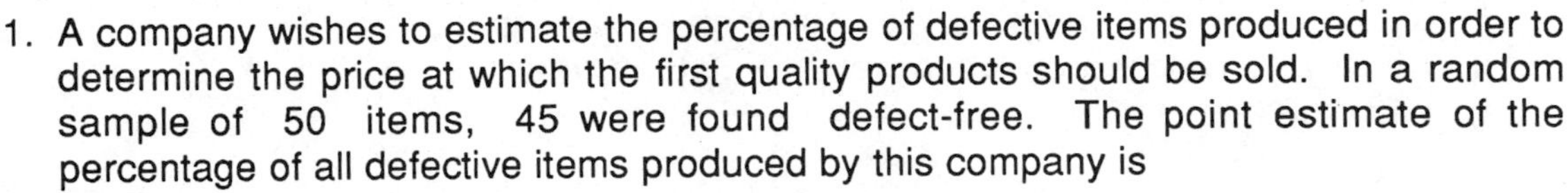

1. A company wishes to estimate the percentage of defective items produced in order to determine the price at which the first quality products should be sold. In a random sample of 50 items, 45 were found defect-free. The point estimate of the percentage of all defective items produced by this company is

   (a) .90
   (b) .10
   (c) .30
   (d) none of these.

2. A confidence interval for a certain population proportion is $.345 < p < .628$. The degree of confidence that can be placed in this interval is

   (a) .95
   (b) .90
   (c) .99
   (d) There is not enough information given to determine the degree of confidence.

3. The credit manager of a store wishes to estimate the proportion of customers who charge purchases for a one month period. How many charge accounts should be randomly sampled in order to be 95% confident that the estimate obtained using this sample will be within .03 of the true proportion if the manager knows from previous data that p will be in the neighborhood of .45?

   (a) 1112
   (b) 978
   (c) 1057
   (d) The sample size cannot be determined from the given information.

4. The probability distribution of the sample proportion

   (a) is approximately normal whenever the sample size is greater than or equal to 30
   (b) is approximately normal whenever $np \geq 5$ and $n(1 - p) \geq 5$
   (c) is normal regardless of the sample size
   (d) is normal only when $p = .5$.

5. In general, the width of a confidence interval for a proportion

   (a) will be wider for 99% confidence than for 95% confidence
   (b) will be wider for a sample of size 100 than for a sample of size 25
   (c) will always be narrower whenever $p = .2$ than whenever $p = .5$
   (d) all of the above.

6. If it is estimated, from a random sample of size 50, that 40% of the viewing audience is watching the new TV serial <u>Happy Doctors</u>. The standard error of the proportion is closest to

   (a) .06
   (b) .005
   (c) .069
   (d) none of the above.

7. Market studies presently indicate that 11% of all bar soap sales are for Zippy Soap. In an attempt to increase the sale of Zippy Soap, an extensive advertising campaign will be conducted. At the end of the campaign, a sample of 400 bar soap sales will be used to estimate Zippy's share of the market and determine if the campaign was successful. State the null and alternative hypotheses that should be used in a test of hypothesis to determine if the campaign was successful.

   (a) H_0: $\bar{p} = .11$ and H_1: $\bar{p} > .11$
   (b) H_0: $p = .11$ and H_1: $p \neq .11$
   (c) H_0: $p = .11$ and H_1: $p \geq .11$
   (d) H_0: $p = .11$ and H_1: $p > .11$

8. When solving for the size of the simple random sample required to estimate the population proportion to within a maximum error e with $(1 - \alpha)100\%$ confidence, under what conditions do we use $p = .5$ in the formula to find the sample size?

   (a) when $\bar{p} = .5$
   (b) when we have no knowledge of what p will turn out to be
   (c) when $e \leq .05$
   (d) when $np \geq 5$.

9. In determining the size of the simple random sample needed to estimate a population proportion, an experimenter came up with $n = 6300$. Due to cost and time limitations, it was impossible for him to take this large a sample. How could he reduce the size of the sample?

   (a) increase the confidence level from the one previously chosen
   (b) decrease the bound on the sampling error from the previously chosen one
   (c) either lower the confidence level or increase the bound on the sampling error (or both) from the ones previously chosen
   (d) none of these - he's stuck with $n = 6300$.

10. For which of the following situations would it be appropriate to use the formula for developing a confidence interval for a proportion?

   (a) $n = 15, \; p = .7$
   (b) $n = 50, \; p = .6$
   (c) $n = 80, \; p = .4$
   (d) none of the above.

Chapter 10

Answers to Problems

1. $n = 1.96^2(.2)(.8)/.05^2 = 245.86$ which rounds up to give $n =$ 246.

2. (a) $H_0: p = .6$ Accept H_0 if $z \leq 1.645$
   $H_1: p > .6$ Reject H_0 if $z > 1.645$

   Using formula [4], obtain $z =$ 2.04

   Thus, reject H_0. "Yes" is the answer to the question posed in the problem.

   (b) p value $= P(z > 2.04) = .5 - .4793 =$ .0207.

3. The characteristic of interest in the population is having Cable USA service, would like to see it expanded, and would pay an extra $2 per month for that expanded service. Thus, we need to count the answers that are "yes" to all three questions. Doing so, we obtain $\bar{p} = 6/20 =$ .30 as the estimate of the population proportion p.

4. $n = 1.96^2 (.5)(.5) / .01^2 = 600.25$. Rounding up, we find the sample size is 601 accounts.

5. Letting x be the number of soldiers who thought they had the enemy outnumbered, $\bar{p} = 30/50 = .60$. Formula [5] gives the confidence interval as

$$.6 \pm 1.96\sqrt{\frac{(.6)(.4)}{50}} = .6 \pm .1358$$

   Thus, the required interval is .4642 to .7358.

Chapter 10

Answers to Multiple Choice Questions

1. b
2. d
3. c
4. b
5. a
6. c
7. d
8. b
9. c
10. c

Chapter 11
INFERENCES ABOUT MEANS AND PROPORTIONS WITH TWO POPULATIONS

WHAT AM I LEARNING?

Chapter Outline and Summary

This chapter gives the statistical methods for *interval estimation* and *hypothesis testing* for the difference between the means of two populations and the difference between the proportions of two populations based on the information contained in two samples. The formulas are different because of the difference in the expected values and standard deviations of the sampling distributions of the sample statistics, but as before, the general form of the confidence interval and hypothesis test remains the same. This chapter extends our coverage of statistical inference to the following:

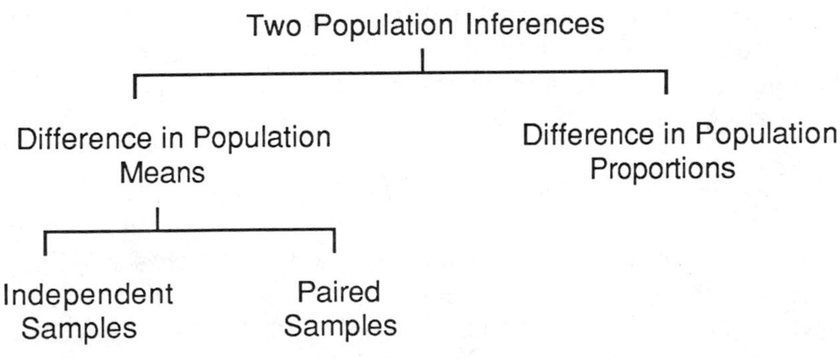

When there are two populations with means μ_1 and μ_2 and variances σ_1^2 and σ_2^2, respectively, the *point estimate of the difference* $\mu_1 - \mu_2$ is given by the statistic $\bar{x}_1 - \bar{x}_2$ where $\bar{x}_1$ is the sample mean of the simple random sample taken from population 1 and $\bar{x}_2$ is the sample mean of the simple random sample taken from population 2. The probability distribution showing all possible values of $\bar{x}_1 - \bar{x}_2$ is called the *sampling distribution of* $\bar{x}_1 - \bar{x}_2$. Using the expected value and standard deviation of the statistic $\bar{x}_1 - \bar{x}_2$, the corresponding confidence interval formula or test of hypothesis statistic can be constructed. The standard deviation of $\bar{x}_1 - \bar{x}_2$ depends on whether the samples are independent or matched, whether or not the population variances are known, the size of the samples which are randomly chosen from each of the two populations, and in some cases, the shape of the parent populations. The forms for confidence intervals and hypothesis tests that arise from these different situations are covered in the formula section of this Guide.

Large sample inferences about the difference between populations means or the difference between population proportions use z statistics. Small sample inferences about the difference between population means can use either an *independent-sample design* (which employs a *pooled variance estimator*) or a *matched-sample design* (employing *difference data*) and use t statistics. Samples are considered *independent* when they are completely separate and unrelated, the results of one sample in no way affecting the results of the other. When observations in one sample are paired or matched with observations in the other sample, the samples are called *paired* or *matched.*

The *point estimator of the difference* $p_1 - p_2$, where p_1 and p_2 are the proportions of success in two populations, is $\bar{p}_1 - \bar{p}_2$, the respective sample proportions of success. Using the standard deviation of this statistic, the corresponding confidence interval or test of hypothesis statistics can be formed. The exact form of the hypothesis testing formula depends on the hypothesized difference of the population proportions. This text considers the case where this hypothesized difference is zero.

Hypothesis tests for differences in means and proportions of two populations once again follow the six steps of a hypothesis test:

Step 1: State, in symbolic form, the null hypothesis.
Step 2: State, in symbolic from, the alternative to the null hypothesis.
Step 3: Determine the test statistic you will use decide whether or not to reject the null hypothesis.
Step 4: Determine the decision rule that provides the appropriate level of significance.
Step 5: Obtain the results of the experiment and use this sample information to calculate the value of the test statistic.
Step 6: Give the conclusion of the test of hypothesis.

Chapter 11

WHICH FORMULA SHOULD I USE?

Formulas

Note: The formulas for confidence intervals and hypothesis tests for each statistic are grouped together in this chapter because of the similar conditions under which they are applicable.

When:

a) working problems about the difference of two population means

b) the two simple random samples are independent

c) σ_1^2 and σ_2^2 are known (Note: s_1^2 and s_2^2 may be used to estimate σ_1^2 and σ_2^2, respectively, when $n_1 \geq 30$ and $n_2 \geq 30$.)

d) both populations are normal (for then, $\bar{x}_1$ and $\bar{x}_2$ have normal distributions regardless of sample size) or $n_1 \geq 30$ and $n_2 \geq 30$ (for then, the Central Limit Theorem applies)

Use:

$$z = \frac{\bar{x}_1 - \bar{x}_2 - (\mu_1 - \mu_2)}{\sqrt{\frac{\sigma_1^2}{n_1} + \frac{\sigma_2^2}{n_2}}} \qquad [1]$$

to test hypotheses about $\mu_1 - \mu_2$

and

$$(\bar{x}_1 - \bar{x}_2) \pm z_{\alpha/2}\sqrt{\frac{\sigma_1^2}{n_1} + \frac{\sigma_2^2}{n_2}} \qquad [2]$$

to give $(1-\alpha)100\%$ confidence intervals for $\mu_1 - \mu$

When:

a) working problems about the difference of two population means

b) the two simple random samples are independent

c) σ_1^2 and σ_2^2 are unknown, but $\sigma_1^2 = \sigma_2^2 = \sigma^2$

d) both populations are normally distributed

Use:

$$t = \frac{\bar{x}_1 - \bar{x}_2 - (\mu_1 - \mu_2)}{\sqrt{s_p^2\left(\frac{1}{n_1} + \frac{1}{n_2}\right)}} \qquad [3]$$

where the t statistic has $n_1 + n_2 - 2$ degrees of freedom to test hypotheses about $\mu_1 - \mu_2$

and

$$(\bar{x}_1 - \bar{x}_2) \pm t_{\alpha/2}\sqrt{s_p^2\left(\frac{1}{n_1} + \frac{1}{n_2}\right)} \qquad [4]$$

where the t statistic has $n_1 + n_2 - 2$ degrees of freedom to give $(1-\alpha)100\%$ confidence intervals for $\mu_1 - \mu_2$

where the pooled variance estimate of σ^2 is

$$s_p^2 = \frac{(n_1-1)s_1^2 + (n_2-1)s_2^2}{n_1 + n_2 - 2} \qquad [5]$$

When:

a) working problems about the difference of two population means

b) the samples are matched (paired)

c) the population of the differences of the data values is normally distributed

Use:

$$t = \frac{\bar{d} - \mu_d}{\frac{s_d}{\sqrt{n}}} \qquad [6]$$

where the t statistic has $n - 1$ degrees of freedom for $n_1 = n_2 = n$ to test hypotheses about the mean difference μ_d

and

$$\bar{d} \pm t_{\alpha/2} \frac{s_d}{\sqrt{n}} \qquad [7]$$

where the t statistic has $n - 1$ degrees of freedom for $n_1 = n_2 = n$ to give $(1-\alpha)100\%$ confidence intervals for the mean difference μ_d

where

$$\bar{d} = \frac{\Sigma d_i}{n} \quad \text{and} \quad s_d^2 = \frac{\Sigma (d_i - \bar{d})^2}{n-1} = \frac{\Sigma d_i^2 - \frac{(\Sigma d_i)^2}{n}}{n - 1} \qquad [8]$$

When:

a) working problems about the difference in two binomial population proportions (percentages)

b) n_1p_1, $n_1(1-p_1)$, n_2p_2, $n_2(1-p_2)$ are all greater than or equal to 5

Use:

$$z = \frac{\bar{p}_1 - \bar{p}_2 - (p_1 - p_2)}{\sqrt{\bar{p}(1-\bar{p})(\frac{1}{n_1} + \frac{1}{n_2})}} \qquad [9]$$

to test the hypothesis H_o: $p_1 - p_2 = 0$

and

$$(\bar{p}_1 - \bar{p}_2) \pm z_{\alpha/2}\sqrt{\frac{\bar{p}_1(1-\bar{p}_1)}{n_1} + \frac{\bar{p}_2(1-\bar{p}_2)}{n_2}} \qquad [10]$$

to give $(1-\alpha)100\%$ confidence intervals for $p_1 - p_2$

where $\bar{p}_1 = x_1 / n_1$ and $\bar{p}_2 = x_2 / n_2$

HERE'S HOW IT'S DONE!

Examples

1. A comparison of the yield of two different varieties of tomatoes, Big Boy and Creole, was obtained by planting and growing 100 acres of each variety under similar growth and soil conditions. The Big Boy plants yielded 80 bushels per acre with a standard deviation of 5 bushels per acre. The Creole plants yielded 76 bushels per acre with a standard deviation of 6 bushels per acre.

   (a) Estimate the mean difference in yield per acre between the two varieties with a 90% confidence interval.

Solution:

(a) Since the samples are independent, use formula [2] to determine the confidence interval for the difference in two population means.

Because the population standard deviations are not known for the large samples, approximate the population standard deviations with the given sample standard deviations.

Letting the population with the Big Boy tomatoes be population 1 and the population with the Creole tomatoes be population 2, we compute the confidence interval, using formula [2], as

$$(80 - 76) \pm 1.645\sqrt{\frac{25}{100} + \frac{36}{100}} = 4 \pm 1.645\sqrt{0.61}$$

$= 4 \pm 1.285$ which gives the interval 2.715 to 5.285.

(b) Interpret this confidence interval.

(b) The person doing the comparison can be 90% confident that the mean yield per acre of land planted with Big Boy tomato plants is between 2.715 and 5.285 bushels higher than the mean yield per acre of land planted with Creole tomatoes.

Out of many such intervals constructed in a manner similar to this one, the difference $\mu_1 - \mu_2$ will be contained in 90% of the intervals; the difference $\mu_1 - \mu_2$ will not be in 10% of the intervals.

2. The length of hospitalization was recorded for patients randomly and independently assigned and subjected to two different surgical procedures. The data, recorded in days, is as follows:

Procedure 1:	$n_1 = 12$	$\bar{x}_1 = 7.3$
Procedure 2:	$n_2 = 16$	$\bar{x}_2 = 8.9$

Using the fact that the two populations from which these samples were drawn are normally distributed with $\sigma_1^2 = 1.5$ and $\sigma_2^2 = 2.4$, construct a 98% confidence interval for the difference in mean time of hospitalization for the two surgical procedures. Interpret this interval estimate.

Solution:

Even though the sample sizes are small, the population variances are known (and unequal). Since both populations are normal, $\bar{x}_1 - \bar{x}_2$ has a normal distribution, and with the independent samples, formula [2] should be used.

The confidence coefficient is $1-\alpha = .98$, giving $\alpha/2 = .01$. Substituting in formula [2], we obtain

$$(7.3 - 8.9) \pm z_{.01}\sqrt{1.5/12 + 2.4/16} = -1.6 \pm 2.33\sqrt{.275} = -1.6 \pm 1.220.$$

Thus, $\mu_1 - \mu_2$ is in the interval (-2.82, -.38).

We are 98% confident that the interval formed in this manner contains the value of $\mu_1 - \mu_2$; that is, 98% of the time that we use this method to estimate the difference in the two population means, the resulting interval actually contains $\mu_1 - \mu_2$. The negative values on the confidence limits indicate that the mean hospitalization time for procedure 1 is estimated to be less than that for procedure 2.

A reminder: The population variances (squared values) are given. Do not square these again when substituting in the formula.

3. Sally Smart obtains the following data on grade-point averages from two independent randomly chosen samples of male and female mathematics majors at State University:

Group 1: Male math majors	$\bar{x} = 3.1$	$s = 0.2$	$n = 10$
Group 2: Female math majors	$\bar{x} = 3.2$	$s = 0.1$	$n = 10$

(a) What is her point estimate of $\mu_1 - \mu_2$?

Solution:

(a) The point estimate of $\mu_1 - \mu_2$ is $\bar{x}_1 - \bar{x}_2 = 3.1 - 3.2 = \underline{-.1}$.

(b) What interval should she give for a 90% interval estimate of $\mu_1 - \mu_2$? Make any necessary assumptions.

Solution:

(b) Assuming that the populations from which these samples were chosen are normally distributed with equal population variances, we use the t confidence interval formula for independent samples, formula [4]. The pooled estimate of the population variance is

$$s_p^2 = \frac{9(.2)^2 + 9(.1)^2}{10 + 10 - 2} = \frac{.45}{18} = .025 .$$

The 90% confidence interval is based on the value of $t_{\alpha/2} = t_{.05} = 1.734$ for $n_1 + n_2 - 2 = 18$ degrees of freedom. The desired confidence interval is then:

$$-.1 \pm 1.734\sqrt{.025(.1 + .1)} = -.1 \pm 1.734(.071) = -.1 \pm .123 \text{ or } (\underline{-.233}, \underline{.023}).$$

(c) Would a 99% confidence interval for $\mu_1 - \mu_2$ be narrower or wider than the 90% confidence interval given in (b)? Why?

Solution:

(c) A 99% confidence would be <u>wider</u> since the confidence is increased and since it is based on the value of $t_{\alpha/2} = t_{.005} = 2.878$.

A reminder: Even though the sample sizes are equal, the number of degrees of freedom of this t statistic is not $n - 1 = 9$, but $n_1 + n_2 - 2 = 18$.

4. The manager of SuperMart Grocery believes that the mean time spent waiting at the checkout counters is more on Sundays (when there are fewer counters open and usually fewer customers) than during weekdays (when there are more counters open). He randomly samples customers during each time period and measures the time spent waiting at the checkout counters. He finds that the mean time on Sundays is 4.50 minutes with a standard deviation of 10 minutes for a sample of 50 customers, and the mean time spent waiting during weekdays is 2.75 minutes with a standard deviation of 12 minutes for a sample of 144 customers.

(a) Does this data provide sufficient evidence to support his belief at the .05 level of significance?

Solution:

(a) Since the samples are large and can be assumed independent of one another, use the z formula for the difference in two population means, formula [1], approximating the population standard deviations with the given sample standard deviations. Letting the population of checkout times on Sundays be population 1 and the population of checkout times on weekdays be population 2, we wish to test:

H_0: $\mu_1 - \mu_2 = 0$ (there is no difference in the mean checkout times)

H_1: $\mu_1 - \mu_2 > 0$ (the manager's belief that the mean time on Sundays is more than the mean time on weekdays)

Using $\alpha = .05$, the decision rule is: Accept H_0 if $z \leq 1.645$
Reject H_0 if $z > 1.645$.

Using formula [1] we obtain the test statistic value

$$z = \frac{4.5 - 2.75}{\sqrt{\frac{100}{50} + \frac{144}{144}}} = \frac{1.75}{\sqrt{3}} = \underline{1.01}\,.$$

Thus, since the value of the test statistic z does not fall in the rejection region, we do not reject the null hypothesis. There is insufficient evidence at the .05 level of significance to support the manager's belief.

(b) Does the test of hypothesis prove the conclusion about the null hypothesis?

Solution:

(b) No, we cannot conclusively say "accept H_0" because there is always the possibility of making a Type II error with probability β.

5. A researcher desired to test the claim that daily doses of Vitamin C taken by children will mean they have fewer common colds. Fifty children were randomly and independently selected for each of two groups with group 1 receiving 100 mg daily of Vitamin C and group 2 receiving no vitamin C supplement. The results for a period of one year were as follows:

	Number of Common Colds	
	Group 1	Group 2
Sample size	50	50
Sample mean	1.5	2.9
Sample variance	8.5	11.5

(a) Do the data provide sufficient evidence, using $\alpha = .10$, to conclude that the mean number of colds for all children with a Vitamin C supplement is less than the mean number of colds for children without such a supplement?

Solution:

(a) Since the samples are large, use the z formula for the difference in two population means, formula [1], approximating the population standard deviations with the given sample standard deviations. We wish to test:

H_0: $\mu_1 - \mu_2 = 0$ (there is no difference in the mean number of colds)

H_1: $\mu_1 - \mu_2 < 0$ (there are fewer colds for children taking Vitamin C)

Using $\alpha = .05$, the decision rule is: Accept H_0 if $z \geq -1.28$
Reject H_0 if $z < -1.28$.

Formula [1] gives

$$z = \frac{1.5 - 2.9}{\sqrt{\frac{8.5}{50} + \frac{11.5}{50}}} = \frac{-1.4}{\sqrt{.4}} = \underline{-2.214}.$$

Thus, since the value of the test statistic z falls in the rejection region, we reject the null hypothesis. There is sufficient evidence at the .10 level of significance to believe that daily doses of 100 mg of Vitamin C does reduce the number of common colds in children.

(b) What is the p value for this test?

Solution:

(b) The p value for this test is $P(z < -2.21) = .5 - .4864 = \underline{.0136}$.

6. Given two independent random samples chosen from two approximately normal populations with equal variances, use the following sample results to test the claim that $\mu_1 < \mu_2$ at the .025 level of significance:

$$n_1 = 10 \qquad \bar{x}_1 = 12 \qquad s_1^2 = 60$$
$$n_2 = 8 \qquad \bar{x}_2 = 20 \qquad s_2^2 = 40$$

Solution:

(a) We wish to test:

H_o: $\mu_1 - \mu_2 = 0$ (there is no difference in the population means)

H_1: $\mu_1 - \mu_2 < 0$ ($\mu_1 < \mu_2$)

Because of the given conditions and the small samples, use the formula for the t statistic for independent samples, formula [3], with $n_1 + n_2 - 2 = 16$ degrees of freedom.

The decision rule, for $\alpha = .025$, is: Accept H_o if $t \geq -2.120$

Reject H_o if $t < -2.120$

The pooled estimate of the population variance is

$$s_p^2 = \frac{9(60) + 7(40)}{10 + 8 - 2} = \frac{820}{16} = \underline{51.25}.$$

Use formula [3] to obtain the value of the test statistic:

$$t = \frac{12 - 20}{\sqrt{51.25(.1 + .125)}} = \frac{-8}{3.396} = \underline{-2.356}\ .$$

Thus, reject H_o and conclude that $\mu_1 < \mu_2$ at the .025 level of significance.

7. Four different types of metal were tested for their resistance to heat. The test was designed as follows: the four strips were cut in half and one piece of each strip was placed in group A while the other matched halves of the strips were placed in group B. The strips in group A were coated with a protective film before being subjected to the heat. The test results were measured on a scale of 0 to 4 with 4 indicating the most resistance to heat. The results were:

Strip	Group A	Group B
1	1	2
2	2	1
3	1	2
4	3	1

Do the data present evidence to indicate that the resistance to heat of these metals is different with the coating of protective material than without? Use $\alpha = .05$.

Solution:

We wish to test:

H_o: $\mu_1 - \mu_2 = 0$ (there is no difference in the population means)

H_1: $\mu_1 - \mu_2 \neq 0$ (there is a difference in the population means)

Since this is a two-tailed test, use $\alpha/2 = .025$ to get the decision rule:

Accept H_o if $-3.182 \leq t \leq 3.182$

Reject H_o otherwise.

Since, by design, the samples are matched, assume the population of differences is normally distributed, and use the t statistic for matched samples, formula [6], with 3 degrees of freedom.

Finding the data of differences we have, for d = group A value - group B value:

Strip	Group A	Group B	d
1	1	2	- 1
2	2	1	+1
3	1	2	- 1
4	3	1	+2

For this data, we use formula [8] to find the summary data for the differences:

$$\bar{d} = \frac{\Sigma d_i}{n} \quad \text{and} \quad s_d^2 = \frac{\Sigma (d_i - \bar{d})^2}{n-1} = \frac{\Sigma d_i^2 - \frac{(\Sigma d_i)^2}{n}}{n-1}$$

Since $\Sigma d = 1$ and $\Sigma d^2 = 7$, substitution in the above formula gives

$\bar{d} = 1$ and $s_d^2 = 9/4$ which means $s_d = 1.5$.

Substituting in the formula for the test statistic, formula [6], we obtain

$$t = \frac{\bar{d} - \mu_d}{\frac{s_d}{\sqrt{n}}} = \frac{.25 - 0}{\frac{1.5}{2}} = \frac{.25}{.75} = \underline{.33}$$

Since this value falls does not fall in the rejection region, the conclusion is do not reject H_0. Thus, the protective coating does not seem to make a difference in the metal's resistance to heat at the .05 level of significance.

8. Two different toothpastes are tested on two sets of children carefully matched for age, sex, diet, fluoride treatments, dental checkups, and so on. During the test period, the number of new cavities for the subjects were recorded:

Subject Pair	A	B	C	D
Toothpaste 1	3	1	4	2
Toothpaste 2	2	1	1	0

Find a 98% confidence interval for the difference in the mean number of new cavities when using the two toothpastes.

Solution:

For the confidence coefficient $1 - \alpha = .98$, $\alpha/2 = .01$ giving $t_{.01} = 4.541$ for 3 degrees of freedom.

Since, by design, the samples are matched, assume the population of differences is normally distributed, and use the t formula for matched samples, formula [7].

The data of differences is 1, 0, 3, 2 where
d = # new cavities for Toothpaste 1 – # new cavities for Toothpaste 2.

For this data,

$$\Sigma d = 6 \text{ and } \Sigma d^2 = 14 \text{ giving } \bar{d} = 1.5 \text{ and } s_d^2 = 1.667 .$$

Substituting in the formula for the interval estimate, formula [7], obtain

$$1.5 \pm 4.541(1.291/2) = 1.5 \pm 2.93 \text{ or } \underline{-1.43} < \mu_d < \underline{4.43} .$$

<u>A reminder</u>: Don't forget to take the square root of s_d^2 since the t formula calls for the standard deviation s_d, not the variance s_d^2.

9. A firm manufacturing candy bars distributes two types: bars with nuts (brand A) and bars without nuts (brand B). If it is found that 56 of 200 people surveyed have purchased brand A in the past month and that 29 of 150 people surveyed have purchased brand B in the past month, develop a 95% confidence interval for the difference in the proportions of all people who have bought the two types of candy bars in the past month.

<u>Solution</u>:
With the confidence $1-\alpha = .95$, $\alpha/2 = .025$ giving $z_{.05} = 1.96$.

The characteristic of interest in population 1 is the purchase of a brand A candy bar, and the characteristic of interest in population 2 is the purchase of a brand B candy bar. Then, find the sample proportions

$$\bar{p}_1 = 56/200 = \underline{.28} \quad \text{and} \quad \bar{p}_2 = 29/150 = \underline{.193}.$$

Substitution in formula [10] gives

$$(.28 - .193) \pm 1.96\sqrt{\frac{(.28)(.72)}{200} + \frac{(.193)(.807)}{150}} = .087 \pm 1.96\sqrt{.002}$$

giving the interval ($\underline{-.002}$, $\underline{.1754}$).

10. The records of a certain metropolitan hospital show that 52 men in a sample of 1000 men versus 23 women in a sample of 1000 women were admitted because of heart disease. Do these data present sufficient evidence to indicate a higher proportion of heart disease among men admitted to the hospital than among women admitted to the hospital? Test using a level of significance of 0.10.

Solution:

Using p_m and p_w to indicate, respectively, the proportion of all men and all women who were admitted to the hospital for heart disease, we wish to test

$$H_0: \; p_m - p_w = 0$$
$$H_1: \; p_m - p_w > 0$$

The decision rule is: Accept H_0 if $z \le 1.28$
Reject H_0 if $z > 1.28$.

Using the sample proportions $\bar{p}_1 = 0.52$ and $\bar{p}_2 = 0.023$ in the z formula used to test the hypothesis that there is no difference in the population proportions, formula [9], we obtain

$\bar{p} = (52 + 23) / (1000 + 1000)$. Thus,

$$z = \frac{.052 - .023}{\sqrt{(.0375)(.9625)(\frac{1}{1000} + \frac{1}{1000})}} = \frac{.029}{\sqrt{.000072}}$$

giving $z = \underline{3.413}$.

Since this value falls in the rejection region, reject H_0 and conclude that the proportion of men admitted to this hospital because of heart disease is higher that the proportion of women admitted to this hospital because of heart disease.

A reminder: Because problems with proportions can involve very small decimal quantities, be sure to carry enough decimal places in your computations. If not, the round off error could lead to incorrect results.

Chapter 11

HAVE I LEARNED THE MATERIAL?

Problems

1. The production manager of Valmir, Inc., a company that makes computer disks, wishes to obtain an estimate of the difference in the proportion of defective disks made by Valmir's two plants. By random sampling at each of the plants, he obtains the following data: the number of defective disks in a sample of 100 at the first plant is 10, and the number of defective disks in a sample of 100 disks at the second plant is 20. What interval estimate should he use if he wishes to be 99% confident in his estimate?

2. A consumer wishes to know if she really saves money by buying the cost-cutter VCR tape rather than the leading brand name VCR tape. She obtains the following data from randomly chosen independent samples on the number of hours before bothersome snow or streaks occur in the playback picture for each of the tapes:

Type of VCR tape	Cost-cutter (1)	Leading brand name (2)
Sample size	80	50
Sample mean	76.2	80.3
Sample variance	64.5	49.3

(a) Test the hypothesis that the cost-cutter tape does not last as long (in terms of mean hours of life before snow or streaks occur in the playback picture) as the leading brand name tape. Use $\alpha = .025$.

(b) Are there any assumptions that must be made about the populations for the procedure in problem 2 to be valid?

3. A course in typing is taught to 16 students by the conventional teacher-instructed classroom procedure. A second group of 11 students, chosen independently from the first group, was given approximately the same course using a programmed computer software package. At the end of two weeks, the same typing examination was given to each group. The first group (teacher-instructed) made an average grade of 85 with a standard deviation of 4, while the second group (computer instructed) made an average grade of 81 with a standard deviation of 5.

   (a) Does the conventional classroom procedure produce higher scores on the typing examination than the computer procedure at the .01 level of significance? Consider the populations from which these samples were drawn to be normally distributed.

   (b) What assumption is necessary about the population variances in order for the procedure you used above to be valid?

   (c) Find and interpret the p value for this test of hypothesis problem.

4. A random sample of size $n_1 = 25$ taken from a normal population with $\sigma_1 = 5$ has a mean $\bar{x}_1 = 80$. A second random sample of size $n_2 = 36$ taken from a different normal population with $\sigma_2 = 3$ has a mean $\bar{x}_2 = 75$. Find a 98% confidence interval for the difference $\mu_1 - \mu_2$.

5. A dentist wishes to estimate, with a 90% confidence interval, the difference in the mean number of cavities in children who have a fluoride treatment at the time of the annual dental checkup and the mean number of cavities in children who do not have the treatment. Twelve children who had fluoride treatments over a period of three years were compared to ten children who did not. Of those receiving the treatment the mean number of cavities was $\bar{x}_1 = 2.64$ with $s_1 = 0.66$. For those not using the fluoride treatment $\bar{x}_2 = 4.93$ with $s_2 = 1.14$. Give the confidence interval.

(b) Are there any assumptions that must be made about either the samples and/or the populations in order for this interval to be valid?

6. John Q. Public is running for mayor. The local newspaper has said that the percentage of voters who favor Mr. Public is different for the two precincts in town. Mr. Public's staff randomly surveys a sample of the voters in each precinct and finds 90 voters out of 100 f or him in precinct 1 and 150 voters out of 300 favoring him in precinct 2. Is there evidence of a difference in the percentage of voters in favor of Mr. Public in the two precincts at the .05 level of significance?

7. A sample survey is conducted to compare the mean annual incomes for waiters and waitresses at medium -priced restaurants in New York City. A random sample of 64 is independently selected from each group. The samples show the following results:

<u>Waiters</u>	<u>Waitresses</u>
$\bar{x}$ = \$14,225	$\bar{x}$ = \$15,212
s = 1,800	s = 2,400

Give a 98% confidence interval for the difference in the true mean incomes for the two groups. Interpret this interval estimate.

8. To test the effect of a speed reading course given to three students, a measure of the mean reading score of the three students was taken after and before they took the course. The results are shown below:

Student	Measure after course	Measure before course
1	4	3
2	6	6
3	5	3

Develop a 90% confidence interval for the difference in the mean scores after and before the course is taken.

9. Do blondes have more fun? A college fraternity randomly surveyed 100 women with blonde hair and found they had an average of 2.70 dates per week with a standard deviation of 0.6, while the 100 women with a hair color other than blonde had an average of 2.04 dates per week with a standard deviation of 1.5. These samples were randomly and independently chosen from the student body at their university. Can the fraternity conclude that the mean number of dates per week for all blondes at this university is significantly more than the mean number of dates per week for women who are not blonde?

10. To test the effect of alcohol on reaction time to respond to a certain stimulus, the reaction times of seven persons were measured. After consuming three ounces of a beverage containing 20% alcohol, the reaction time for each of the seven persons was measured again. Do the following data indicate that the mean time of reaction before consuming the alcohol was less than the mean reaction time after consuming alcohol? Use $\alpha = .05$.

	Reaction time (in seconds)	
Person	Before alcohol	After alcohol
A	4	7
B	5	9
C	5	3
D	4	5
E	3	2
F	5	6
G	3	7

Chapter 11

Multiple Choice Questions

For each of the following multiple choice questions, circle the correct answer.

1. When using the t test for the difference between the means of two populations with independent samples, we must have

   (a) equal sample variances
   (b) equal sample sizes
   (c) equal population variances
   (d) all of the above.

2. When using the t test for the difference between the means of two populations with two independent samples, each of size 14, how many degrees of freedom does the t statistic have?

   (a) 14
   (b) 13
   (c) 26
   (d) none of the above - we should be using the z test.

3. When using the t test for the difference between the means of two populations with paired (matched) samples, each of size 14, how many degrees of freedom does the t statistic have?

   (a) 14
   (b) 13
   (c) 26
   (d) none of the above.

4. Generally, matched pair sampling is preferable to independent samples because

   (a) the matched-sampling design is of less cost to the experimenter
   (b) the matched-sampling design allows the experimenter to control some factors to obtain a better measure of others
   (c) the matched-sampling design often leads to smaller sampling error
   (d) both b) and c).

5. The sampling distribution of $\bar{x}_1 - \bar{x}_2$ for large samples

   (a) has a t distribution with center at $\mu_1 - \mu_2$
   (b) has approximately a normal distribution with center at 0
   (c) has approximately a normal distribution with center at $\mu_1 - \mu_2$
   (d) has a distribution that is normal only if $\mu_1 - \mu_2 > 0$.

6. A psychologist is testing random samples of third grade boys and girls for mental dexterity, with each subject being graded "pass" or "fail" on a problem involving logical reasoning. If the samples yielded the results that 84 of 120 boys and 60 of 80 girls passed the test, what alternative hypothesis would she use to test the claim "the proportion of all third grade boys who pass this test differs from the proportion of all third grade girls who pass this test"?

   (a) $\mu_b - \mu_g = 0$
   (b) $\mu_b - \mu_g \neq 0$
   (c) $p_b - p_g \neq 0$
   (d) $\mu_d \neq 0$ in the matched-sample t test.

7. Refer to problem 6 above. The value of the test statistic that is used in making the decision concerning the null hypothesis is

   (a) $z = {}^{-}.7715$
   (b) $z = {}^{-}.7815$
   (c) $t = {}^{-}1.282$
   (d) none of the above.

8. In a matched-sample t test concerning the difference in two population means, the data of differences is: 1, 2, 1, 0 . The calculated values of the mean and standard deviation of this difference data are, respectively,

   (a) 1 and .6667
   (b) 1 and .8165
   (c) 2 and 1.6667
   (d) none of the above.

9. In a one-tailed test of hypothesis concerning the difference in the means of two normally distributed populations with small samples and unknown, but equal, population variances, the calculated value of the test statistic is $t = 1.865$. The number of degrees of freedom is 23. For this problem,

(a) p value = .5 - .4693
(b) p value > .10
(c) .025 < p value < .05
(d) .05 < p value < .10

10. Two independent random samples drawn from normally distributed populations yielded the following results:

$n_1 = 50$	$\bar{x}_1 = 317.8$	$s_1^2 = 116.64$
$n_2 = 60$	$\bar{x}_2 = 301.9$	$s_2^2 = 87.60$

Give a 99% confidence interval for $\mu_1 - \mu_2$:

(a) $(317.8 - 301.9) \pm 2.33\sqrt{(116.64/50) - (87.6/60)}$

(b) $(317.8 - 301.9) \pm 2.33\,[(116.64^2/50) + (87.6^2/60)]$

(c) $(301.9 - 317.8) \pm 2.58\sqrt{(116.64/60) + (87.6/50)}$

(d) $(317.8 - 301.9) \pm 2.58\sqrt{(116.64/50) + (87.6/60)}$.

Answers to Problems

1. The required confidence interval is obtained by substituting in formula [10] with

   $\bar{p}_1 = .10$, $\bar{p}_2 = .20$, and $z_{.005} = 2.58$ obtaining $-.1 \pm .129$ or <u>(−.229, .029)</u>.

2. (a) $H_0\colon \mu_1 - \mu_2 = 0$ Accept H_0 if $z \geq -1.96$

   $H_1\colon \mu_1 - \mu_2 < 0$ Reject H_0 if $z < -1.96$.

   Using formula [1] , we obtain $z = -4.1/1.34 = \underline{-3.06}$ and reject H_0.

   (b) <u>No</u>, because the sample sizes are each over thirty.

3. (a) $H_0\colon \mu_1 - \mu_2 = 0$ Accept H_0 if $t \leq 2.485$

   $H_1\colon \mu_1 - \mu_2 > 0$ Reject H_0 if $t > 2.485$.

   Using $s_p^2 = 19.6$, obtain $t = 4/1.734 = \underline{2.307}$. Thus, do not reject H_0.

   At the .01 level of significance, the conventional teacher-instructed method does not produce higher exam scores than the computer-instructed method.

   (b) $\sigma_1^2 = \sigma_2^2$

   (c) p value = $P(t > 2.307)$ and without interpolation, <u>.01 < p value < .025</u>. Since the null hypothesis is rejected for any $\alpha >$ p value, Ho would be rejected for several standard values of α, but not the α given in this problem.

4. Because the population variances are known and the populations are normal, $\bar{x}_1 - \bar{x}_2$ has a normal distribution. Thus, using formula [2], we obtain

   $5 \pm 2.33(1.118) = 5 \pm 2.60$ or <u>2.4 to 7.6</u>.

5. Using formula [4] (logically, the samples should be independent), we obtain

$s_p^2 = 16.488 / 20 = .8244$. Using $t_{.05}$ for 20 degrees of freedom gives

$$-2.29 \pm 1.725(.3888) = -2.29 \pm 0.67 \quad \text{or} \quad (\underline{-2.96}, \underline{-1.62}).$$

(b) Yes, the assumptions are: both samples are randomly and independently selected from the two normally distributed populations whose variances are equal.

6. H_0: $p_1 - p_2 = 0$ Accept H_0 if $-1.96 \leq z \leq 1.96$

H_1: $p_1 - p_2 \neq 0$ Reject H_0 otherwise.

Using the formula [9] with $\bar{p}_1 = .9$, $\bar{p}_2 = .5$ and $\bar{p} = 0.6$, $z = .4/.0566 = \underline{7.07}$.

Reject H_0 - the newspaper is correct.

7. For these large samples, use formula [2] obtaining

$$-987 \pm 2.33(375) = -987 \pm 873.75 \quad \text{or} \quad (\underline{-\$1860.75}, \underline{-\$113.25}).$$

We can say that if many such intervals were constructed in a manner similar to this one, 98% of them would contain the true difference in the population means; 2% of them would not.

We estimate that μ_2, the mean annual income for the waitresses, is between \$113.25 and \$1860.75 more than μ_1, the mean annual income for the waiters.

8. Because the samples are matched, use the difference data

d = score after course – score before course: 1, 0, 2.

For this difference data, $\bar{d} = 1$ and $s_d = 1$. Using $t_{.05}$ with 2 degrees of freedom, the required confidence interval is found by substituting in formula [7]:

$$1 \pm 2.920(1/\sqrt{3}) = 1 \pm 1.686 \quad \text{or} \quad (\underline{-.686}, \underline{2.686}).$$

9. Letting "1" refer to the population of blondes and "2" refer to the population of non-blondes, we have

H_0: $\mu_1 - \mu_2 = 0$

H_1: $\mu_1 - \mu_2 > 0$.

Using formula [1], we obtain $z = .66/.162 = \underline{4.07}$.

The p value for this problem is $P(z > 4.07) = \underline{0}$.

Thus, because H_0 would be rejected for any $\alpha >$ p value (in this case, H_0 is rejected for <u>all</u> α since the p value is zero), the fraternity should reject H_0 and believe that the mean number of dates for blondes is significantly greater than the mean number of dates for non-blondes at their university.

10. H_0: $\mu_B - \mu_A = 0$ (or H_0: $\mu_d = 0$

H_1: $\mu_B - \mu_A < 0$ H_1: $\mu_d < 0$)

The decision rule is: Accept H_0 if $t \geq -1.943$

Reject H_0 if $t < -1.943$.

Because the samples are matched, use the difference data

−3, −4, +2, −1, +1, −1, −4 where d = reaction time before − reaction time after.

For this difference data, $\bar{d} = -10/7 = -1.429$, and $s_d^2 = 5.619$.

Using $t_{.05}$ with 6 degrees of freedom, $t = -1.429/.896 = \underline{-1.595}$.

Thus, do not reject H_0 using the .05 level of significance.

Chapter 11

Answers to Multiple-Choice Questions

1. c
2. c
3. b
4. d
5. c
6. c
7. a
8. b
9. c
10. d

Chapter 12
INFERENCES ABOUT POPULATION VARIANCES

WHAT AM I LEARNING?

Chapter Outline and Summary

We continue the discussion of statistical inference in this chapter by considering methods for making inferences about *population variances.* We have seen in preceding sections that an estimate of the population variance, σ^2, is fundamental to procedures for making inferences about population means. Moreover there are many practical situations where σ^2 is the primary objective of an experimental investigation.

For inferences about a population variance, we again work with a sampling distribution of a sample statistic. The natural choice of a sample statistic is s^2, the sample variance. However, it is more convenient to work with the sampling distribution of the quantity $(n - 1)\, s^2/\sigma^2$ because for normally distributed populations this quantity has a probability distribution referred to as a *chi-square distribution* with tables of probabilities already formulated. The shape of the chi-square distribution, like that of the t distribution, will vary with the sample size. Thus, Table 3 of Appendix B of the Anderson/Sweeney/Williams text is constructed in a similar manner to the t table, with degrees of freedom shown in the left hand column.

The statistic $(n - 1)\, s^2/\sigma^2$ is called the *chi-square statistic,* denoted by χ^2. Whenever a random sample of size n is selected from a normally distributed population, χ^2 has a chi-square distribution with n - 1 *degrees of freedom.* Notice that the chi-square distribution is, in general, *not* symmetrical. It commences at $\chi^2 = 0$ since the value $(n - 1)\, s^2/\sigma^2$ cannot be negative. As the sample size, n, gets larger, the shape of the chi-square distribution approaches the shape of a normal distribution.

In Table 3, as with t, the value of the symbol χ^2_α is the value of the chi-square distribution such that $P(\chi^2 > \chi^2_\alpha) = \alpha$. However, unlike t, values corresponding to areas in the left tail of the chi-square distribution cannot be obtained by using the symmetry of the distribution since the chi-square distribution is not symmetrical. Thus, the values in Table 3 of χ^2_α for $\alpha > .05$ represent values in the left tail of the chi-square distribution. To use this table, remember that the subscript α in χ^2_α always represents area to the right of the value given in the table for the appropriate number of degrees of freedom.

The chi-square distribution can be used to develop a confidence interval estimate of a population variance σ^2 for a normal population. We use the notation $\chi^2_{1-\alpha/2}$ and $\chi^2_{\alpha/2}$ to mean the points of the chi-square distribution such that the probability the variable χ^2 is between the values $\chi^2_{1-\alpha/2}$ and $\chi^2_{\alpha/2}$ equals $1 - \alpha$. Graphically, this is

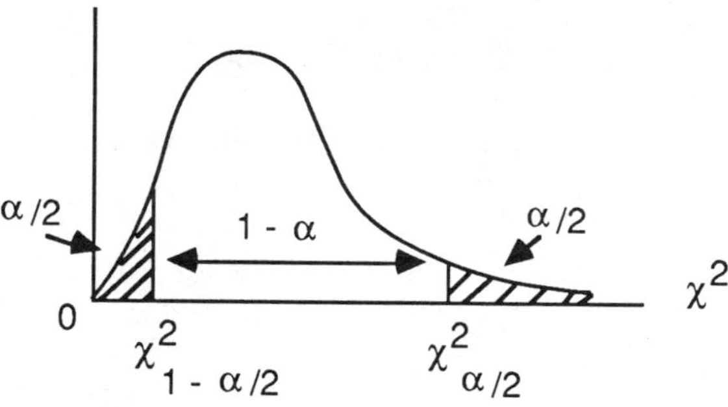

Then, we have a $(1 - \alpha)100\%$ *confidence interval for a variance* σ^2 of a normal population given by the formula

$$\frac{(n-1)s^2}{\chi^2_{\alpha/2}} \leq \sigma^2 \leq \frac{(n-1)s^2}{\chi^2_{1-\alpha/2}}$$

where the chi-square distribution has $n - 1$ degrees of freedom. Note that in this formula, the sense of the inequality has changed from the one presented in the above graph. The larger value of χ^2 now appears in the denominator of the lower endpoint for σ^2, while the smaller value of χ^2 is in the denominator of the term giving the upper endpoint of the confidence interval for σ^2.

Tests of hypothesis involving the population variance σ^2 again use the procedure presented in the six steps of a hypothesis test given in previous chapters. The test is based on the value of χ^2 calculated by the formula $(n - 1)s^2/\sigma^2$ and the chi-square distribution with $n - 1$ degrees of freedom.

In Chapter 11, we looked at procedures for developing confidence intervals and testing hypotheses for the means and proportions of two populations. Situations in which an experimenter may want to test hypotheses about two variances, neither of which are known, frequently arise.

To determine whether or not two population variances, denoted by σ_1^2 and σ_2^2, differ significantly from one another, we refer to yet another distribution: the F distribution. In the hypothesis testing procedure, the test statistic used is the ratio of the two sample variances s_1^2/s_2^2. Whenever the two populations involved both have normal probability distributions with equal variances and we use data collected from two independent random samples, the ratio s_1^2/s_2^2 has the *F probability distribution.*

Since neither s_1^2 nor s_2^2 is negative, values of the F distribution are never negative. The shape of the F distribution depends on the number of degrees of freedom associated with it. Since we are using two sample variances, we must specify two degrees of freedom values. Thus, when using $F = s_1^2/s_2^2$, we say there are $n_1 - 1$ degrees of freedom for the numerator and $n_2 - 1$ degrees of freedom for the denominator.

Again using the notation F_α to denote the point of the F distribution such that the area to the right of the point F_α is α as we did with the other distributions, we use Table 4 of Appendix B of the Anderson/Sweeney/Williams text to find the values of the F distribution associated with certain areas α. In this table only the most commonly used values for α are given because there are so many different combinations of degrees of freedom for the sample sizes. Table 4 provides F values that cut off areas of .05, .025, and .01 in the upper tail of the F distribution. To compute corresponding lower tail values, we use the *inverse relationship* of the F statistic: $F_{1-\alpha} = 1/F_\alpha$ where $F_{1-\alpha}$ is from an F distribution with n_1-1 degrees of freedom in the numerator and n_2-1 degrees of freedom in the denominator and F_α is from an F distribution with n_2-1 degrees of freedom in the numerator and n_1-1 degrees of freedom in the denominator.

Hypothesis testing procedures concerning testing the null hypothesis H_0: $\sigma_1^2 = \sigma_2^2$ are based on the value of the test statistic s_1^2/s_2^2. These procedures follow the six steps outlined in Chapter 9. In one-tail tests of hypotheses, it is convenient (by the way Table 4 is presented) to set up the null hypotheses so that the rejection region is in the upper tail. This can be accomplished by labeling the population with the variance that involves "greater than" in the alternative hypothesis as population 1.

WHICH FORMULA SHOULD I USE?

Formulas

When:

(a) testing a hypothesis about the variance of one population
(b) the population is normally distributed
(c) s^2 is the sample variance for a random sample of size n chosen from the population

Use:

$$\chi^2 = \frac{(n-1)s^2}{\sigma^2} \qquad [1]$$

with $n - 1$ degrees of freedom

When:

(a) determining a $(1 - \alpha)100\%$ confidence interval for the variance of one population
(b) the population is normally distributed

Use:

$$\frac{(n-1)s^2}{\chi^2_{\alpha/2}} \le \sigma^2 \le \frac{(n-1)s^2}{\chi^2_{1-\alpha/2}} \qquad [2]$$

where the values of χ^2 are based on the chi-square distribution with $n - 1$ degrees of freedom

When:

(a) testing a hypothesis about the equality of the variances of two populations
(b) both populations are normally distributed
(c) the samples are independent
(d) s_1^2 is the sample variance for a random sample of size n_1 chosen from the first population and s_2^2 is the sample variance for a random sample of size n_2 chosen from the second population

Use:

$$F = \frac{s_1^2}{s_2^2} \qquad [3]$$

with $n_1 - 1$ degrees of freedom for the numerator and $n_2 - 1$ degrees of freedom for the denominator

When:
determining lower tail values for the F distribution

Use:
Inverse Relationship of the F Statistic

$$F_{(1-\alpha)} = 1/F_{\alpha} \qquad [4]$$

where $F_{(1-\alpha)}$ is a value with "a" degrees of freedom in the numerator and "b" degrees of freedom in the denominator,

and

F_a is a value with "b" degrees of freedom in the numerator and "a" degrees of freedom in the denominator.

$$\frac{(n-1)\,s^2}{\chi^2_{\alpha/2}} \le \sigma^2 \le \frac{(n-1)\,s^2}{\chi^2_{1-\alpha/2}} \quad \text{gives} \quad \frac{19\,(16)}{36.1908} \le \sigma^2 \le \frac{19\,(16)}{7.6327}$$

so $\underline{8.3999} < \sigma^2 < \underline{39.8286}$.

Note: The areas to the right of the points in Table 3 (that is, the values across the top in the table) are the same as the subscript appearing on the chi-square variable.

3. A manufacturer of car batteries claims that the normally distributed life, in years, of his batteries has a variance equal to .81. If a random sample of 10 of these batteries showed a standard deviation of 1.2 years, do you believe that the variance of the life of all the batteries is more than .81? (Use $\alpha = .05$.)

Solution:

Following the six steps of the hypothesis testing procedure, we have:

Steps 1 and 2: We wish to test H_0: $\sigma^2 = .81$ versus H_1: $\sigma^2 > .81$.

Step 3: Because we are testing a hypothesis about the variance of one normally distributed population, the test statistic is χ^2 with 9 degrees of freedom, found in formula [1].

Step 4: The decision rule is: Accept H_0 if $\chi^2 \le 16.919$
(using $\alpha = .05$) Reject H_0 if $\chi^2 > 16.919$.

Step 5: Substituting in formula [1], using the given information $n = 10$ and $s = 1.2$, we have

$$\chi^2 = \frac{(n-1)\,s^2}{\sigma^2} = \frac{(9)\,(1.2)^2}{.81} = \underline{16}\,.$$

Step 6: The value of $\chi^2 = 16$ does not lie in the rejection region, so we do not reject the null hypothesis. No, there is insufficient evidence to conclude that the variance of the life of all the batteries is more than .81.

4. To aid in the of understanding Table 4, find each of the following. For each part, the F statistic is defined as $F = s_1^2/s_2^2$ with n_1-1 degrees of freedom in the numerator and n_2-1 degrees of freedom in the denominator.

   (a) Find the value of the F distribution, say F_o, such that $P(F > F_o) = .05$ for $n_1 = 6$ and $n_2 = 3$.

Solution:

(a) Since Table 4 is set up to give us the point (in the main body of the table) that has a certain amount of area to the right of that point, all we need to do is look in the portion of Table 4 that is for $\alpha = .05$ for the appropriate number of degrees of freedom. Since $F = s_1^2/s_2^2$ has (6 - 1) degrees of freedom for the numerator and (3 - 1) degrees of freedom for the denominator, we look in Table 4 for the number 5 across the top and 2 down the side to obtain the value 19.30.

   (b) Find the value of the F distribution, say F_o, such that $P(F > F_o) = .99$ for $n_1 = 21$ and $n_2 = 8$.

Solution:

(b) If we had a portion of Table 4 for $\alpha = .99$ (as does the χ^2 table), we would find the required value as we did in part a) of this problem. However, Table 4 only gives values of the F distribution for areas (α) of .05, .025, and .01 to the right of the point in the table. Notice, however, that if $\alpha = .01$, $1 - \alpha = .99$. Thus we may use the inverse relationship of the F statistic (formula [4]) to find the required point of the F distribution.

Thus, letting the notation (a, b) represent the degrees of freedom associated with the F statistic as a = number of degrees of freedom for the numerator and b = number of degrees of freedom for the denominator, the statistic we are working with, $F = s_1^2/s_2^2$, has (a,b) = (20, 7) degrees of freedom (dof). Using formula [4], we have

$$F_{.99} \text{ with } (20,7) \text{ dof} = 1/F_{.01} \text{ with } (7,20) \text{ dof} = 1/3.70 = .2703.$$

Note: The above notation for the number of degrees of freedom associated with the F distribution will be used throughout the remainder of this chapter.

5. Two new methods of measuring chemical reaction temperature are tested. Random independent samples of size $n_1 = 13$ and $n_2 = 24$ are taken, and the time to determine the correct temperature is recorded. The time is expected to be normally distributed. The variances of these sample times are $s_1^2 = .32$ and $s_2^2 = .08$. Do these summary data give evidence, at the .01 level of significance, to indicate that the variance of the first population of times is more than that of the second population of times?

Solution:

Following the six steps of the hypothesis testing procedure, we have:

Steps 1 and 2: We wish to test H_0: $\sigma_1^2 = \sigma_2^2$ versus H_1: $\sigma_1^2 > \sigma_2^2$

Step 3: Because we are testing a hypothesis about the variance of two normally distributed populations, the test statistic is F with (12,23) degrees of freedom, found in formula [3].

Step 4: The decision rule is: Accept H_0 if $F \leq 3.07$

(using $\alpha = .01$) Reject H_0 if $F > 3.07$.

Step 5: Substituting in formula [3], using the information given in the problem, we have

$$F = .32/.08 = \underline{4}.$$

Step 6: The value of $F = 4$ falls in the rejection region, so we reject the null hypothesis. Yes, these summary data give evidence, at the .01 level of significance, that the variance of the first population of times is more than that of the second population of times.

6. The temperatures of operation of two paint-drying ovens associated with two manufacturing production lines was recorded, independently, for 21 days for each oven. The sample results are as follows:

	Oven A	Oven B
Mean of sample	164	168
Variance of sample	81	172

Does this data present sufficient evidence to indicate the temperature variability in Oven A is less than the temperature variability for Oven B? The temperatures of operation for each oven are known to be approximately normally distributed. Use a level of significance of .025.

Solution:

If we were to call the temperature of operation for Oven A population 1, we would be faced with the problem of the alternative hypothesis being written with the symbol "<". This is not a serious problem, but it does require some extra work due to the fact that we would need to use the inverse relationship of the F statistic to determine the lower tail critical value. Thus, we will call the temperature of operation for Oven B population 1 which makes the temperature of operation for Oven A population 2. The question asked in the problem now can be stated as:

Does this data present sufficient evidence to indicate the temperature variability of population 1 is <u>more than</u> the temperature variability for population 2?

Following the six steps of the hypothesis testing procedure, we have:

Steps 1 and 2: We wish to test H_0: $\sigma_1^2 = \sigma_2^2$ versus H_1: $\sigma_1^2 > \sigma_2^2$

Step 3: Because we are testing a hypothesis about the variance of two normally distributed populations, the test statistic is F with (20,20) degrees of freedom, found in formula [3].

Step 4: The decision rule is: Accept H_0 if $F \le 2.46$

(using $\alpha = .025$) Reject H_0 if $F > 2.46$.

Step 5: Substituting in formula [3], using the information given in the problem, we have

$$F = 172/81 = \underline{2.123}.$$

Step 6: The value of F = 2.123 does not fall in the rejection region, so we do not reject the null hypothesis. <u>No</u>, there is not sufficient evidence to indicate the temperature variability in Oven A is less than the temperature variability for Oven B at the .025 level of significance.

7. In problem 3 of Chapter 11 of this Guide, you had to make the assumption of equal population variances in order to use the t test for independent samples in order to work the problem. Problem 3 is repeated below for reference:

A course in typing is taught to 16 students by the conventional teacher-instructed classroom procedure. A second group of 11 students, chosen independently from the first group, was given approximately the same course using a programmed computer software package. At the end of two weeks, the same typing examination was given to each group. The first group (teacher-instructed) made an average grade of 85 with a standard deviation of 4, while the second group (computer instructed) made an average grade of 81 with a standard deviation of 5. Does the conventional classroom procedure produce higher scores on the typing examination than the computer procedure at the .01 level of significance? Consider the populations from which these samples were drawn to be normally distributed.

Perform a test of hypothesis, with $\alpha = .02$, to determine if the assumption of equal population variances is a valid one. (If not, the results of problem 3 of Chapter 11 are not valid.)

<u>Solution</u>:

Referring to the grades for the teacher-instructed group as population 1 and the grades for the computer-instructed group as population 2, we again follow the six steps of the hypothesis testing procedure:

Steps 1 and 2: We wish to test H_0: $\sigma_1^2 = \sigma_2^2$ versus H_1: $\sigma_1^2 \neq \sigma_2^2$

Step 3: Because we are testing a hypothesis about the variance of two normally distributed populations, the test statistic is F with (15,10) degrees of freedom, found in formula [3].

Step 4: The decision rule is: Accept H_0 if $.2632 \leq F \leq 4.56$
(using $\alpha = .02$) Reject H_0 otherwise.

<u>Note</u>: The lower tail critical value of .2632 was obtained using formula [4]:

$$F_{.99} \text{ with } (15,10) \text{ dof} = 1/F_{.01} \text{ with } (10,15) \text{ dof} = 1/3.80 = .2632$$

Step 5: Substituting in formula [3], using the information given in the problem, we have

$$F = 16/25 = \underline{0.64}.$$

Step 6: The value of F = .64 does not fall in the rejection region, so we do not reject the null hypothesis. <u>Yes</u>, the assumption of equal population variances is a valid one and the results of problem 3 are therefore valid.

HAVE I LEARNED THE MATERIAL?

Problems

1. (a) Find $\chi^2_{.01}$ for 18 degrees of freedom.

   (b) Find $\chi^2_{.975}$ for 29 degrees of freedom.

   (c) Find χ_o^2 such that $P(\chi^2 < \chi_o^2) = .99$ for 4 degrees of freedom.

2. A television manufacturer is investigating the amount of variation in retail prices of its 19-inch portable black and white sets. In a sample of 25 retailers, the mean price was \$95 with a standard deviation of \$7. Find a 90% confidence interval for the standard deviation of the price of the population of TV sets for this manufacturer.

3. A random sample of 22 observations form a normal population gave a sample variance equal to 37.3. Do these data provide sufficient evidence to indicate that the population variance exceeds 30? Test using $\alpha = .05$.

4. A manufacturer is interested in comparing the variability of the trade-in allowances of two different types of refrigerators. In a sample of 16 Brand A refrigerators the sample variance was found to be 16.40 and in a sample of 9 Brand B refrigerators the sample variance was found to be 4. At the .01 level of significance, does this data indicate the variability of the trade-in allowances for Brand A refrigerators is more than the variability of the trade-in allowance for Brand B refrigerators?

5. (a) Suppose that we want to investigate whether or not men and women earn comparable wages in a certain industry. Sample data show that 10 men earn on the average $282.50 per week with a standard deviation of $15.60 per week while 15 women earn on the average $266.10 per week with a standard deviation of $18.20 per week. If you know that the samples were randomly and independently chosen from their respective populations with the weekly wages being normally distributed for each population, what other condition must hold true for the populations in order to test for the equality of the means of these two populations? (Call the weekly wages of the men population 1.)

(b) Test this condition at the .10 level of significance.

(c) Using a level of significance of .05, test to see if there is a difference in the mean weekly wages for men and women in this industry. (You haven't forgotten how to do this test from Chapter 11, have you?)

6. (a) An experimenter was convinced that his measuring device possessed a variability measured by a standard deviation of $\sigma = 2$. During an experiment, he recorded the measurements 4.1, 5.2, 10.2. Do these data disagree with his assumption? Test using a level of significance of .10.

(b) What must be true about the population in this problem in order for the procedure you used above to be valid?

(c) Find a 95% confidence interval for the population variance using the above sample data.

7. Independent random samples chosen from two normally distributed populations called population A and population B yielded the following results:

	Population A	Population B
Sample size	8	6
Sample mean	25.4	30.6
Sample standard deviation	4	6

Can you conclude, at the .05 level of significance, that the variance of population A is less than the variance of population B?

Chapter 12

Multiple Choice Questions

1. The distribution of $s_1{}^2/s_2{}^2$ for two independent samples chosen from normal populations is the

   (a) χ^2 distribution
   (b) standard normal distribution
   (c) t distribution
   (d) F distribution.

2. For the chi-square distribution with n-1 degrees of freedom, $P(\chi^2 > 40.65)$ for a sample of size 26 is greater than $P(\chi^2 > 40.65)$ for a sample of size

   (a) n = 30
   (b) n = 91
   (c) n = 10
   (d) none of the above.

3. All other things being equal, a 99% confidence interval for the variance of a normally distributed population would be wider if computed from a sample of 50 items than if computed from a sample of

   (a) 20 items
   (b) 30 items
   (c) 75 items
   (d) none of the above.

4. A two-tailed test of hypothesis is to be performed to test the claim $\sigma_1{}^2 = \sigma_2{}^2$ using the ratio $s_1{}^2/s_2{}^2$ for samples of size $n_1 = 16$ and $n_2 = 21$. If the level of significance of the test is .10, which of the following represents the lower tail critical value of the F distribution to which $s_1{}^2/s_2{}^2$ should be compared?

   (a) 1/2.20
   (b) 1/2.33
   (c) The answer cannot be determined since we have no F table for $\alpha = .10$.
   (d) None of these - the χ^2 table should be used.

5. For the chi-square distribution with 11 degrees of freedom, $P(\chi^2 < 40.1133)$ equals

(a) .95
(b) .05
(c) .025
(d) none of these.

6. For the chi-square distribution with 14 degrees of freedom, $P(4.66 < \chi^2 < 26.11)$ equals

(a) .975
(b) .965
(c) .90
(d) none of these.

7. Which of the following variables is most likely to give incorrect results in the hypothesis testing procedure if the assumption of a normally distributed population is not met when dealing with samples of 30 or more?

(a) the chi-square variable used to test hypotheses about a population variance
(b) the t variable used to test the difference in means of two independent samples
(c) the t variable used to test the difference in means of two paired samples
(d) all are equally sensitive to the departure from normality.

8. How does the F distribution compare with the t distribution?

(a) Both distributions have a mean of zero.
(b) Both distributions are symmetric.
(c) Both distributions have a smaller variance than the standard normal distribution.
(d) None of the above.

9. The rejection region used for testing $H_0\colon \sigma_1^2 = \sigma_2^2$ versus $H_1\colon \sigma_1^2 > \sigma_2^2$ where $n_1 = 10$, $n_2 = 16$, $s_1 = 15$, $s_2 = 9$, $\alpha = .025$ is

(a) $\chi^2 > 40.6465$
(b) $F > 3.77$
(c) $F > 3.12$
(d) $F < 1/3.77$.

10. The test statistic used in testing H_0: $\sigma_1^2 = \sigma_2^2$ versus H_1: $\sigma_1^2 > \sigma_2^2$ where $n_1 = 10$, $n_2 = 16$, $s_1 = 15$, $s_2 = 9$, $\alpha = .025$ is

(a) F = 1.67
(b) F = 2.78
(c) F = .625
(d) The test statistic cannot be determined since we are not given the sample means.

Chapter 12

Answers to Problems

1. (a) 34.8053 (b) 16.0471 (c) 13.2767

2. \$5.68 < σ < \$9.22 since

$$\frac{(24)(49)}{36.4151} \le \sigma^2 \le \frac{(24)(49)}{13.8484}$$

3. H_0: $\sigma^2 = 30$ Accept H_0 if $\chi^2 \le 32.6705$
   H_1: $\sigma^2 > 30$ Reject H_0 if $\chi^2 > 32.6705$

   Using formula [1], χ^2 = <u>26.11</u>.

   Therefore, the null hypothesis H_0 is not rejected.
   <u>No</u>, there is not sufficient evidence to indicate the population variance exceeds 30 at the .05 level of significance.

4. H_0: $\sigma_A{}^2 = \sigma_B{}^2$ Accept H_0 if $F \ge 5.52$
   H_1: $\sigma_A{}^2 > \sigma_B{}^2$ Reject H_0 if $F < 5.52$

   Using formula [3], F = 16.4/4 = <u>4.1</u>.

   Therefore, the null hypothesis H_0 is not rejected.
   The answer to the question posed in the problem is "<u>no</u>".

5. (a) $\sigma_1{}^2 = \sigma_2{}^2$

   (b) H_0: $\sigma_1{}^2 = \sigma_2{}^2$ Accept H_0 if $.3322 \le F \le 2.65$
   H_1: $\sigma_1{}^2 \ne \sigma_2{}^2$ Reject H_0 otherwise where F has (9, 14) dof

   Using formula [3], $F = (15.6/18.2)^2$ = <u>.7347</u>.

   Therefore, the null hypothesis H_0 is not rejected and the condition $\sigma_1{}^2 = \sigma_2{}^2$ holds.

(c) H_o: $\mu_1 - \mu_2 = 0$ Accept H_o if $-2.069 \le t \le 2.069$
H_1: $\mu_1 - \mu_2 \neq 0$ Reject Ho otherwise where t has 23 dof

Using formula [3] of Chapter 11, we have t = 2.3316 ($s_p^2 = 296.8522$)

Thus, reject H_o.
Yes, there does appear to be a difference in the weekly wages for the men and women.

6. (a) H_o: $\sigma^2 = 4$ Accept H_o if $.1026 \le \chi^2 \le 5.9915$.
H_1: $\sigma^2 \neq 4$ Reject H_o otherwise

From the 3 sample data values, we calculate $\Sigma x = 19.5$ and $\Sigma x^2 = 147.89$ giving $s^2 = 10.57$.

The value of the test statistic is χ^2 = 5.285. (formula [1])

Thus, H_o is not rejected and the answer to the question is "no".

(b) normal population

(c) A 95% confidence interval for the population variance is:

$2(10.57)/7.3778 < \sigma^2 < 2(10.57)/.0506$ or $2.8654 < \sigma^2 < 417.7866$.

7. Letting population B be called population 1, we have

H_o: $\sigma_1^2 = \sigma_2^2$ Accept H_o if $F \le 3.97$
H_1: $\sigma_1^2 > \sigma_2^2$ Reject H_o if $F > 3.97$ where F has (5, 7) dof

Using formula [3], $F = 36/16$ = 2.25.

Therefore, the null hypothesis H_o is not rejected and the answer to the question is "no".

Chapter 12

Answers to Multiple Choice Questions

1. d
2. c
3. c
4. b
5. a
6. b
7. a
8. d
9. c
10. b

Chapter 13
TESTS OF GOODNESS OF FIT AND INDEPENDENCE

WHAT AM I LEARNING?

Chapter Outline and Summary

Recall the *chi-square distribution* and how we used it to determine confidence interval estimates and perform tests of hypotheses for the variance of one population. This chapter introduces two more hypothesis testing procedures that are based on the use of the chi-square distribution - the goodness-of-fit test and a test for the independence of two variables. The test for independence of two variables employs the use of the contingency table that we discussed as a method of descriptive statistics in Chapter 4.

The relationship between the variable χ^2 used in Chapter 12 and the χ^2 variable in this chapter is that they both are statistics having a chi-square distribution. Thus, we will again use Table 3 of the Anderson/Sweeney/Williams text to find the critical value(s) for accepting or rejecting a null hypothesis based on a particular confidence level $1 - \alpha$.

The *goodness-of-fit* test involves data arising from discrete random variables in which each element of a population is assigned to one and only one of several classes or categories. The random variables of interest are the counts, arising from observed sample data, in each of the categories. The population is described by a *multinomial probability distribution,* an extension of the binomial probability distribution. A goodness-of-fit test is used to test claims concerning the distribution of the values in a population; that is, to determine if a particular multinomial distribution provides a good description of the population. Thus, we are actually comparing the shape of the distribution of a random sample with the "hypothesized" shape of the population from which the sample was chosen.

As we did before with tests of hypothesis, we now formulate the six steps of a goodness-of-fit test:

Step 1: Determine the null and alternative hypotheses for the goodness-of-fit test. These will be of the general form:

H_0: $p_1 = p'_1$, $p_2 = p'_2$, $\cdots$, $p_k = p'_k$

H_1: At least one of the population proportions does not equal to its hypothesized value

where $p'_1, p'_2, \cdots, p'_k$ are the hypothesized population proportions.

Step 2: Obtain the results of a simple random sample of n items from the population and record these *observed frequencies* from the sample in each of the k classes or categories.

Step 3: Under the assumption that the null hypothesis is true, compute the *expected frequency* for each category by the following formula:

$$E_i = n\,p_i \qquad \text{for } i = 1, 2, 3, \cdots, k$$

where E_i = the expected frequency for category i and p_i = hypothesized proportion of category i in the null hypothesis. Note that the observed frequencies will always be *whole number* values and the expected frequencies may either be *integer* or *decimal* (fractional) values.

Step 4: Use the observed (O_i) and expected (E_i) frequencies in the following formula to compute the value of the χ^2 statistic for the test.

$$\chi^2 = \sum_{i=1}^{k} \frac{(O_i - E_i)^2}{E_i}$$

The results of this formula are valid for large samples, "large" meaning that the expected frequency for each category is 5 or more.

For this goodness-of-fit test, the chi-square distribution has $k - 1$ degrees of freedom.

Step 5: The decision rule for the test is: Accept H_o if $\chi^2 \leq \chi^2_\alpha$
Reject Ho if $\chi^2 > \chi^2_\alpha$

where α is the level of significance for the test.

Step 6: Give your conclusion regarding the null hypothesis.

Now that we know how to test "goodness-of-fit", that is, determining if we believe that the distribution of the population from which our sample was obtained fits the distribution of a multinomial population, we can extend these ideas to test for the independence of two variables. The data for this test is usually arranged into an "r by k" (that is, r rows and k columns), *contingency table* and is therefore sometimes referred to as a *contingency table test.* Here, the contingency table consists of qualitative data that has been classified on two scales, or dimensions, with each "box" in the table representing the count, or frequency, for that particular cell.

The contingency table is then used in a test of hypothesis to see if the classifications of the data are independent or dependent. Thus, we formulate the following six steps of the *test of independence:*

Step 1: Determine the null and alternative hypotheses. For the test of independence, these will be of the following general form:

H_o: The classifications of the data are *independent.*
(There is no relation between the categories.)

H_1: The classifications of the data are *dependent.*
(There is a relation between the categories.)

Step 2: Obtain the results of a simple random sample of n items from the population and record these *observed frequencies* from the sample in each of the r rows and k columns of the contingency table. Also, obtain the totals for the rows and columns and place these in the table.

Note that the "total" row and the "total" column are *not* counted when determining the values of r and k.

Step 3: Calculate the expected frequencies under the assumption that the null hypothesis is true (that is, the categories are independent). The rule for calculating theses expected frequencies is:

$$E_{ij} = \frac{(\text{Row } i \text{ Total})(\text{Column } j \text{ Total})}{\text{Sample Size}}$$

where E_{ij} is the calculated expected frequency for the cell in the contingency table that is in the ith row (horizontal) and the jth column (vertical). Record these expected frequencies in the contingency table under the respective observed frequencies for each cell.
Note that it is still the case that the observed frequencies (O_{ij}) will always be whole *number* values and the expected frequencies (E_{ij}) may either be *integer* or *decimal* (fractional) values.

Step 4: Calculate the value of the χ^2 test statistic. The value of the test statistic is again based on the differences between the observed and expected frequencies. It is computed by the following formula with the double summation signs and double subscript notation meaning that the values must be summed for each cell in the contingency table.

$$\chi^2 = \sum_i \sum_j \frac{(O_{ij} - E_{ij})^2}{E_{ij}}$$

The results of this formula are valid for large samples, "large" meaning that the expected frequency for each category is 5 or more.

For this test of independence, the chi-square distribution has $(r-1)(c-1)$ degrees of freedom using a contingency table consisting of r rows and c columns.

Step 5: The decision rule for the test is: Accept H_o if $\chi^2 \le \chi^2_\alpha$
Reject Ho if $\chi^2 > \chi^2_\alpha$

where α is the level of significance for the test.

Step 6: Give your conclusion regarding the null hypothesis.

Although goodness-of-fit tests and tests for independence only allow the conclusion arrived at concerning the null hypothesis, the experimenter can informally compare the observed and expected frequencies to obtain an idea of where significant differences in the data are, thus gaining further insight into the analysis of the sample data.

Chapter 13

WHAT FORMULA SHOULD I USE?

Formulas

When:

a) performing a goodness-of-fit test

b) $E_i \geq 5$ for each category

c) k = number of categories in the multinomial population

O_i = the observed frequency for category i

E_i = the expected frequency for category i where $E_i = n\,p_i$

n = the sample size

p_i = hypothesized proportion of category i in the null hypothesis

Use:

$$\chi^2 = \sum_{i=1}^{k} \frac{(O_i - E_i)^2}{E_i} \qquad [1]$$

where the χ^2 statistic has $k - 1$ degrees of freedom

When:

computing the expected frequency of the cell in the ith row and jth column of the contingency table for use in the test for independence

Use:

$$E_{ij} = \frac{(\text{Row } i \text{ Total})(\text{Column } j \text{ Total})}{\text{Sample Size}} \qquad [2]$$

When:

a) performing a test for independence of classifications

b) $E_i \geq 5$ for each category

c) O_{ij} = the observed frequency for the cell in the ith row and jth column

E_{ij} = the expected frequency for the cell in the ith row and jth column

Use:

$$\chi^2 = \sum_i \sum_j \frac{(O_{ij} - E_{ij})^2}{E_{ij}} \qquad [3]$$

where the χ^2 variable has $(r - 1)(c - 1)$ degrees of freedom for the contingency table consisting of r rows and c columns

HERE'S HOW IT'S DONE!

Examples

1. A company specializing in kitchen products has produced a mixer in five different colors. A random sample of 250 sales of the mixer has produced the following data:

Color	White	Copper	Green	Silver	Yellow
Number Sold	64	48	56	37	45

Does this data indicate that the customer has a preference as to the color of the product? Use the .05 level of significance.

Solution:

The population categories in this problem are the different colors for the mixer. Since there are 5 different colors available, $k = 5$ for this problem.

Next, we follow the 6 steps for a goodness-of-fit test:

Step 1: Determine the null and alternative hypotheses.

Using p_1 = percentage of population who prefers a white-colored mixer, p_2 = percentage of population who prefers a copper-colored mixer, etc., we have

H_0: $p_1 = .2$, $p_2 = .2$, $p_3 = .2$, $p_4 = .2$, $p_5 = .2$
(The customer has no preference as to the color of the mixer.)

H_1: At least one of the percentages is not equal to .2
(The customer has a preference as to the color of the mixer.)

Step 2: Record the observed frequencies from the random sample in each category.

The observed frequencies have been recorded in the categories in the statement of the problem.

Step 3: Compute the expected frequencies.

Using the formula $E_i = n\,p_i = 250(.2) = 50$ for each of the categories, we have:

Category	White	Copper	Green	Silver	Yellow
Observed Frequency	45	64	48	56	37
Expected Frequency	50	50	50	50	50

<u>Note</u>: The expected frequencies are all the same for this example because the population proportions are all hypothesized to be equal. This will not be the case for every goodness-of-fit test.

Step 4: Calculate the value of the χ^2 test statistic.

First, check to see if the large sample condition to use the test is met. Since each expected frequency is at least 5, the condition is met.

Using formula [1], we obtain

$$\chi^2 = \sum_{i=1}^{5} \frac{(O_i - E_i)^2}{E_i} = \frac{(64-50)^2}{50} + \frac{(48-50)^2}{50} + \frac{(56-50)^2}{50} + \frac{(37-50)^2}{50} + \frac{(45-50)^2}{50}$$

$$= \frac{196 + 4 + 36 + 169 + 25}{50} = \underline{8.60}$$

Step 5: Determine the decision rule for the specified level of significance of the test.

One or more large differences between the observed and expected frequencies would lead us to believe that the hypothesized proportions (percentages) are not correct. However, small differences between observed and expected frequencies do not provide sufficient evidence to reject the null hypothesis. Thus, the larger the value of the chi-square variable, the more likely it is that we will reject the null hypothesis. Thus, we always place the rejection region in the <u>upper tail</u> of the chi-square distribution.

We are given a level of significance of .05, and the number of degrees of freedom is $k - 1 = 4$.

The decision rule is therefore: Accept H_o if $\chi^2 \leq 9.48773$

Reject H_o if $\chi^2 > 9.48773$

Step 6: Give the conclusion of the test.

Since $\chi^2 = 8.6 < 9.48773$, we do not reject H_o.

No, there is not sufficient evidence to indicate that the customer has a preference as to the color of the mixer.

2. Consider the contingency table shown below:

	Classification 1			
	20	40	30	10
Classification 2	15	5	25	5
	35	45	45	25

(a) How many rows and columns are in this table?

Solution:

(a) Counting the (horizontal) rows which are the categories for Classification2, we find there are 3 rows.

Counting the (vertical) columns which are the categories for Classification1, we find there are 4 columns.

(b) Assuming these are the observed frequencies to be used in a test for independence of Classification 1 and Classification 2, what are the following values O_{14} and O_{31}?

Solution:

(b) O_{14} is the observed frequency of the cell in the 1st row and 4th column. Thus, O_{14} = 10.

O_{31} is the observed frequency of the cell in the 3rd row and 1st column. Thus, O_{31} = 35.

3. (a) What would the next step be if you were to use the data in the contingency table in problem 2 in order to test for the independence of the two classifications?

Solution:

(a) The next step in the hypothesis testing procedure would be to determine the expected frequencies (E_{ij}), under the assumption of independence, of each of the cells.

To do this, we would need to know the row totals and the column totals. Suppose we find:

	Classification 1				Totals
	20	40	30	10	100
Classification 2	15	5	25	5	50
	35	45	45	25	150
Totals	70	90	110	40	310

(b) Are the above totals correct?

Solution:

(b) One way to double check your arithmetic is, after computing the total for each row and each column, compute the grand total both from the row totals and the column totals. You must get the same numerical value for each!

Note: The grand total is the sample size, n, that is usually given in the problem.

For the table above, the grand total is 310 when computed from the column totals. However, when computed from the row totals, we only get 300. Thus, there is a mistake in arithmetic somewhere.

Checking back over the sums, we see that the total for column 3 is 100, not 110, giving the following corrected table:

	Classification 1				Row Totals
	20	40	30	10	100
Classification 2	15	5	25	5	50
	35	45	45	25	150
Column Totals	70	90	100	40	300

(c) Compute E_{31} and E_{24}.

Solution:

(c) Using formula [2] to find each of these, we have

$$E_{31} = \frac{(\text{Row 3 Total})(\text{Column 1 Total})}{\text{Sample Size}} = \frac{(150)(70)}{300} = \underline{35}.$$

$$E_{24} = \frac{(\text{Row 2 Total})(\text{Column 4 Total})}{\text{Sample Size}} = \frac{(50)(40)}{300} = \underline{6.67}.$$

4. Mary Stebbins, color coordinator for We Plez You Fashions, wished to determine if there is a dependence between hair color and eye color. Two hundred people were randomly sampled to obtain the results shown in the following table. Do the data provide sufficient evidence to indicate a dependence between eye and hair color at the .05 level of significance?

		Eye Color	
		Light	Dark
Hair Color	Blonde	30	20
	Red	15	35
	Brunette	45	55

<u>Solution</u>:

To determine if these sample data indicate a dependence between hair and eye colors, we follow the six steps of the test for independence.

Step 1: Determine the null and alternative hypotheses.

H_0: Hair color and eye color are independent.

H_1: Hair color and eye color are dependent.

Step 2: Record the observed frequencies from the random sample in each category.

These observed frequencies are the ones given in the problem.

Step 3: Determine the expected frequencies.

To determine the expected frequencies, we must first find the row totals and column totals for the contingency table given in the problem. These are:

		Eye Color		
		Light	Dark	Row Totals
Hair Color	Blonde	30	20	50
	Red	15	35	50
	Brunette	45	55	100
	Column Totals	90	110	200 = n

Using formula [2], we find each of the following expected frequencies where $r = 3$, $c = 3$, and $n = 200$.

$E_{11} = (50)(90)/200 = 22.5$, $E_{12} = (50)(110)/200 = 27.5$, and so forth.

It is a good idea to record these in your table for each cell, in parentheses to keep them separate from the observed frequencies, for use in the computation of the χ^2 test statistic.

Notice that each of the expected frequencies is at least 5.

		Eye Color		
		Light	Dark	Row Totals
Hair Color	Blonde	30 (22.5)	20 (27.5)	50
	Red	15 (22.5)	35 (27.5)	50
	Brunette	45 (45)	55 (55)	100
	Column Totals	90	110	200 = n

Step 4: Calculate the value of the χ^2 test statistic.

Use formula [3] to calculate this value, remembering that the double summation signs mean to sum these differences for each cell in the table.

$$\chi^2 = \frac{(30 - 22.5)^2}{22.5} + \frac{(20 - 27.5)^2}{27.5} + \frac{(15 - 22.5)^2}{22.5} + \frac{(35 - 27.5)^2}{27.5} +$$

$$\frac{(45 - 45)^2}{45} + \frac{(55 - 55)^2}{55} = 2.5 + 2.045 + 2.5 + 2.045$$

Thus, $\chi^2 = \underline{9.09}$.

Step 5: Determine the decision rule for the specified level of significance of the test. Using = .05 and (3 - 1)(2 - 1) = 2 degrees of freedom,

The decision rule is: Accept H_o if $\chi^2 \leq 5.99147$

Reject H_o if $\chi^2 > 5.99147$

Step 6: Give the conclusion of the test.

Since the value of 9.09 falls in the rejection region, we reject H_o. Yes, the data indicate that there is a dependence between hair color and eye color.

HAVE I LEARNED THE MATERIAL?

Problems

1. A furniture store is having a sale and wants to determine which modes of advertising are most effective. A random survey of 100 customers gave the following information as to how they learned of the sale: 50 people said they saw it advertised on television, 20 people read about it in the newspaper, 25 people heard it advertised on the radio, and 5 people heard about it from their friends. The store manager believes that for all the customers attending the sale, 38% will see it on television, an equal percentage will read it in the newspaper or hear about it on the radio (28%), and only 6% will hear about it by word of mouth. Do the observed data indicated that the store manager's belief is correct at the .01 level of significance?

2. Develop the expected frequencies that would be used in a test for independence between classifications A and B in the contingency table below.

		B		
		B_1	B_2	
A	A_1	20	40	
	A_2	10	30	

3. A group of 50 people were interviewed to determine their preference of soft drink. Out of these 50 people, 15 preferred Coke, 14 liked 7-Up best, 10 chose Pepsi, 2 preferred an orange drink, and 9 indicated a preference for some other soft drink. Does the data indicate that some soft drinks are preferred over others? Use a level of significance of .10.

4. Do overweight parents tend to have overweight children? Answer this question by performing a test for independence using the following data for a random sample of size 100. (One parent and one child were randomly selected from each family surveyed.) Use $\alpha = .05$.

		Child		
		Overweight	Not Overweight	
Parent	Overweight	34	29	
	Not Overweight	16	21	

5. A random sample of 200 college students were asked to consider the statement: "Every college student have his/her own computer". Each student was asked to give his/her opinion on a scale from 1 - 6 using the following terms:

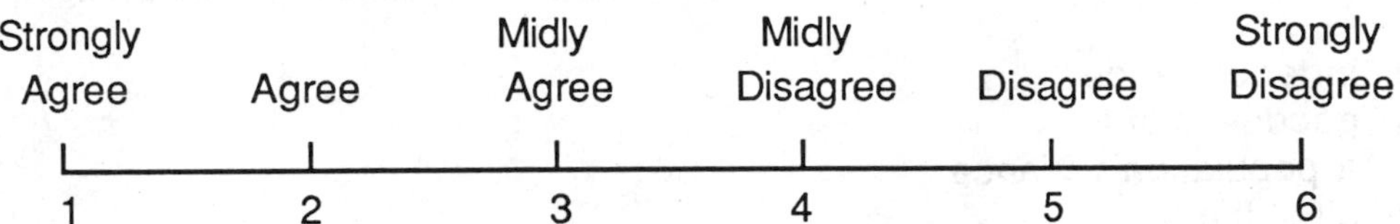

The responses are summarized in the following table:

Opinion of Statement

Sex		1	2	3	4	5	6	
	Male	21	10	7	23	15	21	
	Female	16	22	15	9	18	23	

Is the opinion of the respondent independent of the sex of the person? Test using a level of significance of .05.

Chapter 13

Multiple Choice Questions

1. The chi-square distribution may be used for testing hypotheses concerning

   (a) independence
   (b) goodness of fit
   (c) a population variance
   (d) all of the above.

2. When using formula [1] to determine the value of the chi-square test statistic in a goodness-of-fit test, the numbers E_i that are used

   (a) are the standard deviations of each of the categories
   (b) must all be whole numbers
   (c) are the observed sample data
   (d) none of the above.

3. For the goodness-of-fit test, the number of degrees of freedom associated with the chi-square distribution is

   (a) the number in the sample minus the number of categories
   (b) the number of rows minus one times the number of columns minus one
   (c) the number of categories minus one
   (d) always equal to four.

4. In the test for the independence of two variables, we use the

   (a) normal distribution
   (b) binomial probability distribution
   (c) t distribution
   (d) chi-square distribution.

5. In a test for independence using a 4 by 5 contingency table, the number of degrees of freedom will be

   (a) 20
   (b) 12
   (c) 9
   (d) There is not enough information given to tell.

6. The condition for "large" samples with the goodness-of-fit test is

   (a) the sample size must be at least 30
   (b) each observed frequency, expressed as a percentage, multiplied by the sample size must be at least 5
   (c) each expected frequency must be at least 5
   (d) each observed frequency can be no more than 5.

7. A goodness-of-fit test is used

   (a) to test claims concerning the distribution of values in a multinomial population.
   (b) to test for the independence of two variables
   (c) to determine which of the population categories has the largest expected frequency
   (d) none of the above.

Questions 8 through 10 refer to the following contingency table:

	Classification A		
Classification B	50	70	28
	35	130	72

8. The observed frequency O_{12} equals

   (a) 28
   (b) 70
   (c) 35
   (d) 64.6.

9. The expected frequency E_{23} equals

   (a) 33.9
   (b) 67.7
   (c) 64.6
   (d) 72.0.

10. If the above data were used in a test of independence of the classifications with a significance level of .10, the critical value for the test would be

(a) 4.60517
(b) 9.23635
(c) 5.99147
(d) 5.64463.

Chapter 13

Answers to Problems

1. H_o: $p_1 = .38$, $p_2 = .38$, $p_3 = .38$, $p_4 = .06$

   H_1: At least one of the population proportions is different than specified in H_o

Category	TV	Newspaper	Radio	Word of Mouth
O_i	50	20	25	5
E_i	38	28	28	6

The decision rule is: Accept H_o if $\chi^2 \leq 11.3449$
Reject H_o if $\chi^2 > 11.3449$ (3 dof)

$\chi^2 = 3.7895 + 2.2857 + .3214 + .1667 = \underline{6.5633}$.

Thus, do not reject H_o. Yes, the store manager's belief appears to be true.

2. Use formula [2] to obtain:

A \ B	B_1	B_2	Row Totals
A_1	20 (18)	40 (42)	60
A_2	10 (12)	30 (28)	40
Column Totals	30	70	100

3. H_o: $p_1 = .2$, $p_2 = .2$, $p_3 = .2$, $p_4 = .2$, $p_5 = .2$

   H_1: At least one of the population proportions is different than specified in H_o

Category	Coke	Seven-Up	Pepsi	Orange	Other
O_i	15	14	10	2	9
E_i	10	10	10	10	10

The decision rule is: Accept H_o if $\chi^2 \leq 7.77944$

Reject H_o if $\chi^2 > 7.77944$ (4 dof)

$\chi^2 = (25 + 16 + 0 + 64 + 1)/10 = 106/10 = \underline{10.6}$.

Thus, reject H_o. Yes, it appears that some soft drinks are preferred over others.

4. H_o: A child being overweight is independent of a parent being overweight.

   H_1: A child being overweight is dependent on a parent being overweight.

   The contingency table is

		Child		
		Overweight	Not Overweight	Totals
Parent	Overweight	34 (31.5)	29 (31.5)	63
	Not Overweight	16 (18.5)	21 (18.5)	37
	Totals	50	50	100

The decision rule is: Accept H_o if $\chi^2 \leq 3.84146$

(1 dof) Reject H_o if $\chi^2 > 3.84146$

The value of the test statistic is $\chi^2 = .1984 + .3378 + .1984 + .3378 = \underline{1.0724}$.

Therefore, do not reject Ho. No, there does not seem to be a dependence.

5. H_0: Opinion of respondent and sex of respondent are independent.

H_1: Opinion of respondent and sex of respondent are dependent.

The contingency table is

Opinion of Statement

		1		2	3 4	5	6	Totals
	Male	21 (17.95)	10 (15.52)	7 (10.67)	23 (15.52)	15 (16.01)	21 (21.34)	97
Sex								
	Female	16 (19.06)	22 (16.48)	15 (11.33)	9 (16.48)	18 (17.00)	23 (22.66)	103
	Totals	37	32	22	32	33	44	200

The decision rule is: Accept H_0 if $\chi^2 \leq 11.0705$

(5 dof) Reject H_0 if $\chi^2 > 11.07055$

The value of the test statistic is χ^2 = <u>14.42</u>.

The conclusion is to reject H_0. It appears that the opinion or the respondent and the sex of the respondent are dependent.

Chapter 13

Answers to Multiple Choice Questions

1. d
2. d
3. c
4. d
5. b
6. c
7. a
8. b
9. b
10. a

Chapter 14
EXPERIMENTAL DESIGN AND THE ANALYSIS OF VARIANCE

WHAT AM I LEARNING?

Chapter Outline and Summary

The preceding chapters have presented techniques of descriptive statistics and the methods of inferential statistics. In particular, Chapter 11 discussed how to test whether of not the means of two populations are equal. In this chapter we discuss some of the more widely used tools of statistical analysis and present a statistical hypothesis testing procedure for determining whether or not the means of three or more populations are equal. The technique used in this hypothesis testing procedure is called *analysis of variance.*

The first step in any experimental procedure is to determine the *experimental design*; that is, the process of planning an experiment in order to collect the appropriate data. In experimental design, a *factor,* which can have several *levels,* is the variable of interest in the analysis of variance procedure. The term *treatment* refers to the different independent groups of samples (that is, the different levels of the factor) being compared. The number of measurements in each group is the number of repetitions or *replications.* In experimental design, a treatment is applied to an *experimental unit.* We will apply analysis of variance techniques to two specific types of experimental design: the *completely randomized experimental design* and the *randomized block experimental design.*

A *completely randomized experimental design* is one in which each treatment is randomly assigned to one of the experimental units. Whenever extraneous sources of variation arise in the error term due to factors not considered in the design process, *blocking* results in a better estimate of the error variance and a better test to determine whether or not the population means are equal. Blocking is the process of using the same experimental unit for all treatments of the factor. Within each block, the treatments are randomly assigned. This type of experimental design is called a *randomized block design*. It is appropriate to use a randomized block design when we can cross-classify the experimental units according to two criteria: treatments and *blocks* or when we can apply treatments to different kinds of experimental data.

The second step of the experimental procedure is to collect and summarize the data. We will assume that simple random samples have been selected independently from each of the populations of interest and define the following:

for x_{ij} = jth observation corresponding to the ith treatment

n_T = total sample size for the experiment,

let $\bar{x}_i$ = sample (treatment) mean corresponding to the ith population

where $\bar{x}_i = \sum_j x_{ij} / n$

and

let $\bar{\bar{x}}$ = overall sample mean of the measurements in all the groups for the experiment

where $\bar{\bar{x}} = \sum_i \sum_j x_{ij} / n_T$

The third step of the experimental procedure is to analyze and interpret the data using the technique of *analysis of variance*, commonly referred to as *ANOVA*. The basic idea underlying the analysis of variance is the partitioning of the total variation in a set of data into two or more component parts. Each of these components accounts for a specific source of the variation.

The ANOVA procedure is based upon the following two assumptions:

1) The variable of interest (response variable) for each population must have a normal probability distribution.
2) The variance of the response variable is the same for each population.

While the analysis of variance technique is used to test the equality of three or more population means, the procedure actually centers around the comparison of two independent estimates of σ^2, the common population variance of the response variable. One of these estimates, the *mean square between treatments* (MSTR), is based upon differences *between* the treatment means and the overall sample mean. The other estimate, *the mean square due to error* or *mean square due to treatments* (MSE), is based upon differences of observations *within* each treatment from the corresponding treatment mean. For *balanced designs;* that is, ones in which the sample size is the same for each treatment, the definition of the *between treatments* estimate of σ^2, MSTR, based on the assumption that the population means are all equal and the two assumptions of the ANOVA procedure, is

$$MSTR = \frac{SSTR}{k-1} \quad \text{where} \quad SSTR = n \sum_i (\bar{x}_i - \bar{\bar{x}})^2$$

and k = number of populations
$k - 1$ = number of degrees of freedom of SSTR
n = size of sample selected from each of the k populations
i = number of treatments
SSTR has $k - 1$ degrees of freedom

SSTR is called the *sum of squares between treatments* and is based on the dispersion of the k sample means around the overall sample mean.

For an *unbalanced design,* which is any experimental design for which the sample size is not the same for each treatment,

$$MSTR = \frac{SSTR}{k-1} \quad \text{where} \quad SSTR = \sum_i n_i (\bar{x}_i - \bar{\bar{x}})^2$$

and k = number of populations
$k - 1$ = number of degrees of freedom of SSTR
n_i = size of sample selected from the ith treatment
i = number of treatments
SSTR has $k - 1$ degrees of freedom

The definition of the *within treatment estimate* of σ^2, MSE, is defined as

$$MSE = \frac{SSE}{n_T - k} \quad \text{where} \quad SSE = \sum_i \sum_j (x_{ij} - \bar{x}_i)^2$$

where $n_T = kn$ = total sample size for a balanced design experiment
$n_T = \sum_i n_i$ = total sample size for an unbalanced design experiment.
SSE has $n_T - k$ degrees of freedom

SSE is called the *sum of squares within* or the *sum of squares due to error* and is based upon the variation of the sample observations within each treatment.

The *total sum of squares about the mean,* SST, is defined as

$$SST = \sum_i \sum_j (x_{ij} - \bar{\bar{x}})^2$$

with $n_T - 1$ degrees of freedom

Note that the following condition holds for a completely randomized design:

$$SST = SSTR + SSE.$$

That is, the total sum of squares about the mean can be *partitioned* into two sums - the sum of squares between treatments and the sum of squares due to error. A similar partition holds for the respective associated degrees of freedom

$$n_T - 1 = (k - 1) + (n_T - k).$$

For a randomized block design,

$$SST = SSTR + SSB + SSE.$$

Thus, the total sum of squares about the mean is partitioned into three sums - the sum of squares between treatments (dof = k - 1), the sum of squares due to blocks (dof = b - 1), and the sum of squares due to error [dof = (k - 1)(b - 1)]. In these degrees of freedom, k is the number of treatments, b is the number of blocks, and n = kb is the total sample size.

MSE always is an unbiased estimate of σ^2. MSTR provides an unbiased estimate of σ^2 only under the assumption that the population means are all equal. If this condition is not true, then MSTR overestimates σ^2. The key to the ANOVA procedure is to compare these two estimates of the population variance using an F statistic.

This comparison is done in the six steps of the analysis of variance procedure for testing the hypothesis of the equality of three or more population means under the assumptions made to define MSR and MSTR.

Step 1: <u>State the null and alternative hypotheses</u>. For ANOVA, these are:

H_0: $\mu_1 = \mu_2 = \ldots = \mu_k$
H_1: Not all μ_i are equal.

(for k = the number of population treatments)

Step 2: Develop the two independent estimates of the population variance σ^2: MSTR and MSE .

See the formula section of this Guide for the computational procedures involved in obtaining the values of MSTR and MSE for each of the two designs studied in this chapter.

Step 3: Determine the test statistic.

Recall from Chapter 12 that the sampling distribution of the ratio of two independent estimates of σ^2 from normal populations follows an F probability distribution. In this chapter the two independent estimates of σ^2 from normal populations are MSTR and MSE. Thus, the statistic used for this test is

$$F = \frac{MSTR}{MSE}$$

with numerator degrees of freedom given by the degrees of freedom for SSTR and denominator degrees of freedom given by the degrees of freedom for SSE.

Step 4: Determine the decision rule:

If the sample means are all nearly equal, the F statistic is small. The more the sample means differ, the larger the F statistic becomes. Hence, we reject H_0 if F is large. Therefore, for a level of significance equal to α, the decision rule is:

Do not reject H_0 if $F \leq F_\alpha$

Reject H_0 if $F > F_\alpha$.

Step 5: Calculate the value of the F statistic in step 3.

Step 6: Give the conclusion of the test.

A convenient way to summarize the computation and results of the analysis of variance procedure is to develop an *ANOVA table.* For a completely randomized design, the ANOVA table is of the form:

ANOVA Table for a Completely Randomized Design

Source of Variation	Sum of Squares	Degrees of Freedom (dof)	Mean Square	F
Between treatments	SSTR	k - 1	MSTR = $\frac{SSTR}{k-1}$	$\frac{MSTR}{MSE}$
Error (within treatments)	SSE	$n_T - k$	MSE = $\frac{SSE}{n_T - k}$	
Total	SST	$n_T - 1$		

For a randomized block design with k treatments and b blocks, the ANOVA table is of the form:

ANOVA Table for the Randomized Block Design with k Treatments and b Blocks

Source of Variation	Sum of Squares	Degrees of Freedom (dof)	Mean Square	F
Between treatments	SSTR	k - 1	MSTR = $\frac{SSTR}{k-1}$	$\frac{MSTR}{MSE}$
Between blocks	SSB	b - 1	MSB = $\frac{SSB}{b-1}$	
Error (within treatments)	SSE	(k - 1)(b - 1)	MSE = $\frac{SSE}{(k-1)(b-1)}$	
Total	SST	$n_T - 1$		

A procedure for further analysis of the data is obtained using a t test to conduct statistical comparisons between pairs of the treatment means when the null hypothesis of equality between the populations means is rejected. This test consists of three steps:

Step 1: Determine the null and alternative hypotheses for the two population means of interest, say, μ_1 and μ_2. This test will be of the form:

$$H_0: \mu_1 = \mu_2$$
$$H_1: \mu_1 \neq \mu_2$$

Step 2: Develop a confidence interval estimate for the difference in the two population means. See the formula section of this Guide for the computational formula.

Step 3: Give the conclusion of the test.

If this confidence interval includes the value 0, conclude that there is no significant difference between the treatment means (do not reject H_0). If the confidence interval does not contain the value 0, conclude there is a difference (reject H_0).

Note that this procedure should only be applied when we *reject* the null hypothesis of equal population means. Caution is advised in using this test, however, due to the increasing probability of making a Type I error when conducting several tests for individual differences. There are specialized tests available that should be used when making multiple comparisons to eliminate this problem.

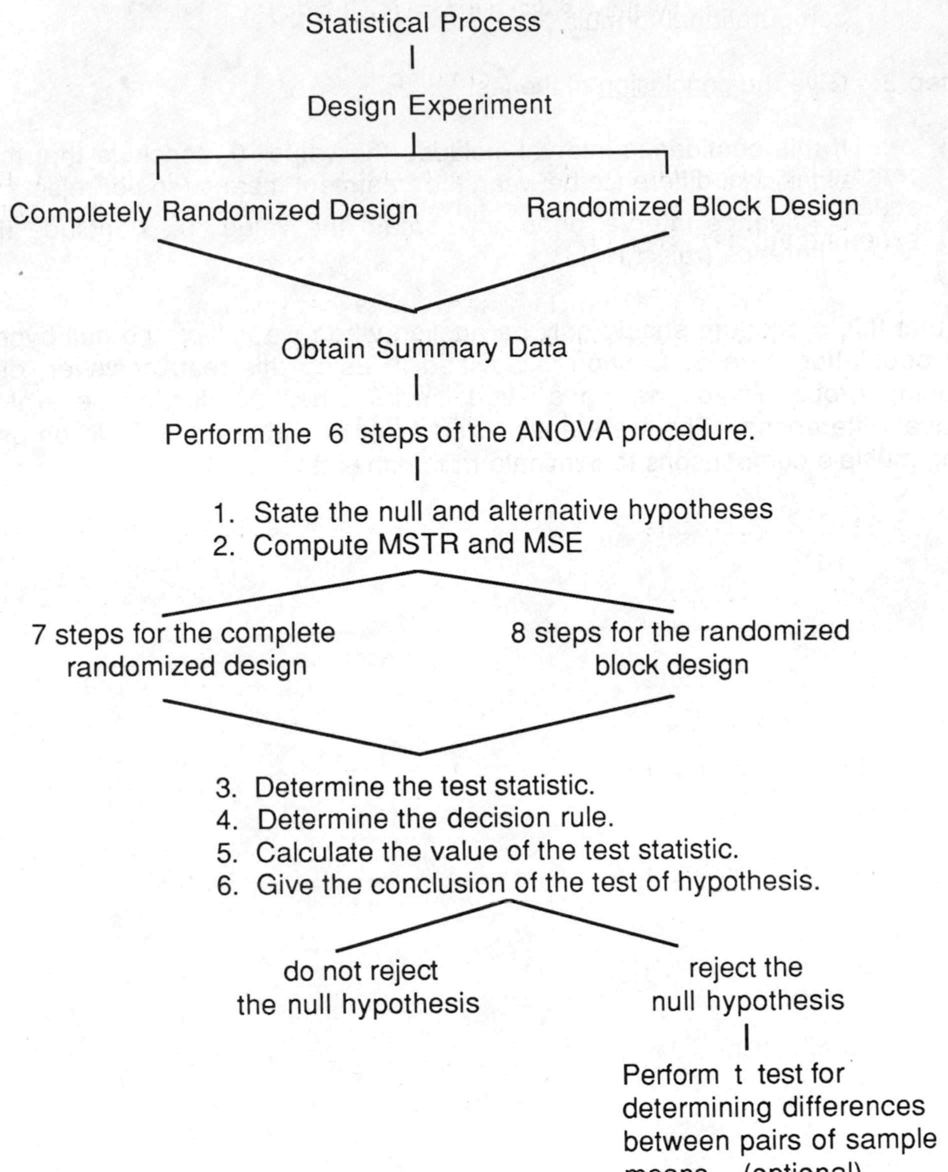
Statistical Process
Design Experiment
Completely Randomized Design
Randomized Block Design
Obtain Summary Data
Perform the 6 steps of the ANOVA procedure.
1. State the null and alternative hypotheses
2. Compute MSTR and MSE
7 steps for the complete randomized design
8 steps for the randomized block design
3. Determine the test statistic.
4. Determine the decision rule.
5. Calculate the value of the test statistic.
6. Give the conclusion of the test of hypothesis.
do not reject the null hypothesis
reject the null hypothesis
Perform t test for determining differences between pairs of sample means. (optional)

WHICH FORMULA SHOULD I USE?

Formulas

When:

computing the values of MSTR and MSE used in the ANOVA test of the equality of the means of three or more populations in the completely randomized experimental design where

x_{ij} = the value of the jth observation under treatment i
T_i = the sum of all observations in treatment i
T = the sum of all the observations
n_i = the sample size for the ith treatment
n_T = the total sample size for the experiment

Step 1: Compute $T_i = \sum_j x_{ij}$ for $i = 1, 2, 3, \ldots, k$
Compute $T = \sum_i T_i$ [1]

Step 2: Compute $\sum_i \sum_j x_{ij}^2$

Step 3: Compute $SST = \left(\sum_i \sum_j x_{ij}^2\right) - \frac{T^2}{n_T}$ [2]

Step 4: Compute $SSTR = \left(\sum_i \frac{T_i^2}{n_i}\right) - \frac{T^2}{n_T}$ [3]

Step 5: Compute $SSE = SST - SSTR$ [4]

Step 6: Compute $MSTR = \frac{SSTR}{k-1}$ [5]

Step 7: Compute $MSE = \frac{SSE}{n_T - k}$ [6]

When:

testing the hypothesis in the ANOVA test for the equality of three or more population means in the completely randomized design experiment

Use:

$$F = \frac{MSTR}{MSE}$$

with numerator degrees of freedom equal to $k - 1$ [7]

and denominator degrees of freedom equal to $n_T - k$

When:

computing the values of MSTR and MSE used in the ANOVA test of the equality of the means of three or more populations in the randomized block experimental design where

x_{ij} = the value of the observation under treatment i in block j
$T_{i\cdot}$ = the total of all observations in treatment i
$T_{\cdot j}$ = the total of all observations in block j
T = the total of all observations
$\bar{x}_{i\cdot}$ = sample mean of the ith treatment
$\bar{x}_{\cdot j}$ = sample mean of the jth block
$\bar{\bar{x}}$ = overall sample mean

Step 1: Compute $T_{i\cdot} = \sum_j x_{ij}$, $T_{\cdot j} = \sum_i x_{ij}$ [8]

Compute $T = \sum_i \sum_j x_{ij}$

Step 2: Compute $\sum_i \sum_j x_{ij}^2$

Step 3: Compute $SST = \left(\sum_i \sum_j x_{ij}^2\right) - \frac{T^2}{n_T}$ [9]

Step 4: Compute $SSTR = \left(\frac{\sum_i T_{i\cdot}^2}{b}\right) - \frac{T^2}{n_T}$ [10]

Step 5: Compute $SSB = \left(\frac{\sum_j T_{\cdot j}^2}{k}\right) - \frac{T^2}{n_T}$ [11]

Step 6: Compute $SSE = SST - SSTR - SSB$ [12]

Step 7: Compute $MSTR = \frac{SSTR}{k - 1}$ [13]

Step 8: Compute $MSE = \frac{SSE}{(k - 1)(b - 1)}$ [14]

When:

testing the hypothesis in the ANOVA test for the equality of three or more population means in the randomized block design experiment

Use:

$$F = \frac{MSTR}{MSE}$$

with numerator degrees of freedom equal to $k - 1$ [15]
and denominator degrees of freedom equal to $(k - 1)(b - 1)$

When:

computing the interval estimate for $\mu_1 - \mu_2$ to be used in testing the hypotheses

H_0: $\mu_1 = \mu_2$
H_1: $\mu_1 \neq \mu_2$

Use:

$$\bar{x}_1 - \bar{x}_2 \pm t_{\alpha/2}\sqrt{MSE\left(\frac{1}{n_1} + \frac{1}{n_2}\right)} \qquad [16]$$

where $\bar{x}_1$ = sample mean for the first treatment
$\bar{x}_2$ = sample mean for the second treatment
n_1 = sample size for the first treatment
n_2 = sample size for the second treatment

and the $t_{\alpha/2}$ value is obtained using the number of degrees of freedom for error (MSE) given in the ANOVA table.

Note: For the case of more than two independent variables, similar tests may be conducted by replacing the subscripts in this formula with the appropriate values.

Chapter 14

HERE'S HOW IT'S DONE!

Examples

1. A class in marketing is given the assignment of creating a new poster to promote sales of tickets for a charity event. They have developed five distinct advertising designs and decide to test the effectiveness of these designs on a group of 20 people randomly selected from the population of the city where the charity event is to take place. These 20 people are randomly divided into 5 groups of 4 people each for the test that will be conducted to see if the mean sales of tickets are the same for each of the five advertising designs.

   (a) What is the factor of interest in this test?

   Solution:
   (a) The factor of interest is the advertising design of the poster.

   (b) How many levels are there for the factor?

   Solution:
   (b) Since there are five distinct advertising designs, there are 5 levels.

   (c) What are the treatments?

   Solution:
   (c) There are five treatments for this experiment, one corresponding to each of the 5 different advertising designs. Recall that the treatments are the different levels of the factor.

   (d) How many experimental units are there for this experiment?

   Solution:
   (d) The treatments are applied to the experimental units. Hence, the experimental units are the people who are selected from the city. There are 20 people involved in this experiment.

   (e) Is this experiment a completely randomized experimental design experiment or a randomized block experiment?

   Solution:
   (e) Since the 20 people were randomly selected from the city and divided into the 4 groups at random, this is a problem using a completely randomized experimental design.

2. On a test of small-motor skills administered to three independent randomly selected groups of preschool children, the following results were obtained for the scores on the test under three different environmental conditions, one group being assigned to each condition:

Group 1	Group 2	Group 3
9	6	8
6	7	7
8	5	9
8	6	7
9	6	7

(a) Discuss the following terms as applied to this problem: *treatments, response variable, statistical objective, experimental units, experimental design.*

Solution:

(a) The treatments in this example are the three groups of preschool children to who the test is administered. The variable of interest, the response variable, is the score on the small-motor skills test, and the statistical objective is to determine whether or not the mean test scores are the same for all three groups. The children are the experimental units. The experimental design is the completely randomized experimental design since the experimental units (the children) are randomly assigned to the treatments (the groups). It is a balanced design since there is the same sample size for each treatment.

(b) Conduct an analysis of variance on the data using a level of significance of .05 to determine if there is a significant difference in the mean test scores for the three groups.

Solution: (b)

First, let us define what we wish to do. Let

μ_1 = the small-motor skills test score for the population of all preschool children chosen for group 1,

μ_2 = the small-motor skills test score for the population of all preschool children chosen for group 2, and

μ_3 = the small-motor skills test score for the population of all preschool children chosen for group 3.

We wish to test: H_o: $\mu_1 = \mu_2 = \mu_3$
H_1: Not all means are equal.

Notice, for the data, we have:

k = number of treatments = 3
n = sample size of each group in the balanced design = 5
n_T = total sample size = kn for the balanced design = 15.

The way these data are presented, we have the treatments being the columns. Thus, the subscript "i " in the formulas represents the column number. The subscript "j" represents the particular row the data is in. If you do not like the data arranged this way, simply rotate it to the way you wish. The important thing to remember is that the treatment means $\bar{x}_i$ are for i = 1, 2, 3 since we have 3 treatments, however the data are arranged.

The sample means for each group, that is, the treatment means, are obtained by summing the values in each group and dividing by 5. Thus, we obtain

$$\bar{x}_1 = (9 + 6 + 8 + 8 + 9)/5 = 40/5 = \underline{8};\ \bar{x}_2 = 30/5 = \underline{6};\ \bar{x}_3 = 38/5 = \underline{7.6}.$$

The overall sample mean is (40 + 30 + 38)/15 = 108/15 = 7.2.

The assumptions that must hold true in this analysis of variance procedure are:

1) The test score for each population has a normal probability distribution
2) The variance, σ^2, of the test scores is the same for each population.

The between treatments estimate of σ^2 is MSTR = SSTR/(k-1) where SSTR is n times the sum of the squared differences in the treatment means and the overall sample mean. Now,

$$SSTR = 5\,[(8 - 7.2)^2 + (6 - 7.2)^2 + (7.6 - 7.2)^2] = 5(2.24) = \underline{11.2}.$$

Thus,

$$MSTR = 11.2/2 = \underline{5.60} \text{ with 2 dof.}$$

The within-treatments estimate of σ^2 is MSE = SSE/(n_T - k) where SSE is the sum of the squared differences of each observation from its corresponding sample mean. Now,

$$SSE = (9-8)^2 + (6-8)^2 + (8-8)^2 + (8-8)^2 + (9-8)^2 + (6-6)^2 + (7-6)^2 + (5-6)^2 + (6-6)^2 + (6-6)^2 + (8-7.6)^2 + (7-7.6)^2 + (9-7.6)^2 + (7-7.6)^2 + (7-7.6)^2 = 6 + 2 + 3.2 = \underline{11.2}.$$

Thus,

$$MSE = 11.2/(15-3) = 11.2/12 = \underline{.933} \text{ with 12 dof.}$$

Note: Due to inaccuracies that may arise from round-off errors, it is a good idea to keep at least three decimal places in all calculations.

Finally, to test the hypothesis of the equality of the three population means, we use F = MSTR/MSE with numerator degrees of freedom equal to 2 and denominator degrees of freedom equal to 12.

Note: These degrees of freedom are the respective degrees of freedom of the numerator and denominator of the quantities in the F statistic.

The decision rule for the test of hypothesis is:

Do not reject H_0 if $F \leq F_{.05} = 3.89$
Reject H_0 if $F > F_{.05} = 3.89$.

Since $F = 5.6/.933 = \underline{6.002}$, we reject H_0 and conclude that there is sufficient evidence to believe that at least one of the population means differs from the others.

3. In an effort to establish consistency in attendance policies throughout a university for entering freshmen, random samples of four freshman courses, each meeting three times a week during the semester, were selected from each of the five colleges of the university. The number of allowed absences for each course selected is recorded below.

College of Liberal Arts	College of Agriculture	College of Business	College of Education	College of Sciences
5	6	3	6	3
3	5	3	4	4
8	4	4	8	3
3	4	3	5	5

Can the mean number of allowed absences per course for each of the five colleges be considered the same at the .05 level of significance?

Solution:

Letting μ_1 = mean number of allowed absences per course in the College of Liberal Arts, μ_2 = mean number of allowed absences per course in the College of Agriculture, and so forth, we want to use the above sample results to test the hypotheses:

$$H_0: \mu_1 = \mu_2 = \mu_3 = \mu_4 = \mu_5$$
$$H_1: \text{Not all } \mu_i\text{'s are equal.}$$

Having completed step 1 in the ANOVA procedure, we now must proceed to step 2 in which we have to decide which type of experimental design was used in the experiment. Since we are looking at the mean number of allowed absences per college, the treatments are the colleges. The experimental units are the courses which were randomly chosen from the colleges. Thus, this is a problem using a complete randomized design.

We now proceed with step 2, the 7 steps of the computational procedure to determine MSTR and MSE. (Refer to the formula section of this chapter for the exact formulas needed for computation.)

Step 1: Compute $T_i = \Sigma x_{ij}$ for each of the k treatments. Since the data is arranged for the treatments by columns, the T_i are simply the column totals. (If the treatments were the rows of the data, then the T_i would be the row sums.) Thus, we have

$T_1 = 5+3+8+3 = \underline{19}$, $T_2 = \underline{19}$, $T_3 = \underline{13}$, $T_4 = \underline{23}$, and $T_5 = \underline{15}$.

Also, $T = \Sigma T_i = 19 + 19 + 13 + 23 + 15 = \underline{89}$.

Step 2: Compute $\Sigma\Sigma x_{ij}^2$. This double sum is the square of each of the data values (corresponding to the experimental units) in the table. Thus,

$\Sigma\Sigma x_{ij}^2 = 5^2 + 6^2 + 3^2 + ... + 5^2 + 5^2 = \underline{443}$.

Step 3: Compute SST = $443 - (89)^2/20 = 443 - 396.05 = \underline{46.95}$.

Step 4: Compute SSTR.

$$SSTR = (19)^2/4 + (19)^2/4 + (13)^2/4 + (23)^2/4 + (15)^2/4 - (89)^2/20 = \underline{15.2}$$

Step 5: Compute SSE = SST - SSTR = $46.95 - 15.2 = \underline{31.75}$.

Step 6: Compute MSTR = 15.2/4 = 3.80.

Step 7: Compute MSE = 31.75/(20 - 5) = 2.117.

The third step is to determine the test statistic to be used. This is F = MSTR/MSE with numerator degrees of freedom equal to k - 1 = 4 and denominator degrees of freedom equal to n_T - k = 15.

Next, we determine the decision rule for the test at α = .05. It is

Do not reject H_o if $F \le 2.90$
Reject H_o if $F > 2.90$.

The fifth step of the procedure is to calculate the value of F.

F = 3.8/2.117 = 1.795.

In the final step, we give the conclusion. Since 1.795 does not fall in the rejection region, we do not reject the null hypothesis. It appears that the mean number of allowable absences is the same for all the five colleges.

4. The following questions refer to Example 3:

(a) Are there any conditions that must hold true for the ANOVA procedure to be valid?

Solution:
(a) The conditions are that the response variable, the number of allowed absences per course, follows a normal probability distribution and that the variance of the response variable is the same for each of the five colleges.

(b) Is the design balanced or unbalanced?

Solution:
(b) Since the number of sampled courses per college is the same for each college, this is a balanced design.

5. Refer to the information obtained as a result of example 2 with the preschool children and the small-motor skills test. In many instances, girls develop skills faster than boys during the preschool ages. Suppose, in considering the different group environments, we wished to control the source of variation in the MSE term due to the sex of the child. To determine if there is a significant difference in the mean test scores between the three groups, two children are chosen at random, one boy and one girl, and they are each assigned to the three environmental groups in a random order to take the small-motor skills test. The resulting scores are

		Environment		
		Group 1	Group 2	Group 3
Sex	Male	7	6	6
	Female	9	8	9

(a) Discuss the terms *treatments, blocks, experimental units,* and *experimental design* as they apply to this problem.

Solution:

(a) The treatments are once again the three different groups since they are the groups for which we wish to compare the means. However, the students are not randomly assigned to the groups here as was done in example 2, but they are randomly assigned within each group. The experimental units are again the preschool children. Since the same experimental unit (child) is used for all treatments (environmental groups), blocking has occurred and this is a problem using the randomized block experimental design. The two sexes constitute the blocks.

(b) Test the hypothesis of no difference between the mean scores of the three groups using the eight-step procedure for a randomized block designed experiment. Use $\alpha = .05$.

Solution:

(b) For these data, k = number of treatments = 3

b = number of blocks = 2

n_T = total sample size = kb = 6

i = number of the treatment in which the observation lies
i ranges from 1 to 3

j = number of the block in which the observation lies
j ranges from 1 to 2.

We wish to test: H_o: $\mu_1 = \mu_2 = \mu_3$
H_1: Not all means are equal.

Following the six steps of the computational procedure for a randomized block design given in the formula section of this Guide, we have

Step 1: Compute the $T_{i.}$ values. For these data, the treatments are the columns and the blocks are the rows. Thus, $T_{i.}$ is simply the sum of the observations in the ith treatment (column) for all the blocks (rows).

$T_{1.} = 7 + 9 = \underline{16}$; $T_{2.} = 6 + 8 = \underline{14}$; $T_{3.} = 6 + 9 = \underline{15}$.

Compute the $T_{.j}$ values. For these data, these values are the sums of the observations in the blocks for all the treatments.

$T_{.1} = 7 + 6 + 6 = \underline{19}$; $T_{.2} = 9 + 8 + 9 = \underline{26}$.

The overall total is $T = 7 + 6 + 6 + 9 + 8 + 9 = \underline{45}$.

Step 2: Compute $\Sigma\Sigma x_{ij}^2$ = the sum of the squares of all the individual observations. Thus, $\Sigma\Sigma x_{ij}^2 = 7^2 + 6^2 + 6^2 + \cdots + 9^2 = \underline{347}$.

Step 3: Compute $SST = (\Sigma\Sigma x_{ij}^2) - T^2/n_T = 347 - (45)^2/6 = 347 - 337.5 = \underline{9.5}$.

Step 4: Compute $SSTR = \Sigma T_{i.}^2/b - T^2/n_T = (16^2 + 14^2 + 15^2)/2 - 337.5 = \underline{1}$.

Step 5: Compute $SSB = \Sigma T_{.j}^2/k - T^2/n_T = (19^2 + 26^2)/3 - 337.5 = \underline{8.167}$.

Step 6: Compute $SSE = SST - SSTR - SSB = 9.5 - 1 - 8.167 = \underline{.333}$.

Step 7: Compute $MSTR = SSTR/2 = 1/2 = \underline{.5}$ with 2 degrees of freedom

Step 8: Compute $MSE = SSE/2 = .333/2 = \underline{.167}$ with 2 degrees of freedom.

Finally, completing the ANOVA procedure, for the decision rule

Do not reject H_o if $F \le F_{.05} = 19.00$
Reject H_o if $F > F_{.05} = 19.00$,

we compute

$$F = MSTR/MSE = .5/.167 = \underline{2.994}.$$

Hence, since 2.994 < 19, we <u>do not reject the null hypothesis</u> and conclude that there is no significant difference between the means of the three groups.

6. A consumer group wishes to compare the mean prices of each of three brands of a 12 fluid ounce can of orange juice in a state. Fifteen supermarkets were randomly selected from the state such that 5 supermarkets were assigned to each brand of orange juice. The price per can was recorded for each of the three brands in the supermarkets and the analysis of variance procedure was applied to the data. The following results were obtained: SSE = 0.1 and SST = 0.489.

   (a) Set up the ANOVA table for this procedure.

   <u>Solution</u>:

   (a) For this completely randomized experimental design, we need to compute the following quantities in order to complete the ANOVA table using

$$k = \text{number of treatments} = 3$$
$$n_T = kn = 3(5) = 15$$

Solving formula [4] for SSTR, we obtain

$$SSTR = SST - SSE = .489 - .1 = \underline{.389}.$$

The number of degrees of freedom for SSTR is $k - 1 = \underline{2}$,
the number of degrees of freedom for SSE is $n_T - k = 15 - 3 = \underline{12}$, and
the number of degrees of freedom for SST is $n_T - 1 = 15 - 1 = \underline{14}$.

(Notice that the partitioning of the degrees of freedom gives us a check on these values since 14 = 2 + 12.)

Formula [5] gives $MSTR = SSTR/(k - 1) = .389/2 = \underline{.195}$, and

formula [6] gives $MSE = SSE/(n_T - k) = .1/12 = \underline{.008}$.

The F ratio, $MSTR/MSE = .195/.008 = \underline{24.38}$.

Filling these results in the ANOVA table, we have

ANOVA Table for a Completely Randomized Design

Source of Variation	Sum of Squares	Degrees of Freedom (dof)	Mean Square	F
Between treatments	.389	2	.195	24.38
Error (within treatments)	.1	12	.008	
Total	.489	14		

(b) Is there a difference, using a significance level of .05, in the mean prices of the three brands?

<u>Solution</u>:

(b) We wish to test: H_0: $\mu_1 = \mu_2 = \mu_3$
H_1: Not all means are equal.

The decision rule for the test of hypothesis is:

Do not reject H_0 if $F \le F_{.05} = 3.89$
Reject H_0 if $F > F_{.05} = 3.89$.

Using the results from part (a), $F = 24.38$ falls in the rejection region, so we <u>reject the null</u> hypothesis and conclude that not all the population means are equal.

(c) Test for any significant difference in the mean price of Brand 1 and Brand 2 the using a level of significance of .01 given the following information:

$n_1 = n_2 = 5$ $\quad \bar{x}_1 = .97$ $\quad \bar{x}_2 = 1.26$

<u>Solution</u>:

(c) We wish to perform the tests of hypothesis:

H_0: $\mu_1 = \mu_2$ (there is no difference in treatment means 1 and 2)
H_1: $\mu_1 \ne \mu_2$ (there is a difference in treatment means 1 and 2)

Using the procedure described in the outline and summary for this chapter, we must first calculate a 99% (since $\alpha = .01$) interval estimate of the difference $\mu_1 - \mu_2$ using formula [16]:

(Recall that the number of degrees of freedom to find $t_{.005}$ is obtained by the number of degrees of freedom of MSE)

$$\overline{x}_1 - \overline{x}_2 \pm t_{\alpha/2}\sqrt{MSE\left(\frac{1}{n_1} + \frac{1}{n_2}\right)} = (.97 - 1.26) \pm 3.055\sqrt{(.008)(2/5)}$$

$= -.29 \pm 3.055(.0566) = -.29 \pm .17$ which gives the interval (-.46, -.12).

Since this interval does not include the value 0, we conclude that there is a significant difference in the mean price of Brand 1 and Brand 2.

HAVE I LEARNED THE MATERIAL?

Problems

1. A nationally advertised cosmetics firm sells its products through home demonstrations. Persons desiring to sell the firm's cosmetics are given a training program before being assigned a sales area. Three groups of applicants are chosen randomly from the population of applicants, with 4 women in each group. These groups are randomly assigned to three distinct training programs. After completing their respective training programs, the salespersons are assigned sales areas which are judged to have equivalent sales potentials. The number of individual item sales made by each salesperson during the first two weeks after completing the program is recorded below.

Number of Individual Item Sales in Two Week Period

Sales Training Program A	Sales Training Program B	Sales Training Program C
75	62	48
78	73	76
65	81	54
90	70	88

(a) Discuss the following terms as they apply to this problem: factor, level of the factor, treatment, number of replications, experimental unit, and experimental design.

(b) Do the data indicate a significant difference in the mean sales resulting from each of the three training programs? Use a level of significance of .05.

2. Four questions on a standardized calculus examination are graded by each of three teaching assistants in an experiment to assess differences in grading techniques. The order in which each question was graded by the teaching assistant was selected at random Each question was graded on with a score ranging from 0 (no credit) to 10 (full credit). To what extent do the three teaching assistants differ in terms of mean grades assigned to the four questions? Use a significance level of .05.

		Question			
		A	B	C	D
Teaching Assistant	1	8	7	10	5
	2	9	6	9	4
	3	10	8	10	8

3. In Big City, USA, there are 4 different secretarial schools. Twenty eight students at these schools are selected at random near the completion of their course, seven from each school, to participate in a typing test to measure their typing speeds (words per minute). Unfortunately, due to bad weather the day of the test, not all twenty eight showed up to take the test. The following typing speeds were obtained:

School 1	School 2	School 3	School 4
75	70	60	65
80	60	50	65
75	55	45	70
78	50	65	55
82	65	70	75
70	60		54
65			76

Is there a significant difference, using $\alpha = .10$, in the mean typing speeds at the four schools?

4. For the data on the secretarial school in problem 3, test to see if there is a difference in treatment means μ_1 and μ_4 using $\alpha = .10$.

5. A newly designed pain reliever, Brand XX, was tested for effectiveness against the three leading brands, Brands A, B, and C. Three people who regularly suffer the various degrees of headaches of interest were selected for the test and asked to take the four brands in a random order when a headache occurred. They were also asked to record the time until relief for each brand of pain reliever for each type of headache. Use the following data (which records the number of minutes until relief for each brand) to compare the mean time until relief for the four brands at the .025 level of significance.

		Degree of Headache		
		Mild	Severe	Migraine
Brand	A	10	12	14
	B	8	15	30
	C	3	8	10
	XX	4	10	15

Chapter 14

Multiple Choice Questions

1. For the analysis of variance procedure discussed in this chapter, which of the following is a general statement of the correct null hypothesis?

   (a) The means of two population treatments are equal.
   (b) The variances of k population treatments are equal for $k \geq 3$.
   (c) The means of k sets of sample data are equal for $k \geq 3$.
   (d) The means of k population treatments are equal for $k \geq 3$.

2. In the analysis of variance procedure to test H_0: the k treatment means are equal, the estimate of the common population variance σ^2 using the difference between the treatment means, MSTR, overestimates σ^2 when

   (a) the null hypothesis is true
   (b) the null hypothesis is false
   (c) the computed F statistic is near 0
   (d) MSTR never overestimates σ^2.

3. In the analysis of variance procedure for the randomized block design,

   (a) SSE = SSTR - SST
   (b) SSTR = SSB + SST + SSE
   (c) SST = SSTR + SSB + SSE
   (d) none of the above are true.

4. In the analysis of variance procedure using the completely randomized experimental design, the test of significance at level α is based on a statistic following the

   (a) normal distribution
   (b) chi-square distribution
   (c) t distribution
   (d) F distribution.

5. In the analysis of variance procedure using the randomized block experimental design, the test of significance at level α is based on the statistic

   (a) F = MSTR/MSE
   (b) F = SSTR/SSB
   (c) F = MSB/MSTR
   (d) F = MSTR/MSB.

6. A chamber of commerce has the following data on the scores of potential managers completing a one week seminar in management science that was taught using three different programs: (The test taken was scored on a scale of 0 - 100 points.)

Program 1	Program 2	Program 3
85	75	94
80	70	82
76	81	79
95	64	98
90	70	88

Analysis of variance will be used to test whether or not the mean score is the same for each of the programs. For this problem, there are

(a) 5 treatment levels with 3 replicates each
(b) 3 treatment levels with 5 replicates each
(c) 15 treatment levels with 1 experimental unit in each
(d) 1 treatment level with 20 replicates.

Questions 7 - 10 refer to the following partially completed ANOVA table for a problem in regression analysis using the randomized block experimental design:

Source of Variation	Sum of Squares	Degrees of Freedom	Mean Squares	F
Between treatments	3.5	2		
Between blocks	1.667	3		
Error	3.833			
Total				

7. The number of degrees of freedom corresponding to error and total are, respectively

(a) 5 and 10
(b) 12 and 16
(c) 6 and 11
(d) 8 and 13.

8. The value of the mean square between treatments term is

(a) 0.583
(b) 1.75
(c) 0.556
(d) 4.50.

9. The value of the mean square within treatments term is

   (a) 0.639
   (b) 0.556
   (c) 1.916
   (d) none of these.

10. The conclusion of the test of hypothesis, testing that H_0: the treatment means are equal, using the .025 level of significance, is

   (a) F = .365, which is smaller than the critical value of 39.33, so accept H_0
   (b) F = 3.147, which is larger than the critical value of 2.99, so reject H_0
   (c) F = 2.739, which is smaller than the critical value of 7.26, so do not reject H_0
   (d) There is not enough information given to complete the test.

Chapter 14

Answers to Problems

1. (a) factor - the sales resulting from the sales training programs
level of the factor - there are 3 levels of the factor corresponding to the three sales programs
treatment - there are 3 treatments, one corresponding to each of the three sales training programs
number of replications - there are 4 replications since there are 4 trainees in each group (treatment)
experimental unit - the individual trainees (salespersons) are the experimental units.

(b) To test the hypotheses

H_0: $\mu_A = \mu_B = \mu_C$
H_1: Not all μ_i are equal

The decision rule is
F has (2,9) dof

Accept H_o if $F \leq 4.26$
Reject H_o if $F > 4.26$

ANOVA Table for a Completely Randomized Design

Source of Variation	Sum of Squares	Degrees of Freedom (dof)	Mean Square	F
Between treatments	220.667	2	110.333	.639
Error (within treatments)	1554	9	172.667	
Total	1774.667	11		

Thus, since .639 < 4.26, we do not reject the null hypothesis that the means are equal.

2. To test the hypotheses

H_0: $\mu_1 = \mu_2 = \mu_3$
H_1: Not all μ_i are equal

The decision rule is
F has (2, 6) dof

Accept H_o if $F \leq 5.14$
Reject H_o if $F > 5.14$

ANOVA Table for the Randomized Block Design with 3 Treatments and 4 Blocks

Source of Variation	Sum of Squares	Degrees of Freedom (dof)	Mean Square	F
Between treatments	8.667	2	4.333	5.571
Between blocks	30.333	3	10.111	
Error (within treatments)	4.667	6	.778	
Total	43.667	11		

Thus, since 5.571 > 5.14, we reject the null hypothesis and conclude that the mean grade assigned on the 4 questions is not the same for the 3 teaching assistants.

3. To test the hypotheses H_0: $\mu_1 = \mu_2 = \mu_3 = \mu_4$
H_1: Not all μ_i are equal

The decision rule is Accept H_0 if $F \leq 3.07$
F has (3, 21) dof Reject H_0 if $F > 3.07$

ANOVA Table for a Completely Randomized Design (Unbalanced Design)

Source of Variation	Sum of Squares	Degrees of Freedom (dof)	Mean Square	F
Between treatments	1094.571	3	364.857	5.67
Error (within treatments)	1351.429	21	64.354	
Total	2446	24		

Since F = 5.67 > 3.07, we reject H_0 and conclude that there is a difference in the mean typint scores obtained by students going to the 4 different schools.

4. From the data in the problem, we calculate $\bar{x}_1 = 525/7 = 75$ for $n_1 = 7$ and
$\bar{x}_2 = 460/7 = 65.71$ for $n_2 = 7$.

The confidence interval obtained from formula [16] uses MSE = 64.354 and $t_{.05} = 1.721$ (21 degrees of freedom). The interval is $9.29 \pm 1.721(4.288) = 9.29 \pm 7.38$ or <u>1.91 to 16.67</u>. Since this interval does not contain 0, we conclude that μ_1 is significantly different from μ_4 at the .10 level of significance.

5. To test the hypotheses H_o: $\mu_A = \mu_B = \mu_C = \mu_{XX}$
H_1: Not all μ_i are equal

The decision rule is F has (3, 6) dof
Accept H_o if $F \le 6.60$
Reject H_o if $F > 6.60$

ANOVA Table for the Randomized Block Design with 4 Treatments and 3 Blocks

Source of Variation	Sum of Squares	Degrees of Freedom (dof)	Mean Square	F
Between treatments	185.583	3	61.861	3.546
Between blocks	242.667	2	121.333	
Error (within treatments)	104.667	6	17.444	
Total	532.917	11		

Since F = 3.546 < 6.60, we do not reject the null hypothesis and conclude there is no difference in the mean time until relief from headache pain for the 4 brands.

Chapter 14

Answers to Multiple Choice Questions

1. d
2. b
3. c
4. d
5. a
6. b
7. c
8. b
9. a
10. c

Chapter 15
LINEAR REGRESSION AND CORRELATION

WHAT AM I LEARNING?

Chapter Outline and Summary

Recall that the role of correlation and regression analyses in investigating the relationship between two variables was discussed in Chapter 4. In this chapter, we extend the study of regression and correlation analyses to include the consideration of statistical inference. We limit our discussion to simple (as opposed to multiple) models of regression and correlation analysis; that is, we will be working with mathematical equations relating two variables - one independent and one dependent variable. We also are working only with models where the relationship between the variables can be described by a straight line. Thus, the equations in this chapter will be linear. Multiple models for regression and correlation analyses will be discussed in the next chapter.

The purpose of *regression analysis* is to estimate the value of one variable given knowledge of another quantitative variable. The purpose of *correlation analysis* is to measure the degree of the relationship (association) between the variables. When two variables are being used, the variable that is being predicted is called the *dependent variable.* The variable being used to predict the value of the dependent variable is called the *independent variable.*

When the values of the two variables are plotted, the resulting graph is called a *scatter diagram.* The independent variable, usually denoted by x, is measured along the horizontal axis, and the dependent variable, denoted by y, is measured along the vertical axis. The resulting points compose the scatter diagram of the data. The scatter diagram provides a check on the reasonableness of the linearity assumption and gives an overview of the data.

Recall from Chapter 4 that the straight line that is fitted to the data is called the *estimated regression line* with equation $\hat{y} = b_0 + b_1x$ where b_0 equals the y-intercept of the estimated regression line and b_1 equals the slope of the estimated regression line. The equations for finding b_0 and b_1 were developed through the *method of least squares.* The least squares method is a procedure for determining, using differential calculus, the equations that give the minimum value of $\Sigma (y_i - \hat{y}_i)^2$ where y_i is an observed value of the dependent variable y (that is, a data value) and $\hat{y}_i$ is the corresponding value on the estimated regression line. Solving these equations for the statistics b_0 and b_1 give the computational formulas for finding b_0 and b_1 (See formulas [2] and [3] in the formula section of this Guide).

The sample statistics b_0 and b_1 provide estimates of the population parameters β_0 and β_1, respectively. The equation of the *population regression line* is

$$E(y) = \beta_0 + \beta_1x$$

where E(y) is the mean value of y for a given value of x, β_0 equals the y-intercept of the regression line, and β_1 is the slope of the regression line.

In order for the least squares estimators b_0 and b_1 to be reliable at the chosen level of significance, the following *assumptions of regression analysis* must be made:

1. For a particular value of x, the values of y are normally distributed about the regression line $E(y) = \beta_0 + \beta_1x$.
2. The variance of y, denoted by σ^2, is the same for each value of x.
3. The values of y are independent.

Various techniques are available for checking the validity of these assumptions, but they will not be discussed in this text.

The error in using $\hat{y}$ to estimate y with the regression line is the difference between y and $\hat{y}$ for any data point (x,y). This (vertical) difference, $y - \hat{y}$, is called a *residual.* The resulting sum of squares, which is the one that the least squares method minimizes, is called the *sum of squares due to error,* or the *residual sum of squares,* denoted by SSE.

Recall from Chapter 9 that when data were available for just one variable, whether it be called x or y, the value of the sample mean is the point estimate of the population mean. If $\bar{y}$ were being used to predict y instead of using the estimated regression line value $\hat{y}$, the error would be given by $y - \bar{y}$. The corresponding total sum of squares is denoted by SST and called the *sum of squares about the mean.* To help answer the question "Is $\hat{y}$ a better predictor of y, or is it really no better than using $\bar{y}$?", a measure of the deviation of the estimated regression line from the line $y = \bar{y}$, denoted by SSR, can be computed. SSR is called the *sum of squares due to regression.* The relationship between these three sums of squares is

$$SST = SSR + SSE$$

or, total sum of squares about the mean = sum of squares due to regression + sum of squares due to error. A corresponding relationship also holds for their respective degrees of freedom.

$$\text{Total dof} = \text{Regression dof} + \text{Error dof}$$

Computational formulas for these sums of squares are given in the formula section of this Guide.

These sums of squares can be used to provide a measure of the strength of the regression relationship. The ideal case, or strongest possible relationship, is achieved when all the data values fall on the least squares fitted line. In this case, SSE = 0 or equivalently, SSR/SST = 1. The poorest fit occurs for the largest possible value of SSE, or equivalently, when SSR = 0. In the case of the poorest fit, the estimated regression does not help predict y. The quantity SSR/SST is called the *coefficient of determination* and is denoted by the symbol r^2. When expressed as a percentage, r^2 can be interpreted as the total sum of squares (that is, a measure of the variation in y) that can be explained using the estimated regression line. Thus, r^2 is a measure of the *goodness-of-fit* of the estimated regression line.

The value of r^2 indicates the strength of the regression relationship, but it does not tell us whether or not the relationship is statistically significant. In other words, we wish to know if the estimated regression line is the predictor we should be using or if another model is appropriate. To test for the significance of a relationship between x and y, we test the hypotheses H_0: $\beta_1 = 0$ (there is not a significant relationship between x and y) versus H_1: $\beta_1 \neq 0$ (there is a significant relationship between x and y). These hypotheses can be tested using either a test based on a statistic with a t distribution or a test based on a statistic with an F distribution. (See the formula section for the exact form of the test statistics.) These tests are equivalent for regression analysis with only one independent variable. Both tests use the quantity MSE = SSE/(n - 2), called the *mean square due to error.* MSE is an unbiased estimate of the variance of y, σ^2, mentioned in the assumptions for regression analysis. The F test also uses the quantity MSR, called the *mean square due to regression,* defined as SSR divided by the number of regression degrees of freedom. For one independent variable, the number of regression degrees of freedom is one, so in this chapter, MSR = SSR.

Once the estimated regression equation based on sample data has been developed, it may be desired to estimate either an individual value of y given a specific value of x or the mean value of y given a specific value of x. To distinguish between these two, the confidence interval estimate for the individual value of y is called a *prediction interval* and the interval estimate for the mean value of y is called a *confidence interval.* The corresponding computational formulas are given in the formula section of this Guide.

The results of regression analysis can be summarized conveniently in the form of the

ANOVA table as was done for the computations for analysis of variance in the last chapter. Computer outputs are normally given in this form. The general form of the ANOVA table for two-variable regression analysis is:

Source of Variation	Sum of Squares	Degrees of Freedom	Mean Square
Regression	SSR	1	$MSR = \frac{SSR}{1}$
Error	SSE	n - 2	$MSE = \frac{SSE}{n-2}$
Total (about the mean)	SST	n - 1	

In the case where x and y are both normally distributed random variables, correlation analysis can be used to determine the strength of the relationship between these variables. The sample correlation coefficient, r, was used in Chapter 4 for such a determination. Recall that the values of r always fall between -1 and +1 with the following interpretation:

a) If $r = 1$, there is a perfect positive linear relationship between x and y with all the data points falling on a straight line with positive slope.
b) If $r > 0$, there is a positive linear relationship between x and y that gets stronger as r gets closer to 1.
c) If $r = 0$, there is no linear relationship between x and y.
d) If $r < 0$, there is a negative linear relationship between x and y that gets stronger as r gets closer to -1.
e) If $r = -1$, there is a perfect negative linear relationship between x and y with all the data points falling on a straight line with negative slope.

Using the results of regression analysis and the estimated regression line $\hat{y} = b_0 + b_1x$, the sample correlation coefficient can be computed by more convenient formulas that the one presented in Chapter 4. These formulas are given in the formula section of this Guide. The sample correlation coefficient is a point estimator of the population correlation coefficient, ρ. A statistical test for the significance of a linear relationship between x and y can be performed by testing the hypotheses:

$$H_0: \rho = 0 \quad \text{versus} \quad H_1: \rho \neq 0.$$

The appropriate t test is given by formula [20] in this Guide.

Chapter 15

WHICH FORMULA SHOULD I USE?

Formulas

When:

developing the estimated regression with y-intercept b_0 and slope b_1,

Use:

$$\hat{y} = b_0 + b_1 x \qquad [1]$$

When:

calculating the least squares values for the slope b_1 and the y-intercept b_0 of the estimated regression line for a set of sample data points (x,y) where $\bar{x}$ is the mean of the x values and $\bar{y}$ is the mean of the y values,

Use:

$$b_1 = \frac{\Sigma x_i y_i - (\Sigma x_i \Sigma y_i)/n}{\Sigma x_i^2 - (\Sigma x_i)^2/n} \qquad [2]$$

$$b_0 = \bar{y} - b_1 \bar{x} \qquad [3]$$

When:

defining the population regression line with y-intercept β_0 and slope β_1

Use:

$$E(y) = \beta_0 + \beta_1 x \qquad [4]$$

When:

defining the sum of squares due to error

Use:

$$SSE = \Sigma (y_i - \hat{y}_i)^2 \qquad [5]$$

When:
defining the total sum of squares

Use:

$$SST = \Sigma (y_i - \bar{y})^2 \qquad [6]$$

When:
<u>computing</u> the total sum of squares about the mean

Use:

$$SST = \Sigma y_i^2 - (\Sigma y_i)^2/n \qquad [7]$$

When:
defining the sum of squares due to regression

Use:

$$SSR = \Sigma (\hat{y}_i - \bar{y})^2 \qquad [8]$$

When:
<u>computing</u> the sum of squares due to regression

Use:

$$SSR = \frac{\left[\Sigma x_i y_i - (\Sigma x_i \Sigma y_i)/n\right]^2}{\Sigma x_i^2 - (\Sigma x_i)^2/n} \qquad [9]$$

When:
<u>computing</u> the value of the sum of squares due to error

Use:

$$SSE = SST - SSR \qquad [10]$$

When:

computing the value of the coefficient of determination

Use:

$$r^2 = \frac{SSR}{SST} \qquad [11]$$

When:

computing the mean square due to error, the estimate of σ^2

Use:

$$MSE = \frac{SSE}{n - 2} \qquad [12]$$

When:

testing the hypotheses H_0: $\beta_1 = 0$ versus H_1: $\beta_1 \neq 0$ to determine the significance of the regression relationship between x and y at a specified significance level α

Use:

$$t = \frac{(b_1 - \beta_1)\sqrt{\sum x_i^2 - (\sum x_i)^2/n}}{\sqrt{MSE}} \qquad [13]$$

where the t statistic has n - 2 degrees of freedom

with the decision rule: Accept H_0 if $-t_{\alpha/2} \leq t \leq t_{\alpha/2}$; Reject otherwise.

When:

testing the hypotheses H_0: $\beta_1 = 0$ versus H_1: $\beta_1 \neq 0$ to determine the significance of the regression relationship between x and y at a specified significance level α

Use: [14]

$$F = MSR/MSE = SSR/MSE \quad \text{with one independent variable}$$

where the F statistic has 1 degree of freedom for the numerator and n - 2 degrees of freedom for the denominator

with the decision rule: Accept H_0 if $F \leq F_\alpha$; Reject H_0 if $F > F_\alpha$.

When:

determining a $(1 - \alpha)100\%$ confidence interval for $E(y_p)$ = the mean value of y at a particular value of x, x_p

Use:

$$(b_0 + b_1 x_p) \pm t_{\alpha/2} \sqrt{MSE\left[\frac{1}{n} + \frac{(x_p - \bar{x})^2}{\Sigma x_i^2 - (\Sigma x_i)^2/n}\right]} \qquad [15]$$

When:

determining a $(1 - \alpha)100\%$ prediction interval for y_p = the value of y at a particular value of x, x_p

Use:

$$(b_0 + b_1 x_p) \pm t_{\alpha/2} \sqrt{MSE\left[1 + \frac{1}{n} + \frac{(x_p - \bar{x})^2}{\Sigma x_i^2 - (\Sigma x_i)^2/n}\right]} \qquad [16]$$

When:

determining the sample correlation coefficient from the original data points

Use:

$$r = \frac{\Sigma x_i y_i - (\Sigma x_i \Sigma y_i)/n}{\sqrt{\Sigma x_i^2 - (\Sigma x_i)^2/n}\ \sqrt{\Sigma y_i^2 - (\Sigma y_i)^2/n}} \qquad [17]$$

When:

calculating the sample correlation coefficient using the regression analysis output

Use:

$$r = \pm\sqrt{\text{Coefficient of Determination}} \qquad [18]$$

the sign being determined by the sign of b_1, the slope of the estimated regression line

or

$$r = b_1 \left(\frac{s_x}{s_y}\right) \qquad [19]$$

where

$$s_x = \sqrt{\frac{\Sigma x_i^2 - (\Sigma x_i)^2/n}{n - 1}}$$

and

$$s_y = \sqrt{\frac{\Sigma y_i^2 - (\Sigma y_i)^2/n}{n - 1}}$$

When:

testing the hypothesis that x and y are not linearly related against the hypothesis that x and y are linearly related; that is, when testing the hypotheses H_0: $\rho = 0$ versus $H_1: \rho \neq 0$ for the population correlation coefficient, use the equivalent test of hypothesis for testing H_0: $\beta_1 = 0$ versus H_1: $\beta_1 \neq 0$ given in formula [13] or

Use:

$$t = r\sqrt{\frac{n-2}{1-r^2}} \qquad [20]$$

where the t statistic has n - 2 degrees of freedom

with the decision rule: Accept H_0 if $-t_{\alpha/2} \leq t \leq t_{\alpha/2}$; Reject otherwise.

Chapter 15

HERE'S HOW IT'S DONE!

Examples

Parents and doctors are very concerned with the increasing number of hearing difficulties for children. Do the levels of noise at rock concerts and the volume at which a child listens to music on headsets for radios cause problems in a child's hearing? To help answer these questions, an index of exposure to noise was calculated for each of five randomly chosen groups of children. Higher index values represent higher levels of noise. The table below shows these index values and the resulting rate of noticeable hearing difficulties (per 100).

Index of Exposure to Noise	Rate of Hearing Difficulties (per 100)
1	10
2	16
3	14
4	16
5	24

1. (a) Determine the independent variable and the dependent variable.

Solution:

(a) Since the noise level index will be used to predict the rate of hearing difficulties per 100 children, the index of exposure to noise, x, is the independent variable and the rate of hearing difficulties is the dependent variable, y.

(b) Develop a scatter diagram for these data. Are there any preliminary conclusions about a possible relationship between x and y that can be drawn from this graph?

Solution:

(b) Plotting the independent variable, x, on the horizontal axis and the dependent variable, y, on the vertical axis, the scatter diagram is obtained. Looking at this graph, it appears that x and y are related in a positive sense. That is, it appears that as the noise level increases, so does the rate of hearing difficulties. The relationship appears to be such that a straight line may give a good fit. Before being able to justify these conclusions statistically, however, we must perform several procedures of statistical inference.

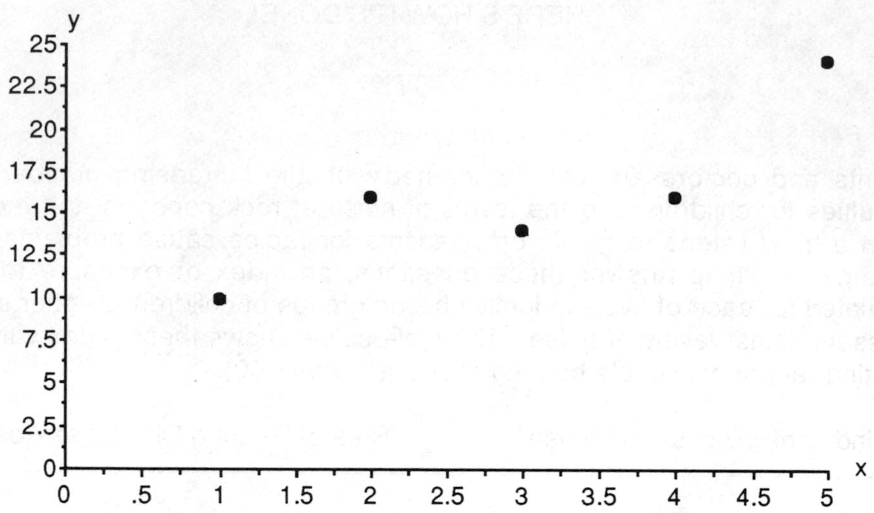

2. (a) Use the method of least squares to develop the estimated regression line.

Solution:

(a) Recall from Chapter 4 that the following quantities are needed to find b_0 and b_1:

	x_i	y_i	x_iy_i	x_i^2
	1	10	10	1
	2	16	32	4
	3	14	42	9
	4	16	64	16
	5	24	120	25
Totals:	15	80	268	55

Substituting in formulas [1], [2], and [3], we obtain

$$b_1 = \frac{\sum x_iy_i - (\sum x_i \sum y_i)/n}{\sum x_i^2 - (\sum x_i)^2/n} = \frac{268 - \frac{(15)(80)}{5}}{55 - \frac{(15)^2}{5}} = \frac{268 - 240}{55 - 45} = 2.80$$

$$b_0 = \bar{y} - b_1\bar{x} = \frac{80}{5} - (2.8)\frac{15}{5} = 16 - 2.8(3) = 7.60$$

Thus, the equation of the estimated regression line is $\hat{y} = 7.6 + 2.8x$.

(b) Plot this line on the scatter diagram in example 1 to visually check the reasonableness of the fit.

Solution:

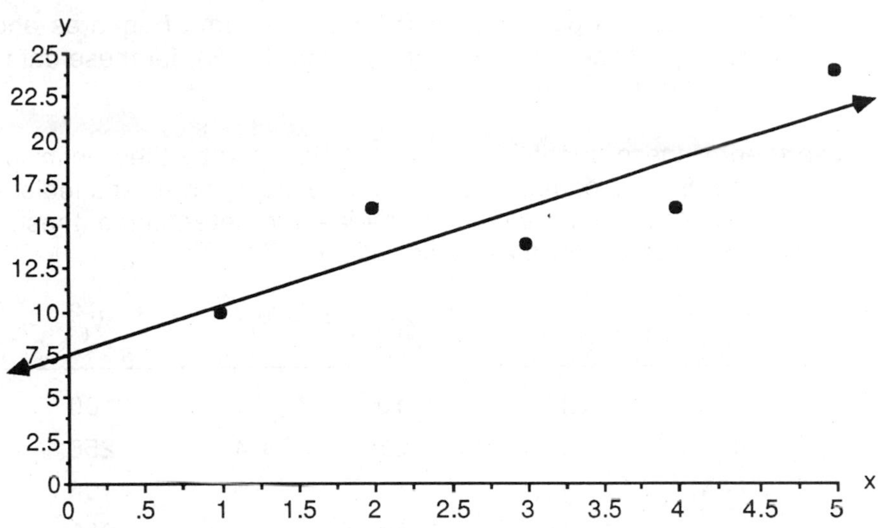

(c) Provided the proper conditions hold true for the estimated regression line to be valid, what rate of hearing difficulties would you predict for children attending a concert with a noise level index of 3.5?

Solution:

(c) Substituting $x = 3.5$ in $\hat{y} = 7.6 + 2.8x$, we obtain a predicted rate of hearing difficulties of

$$\hat{y} = 7.6 + 2.8x = 7.6 + 2.8(3.5) = \underline{17.4}.$$

3. In the regression model $\hat{y} = 7.6 + 2.8x$, what assumptions must hold true?

Solution:

The assumptions are:

(1) for a particular value of the noise level index (x), the values of the rate of hearing difficulty (y) are normally distributed about the population regression line,

(2) the variance of the rate of hearing difficulty, σ^2, is the same for each noise level index, and

(3) the values of the rate of hearing difficulty are independent.

4. Find the sum of squares due to error (SSE), the sum of squares about the mean (SST), and the sum of squares due to regression (SSR) for these data.

Solution:

Even though these quantities could be calculated by their definitions, formulas [5], [6], and [8], the computations can be quite involved and tedious. Therefore, we will use the computational formulas for determining these values. The following are needed for these calculations:

	x_i	y_i	x_iy_i	x_i^2	y_i^2
	1	10	10	1	100
	2	16	32	4	256
	3	14	42	9	196
	4	16	64	16	256
	5	24	120	25	576
Totals:	15	80	268	55	1384

Substituting in formulas [7], [9], and [10], we obtain

$$SST = \Sigma y_i^2 - \frac{(\Sigma y_i)^2}{n} = 1384 - \frac{(80)^2}{5} = 1384 - 1280 = \underline{104}.$$

$$SSR = \frac{\left[\Sigma x_i y_i - (\Sigma x_i \Sigma y_i)/n\right]^2}{\Sigma x_i^2 - (\Sigma x_i)^2/n} = \frac{[268 - (15)(80)/5]^2}{55 - 225/5} = \frac{784}{10} = \underline{78.4}.$$

$$SSE = SST - SSR = 104 - 78.4 = \underline{25.6}.$$

5. Find and interpret r^2, the coefficient of determination, for these sample data.

Solution:

Substituting in formula [11], we obtain

$$r^2 = SSR/SST = 78.4/104 = \underline{.754}.$$

Thus, we conclude that the estimated regression line has accounted for 75.4% of the total sum of squares (SST). Since a perfect fit occurs when $r^2 = 1$ and the worst fit occurs when $r^2 = 0$, the estimated regression gives a very good fit to the data.

6. How significant is the regression relationship? (Use $\alpha = .10$)

Solution:

To answer this question, we test the hypotheses

H_0: $\beta_1 = 0$ (there is not a significant relationship between x and y)

H_1: $\beta_1 \neq 0$ (there is a significant relationship between x and y)

To test these hypotheses, we use formula [13] where the t statistic has 5 - 2 = 3 degrees of freedom.

The decision rule is Accept H_0 if $-2.353 \leq t \leq 2.353$
Reject H_0 otherwise.

Substituting in formula [13], we obtain

$$t = \frac{(b_1 - \beta_1)\sqrt{\Sigma x_i^2 - (\Sigma x_i)^2/n}}{\sqrt{MSE}} = \frac{(2.8 - 0)\sqrt{55 - 225/5}}{\sqrt{8.533}} = \underline{3.031}$$

since MSE = SSE/(5 - 2) = 25.6/3 = 8.533 by formula [12].

Thus, since the value of t = 3.031 falls in the rejection region, we reject the null hypothesis and conclude that there is a significant relationship between the index of exposure to noise and the rate of hearing difficulty in children.

Note: We could have just as well (in fact, more easily) used the F test in formula [14] to test these hypotheses where the F statistic has 1 degree of freedom for the numerator and 5 - 2 = 3 degrees of freedom for the denominator. To perform this test,

The decision rule is Accept H_0 if $F \leq 5.54$
Reject H_0 if $F > 5.54$.

Note: This value of $F_{.10}$ was obtained from a more complete listing of the critical values of the F distribution than given in your text.

Substituting in formula [14], for the case of one independent variable, x, we obtain

$$F = MSR/MSE = SSR/MSE = 78.4/8.533 = \underline{9.188}.$$

The same conclusion is reached as in the t test above.

7. (a) There is a planned rock concert in Springfield tonight with an estimated noise level index of 4.2. Obtain a 98% confidence interval for the mean rate of hearing difficulty for the children attending the concert.

Solution:

(a) Since we are asked for a confidence interval for the mean value of y at a particular value of x, x = 4.2, we substitute in formula [15] with $1-\alpha = .98$ to obtain

$$(b_0 + b_1 x_p) \pm t_{\alpha/2} \sqrt{MSE\left[\frac{1}{n} + \frac{(x_p - \bar{x})^2}{\Sigma x_i^2 - (\Sigma x_i)^2/n}\right]} =$$

$$[7.6 + 2.8(4.2)] \pm 4.541 \sqrt{8.533\left[0.2 + \frac{(4.2 - 3)^2}{55 - 225/5}\right]}$$

$$= 19.36 \pm 4.541(1.713) = 19.36 \pm 7.778 \quad \text{or} \quad (11.582,\ 27.138)$$

Thus, the mean rate of hearing difficulty (per 100) is estimated with 98% confidence to be between 11.582 and 27.138.

(b) Tim Kneafson, age 14, will be attending the Springfield concert. Give a 98% prediction interval for the rate of hearing difficulty of the group of children to which Tim belongs.

Solution:

Notice that the only difference in formulas [15] and [16] is the "1" under the square root. Thus, using the $x_p = 4.2$ and the confidence of 98%, the prediction interval is obtained from formula [16].

$$19.36 \pm 4.541(3.386) = 19.36 \pm 15.378 = (\underline{3.982}, \underline{34.738}).$$

8. Show the results of this regression analysis in the form of an ANOVA table for the two-variable regression analysis.

Solution:

Referring to the chapter summary and outline, we obtain the proper form of the ANOVA table. Substituting in the correct values, we have

Source of Variation	Sum of Squares	Degrees of Freedom	Mean Square
Regression	78.4	1	78.4
Error	25.6	3	8.533
Total (about the mean)	104	4	

9. Find the sample correlation coefficient by three different methods.

Solution

(a) The simplest way to find the sample correlation coefficient, r, is to use formula [18]:

$$r = \pm\sqrt{r^2} = \pm\sqrt{.754} = \pm .868 .$$

Since the sign of r is determined by the sign of b_1, which is positive, $r = \underline{.868}$.

Solution

(b) Using the methods of Chapter 4, formula [17] gives

$$r = \frac{\Sigma x_i y_i - (\Sigma x_i \Sigma y_i)/n}{\sqrt{\Sigma x_i^2 - (\Sigma x_i)^2/n}\ \sqrt{\Sigma y_i^2 - (\Sigma y_i)^2/n}} = \frac{268 - (15)(80)/5}{\sqrt{10}\ \sqrt{104}}$$

$$= \frac{28}{32.249} = \underline{.868}.$$

Solution

(c) A third method for finding r is to use formula [19]. Finding $s_x^2 = 2.5$ and $s_y^2 = 26$, we obtain

$$r = 2.8\left(\frac{\sqrt{2.5}}{\sqrt{26}}\right) = 2.8(.310) = \underline{.868}.$$

10. Use formula [20] to determine whether or not the relationship between x and y is linear. Use a level of significance of .10.

Solution:

We wish to test the hypotheses: H_0: $\rho = 0$ (x and y are not linearly related)

H_1: $\rho \neq 0$ (x and y are linearly related)

The decision rule for the t statistic in formula [20] with 5 - 2 = 3 degrees of freedom is

Accept H_0 if $-2.353 \leq t \leq 2.353$

Reject H_0 otherwise.

Substituting in formula [20], we obtain

$$t = r\sqrt{\frac{n-2}{1-r^2}} = .868\sqrt{\frac{3}{1-.754}} = .868\,(3.492) = \underline{3.031}.$$

Thus, since t = 3.031 falls in the rejection region, we conclude that the population correlation coefficient is not 0 and thus the index of exposure to noise and the rate of hearing difficulty (per 100) are linearly related.

Chapter 15

HAVE I LEARNED THE MATERIAL?

Problems

Henry Howard, a student in Professor Jover's English class, has a theory that grades in Professor Jover's courses are related to where the students have been sitting during the term. Harry takes a random sample of students and records their grade and the distance between the students' desks and Professor Jover's lectern.

Distance of Desk from Lectern (in feet)	Grade in Course (on a scale of 1 to 10)
1	10
4	7
6	8
9	5

The following problems all pertain to this set of data.

1. (a) Which variable is the independent variable? the dependent variable?

   (b) Develop a scatter diagram of these data. Comment on any possible relationship between the two variables.

2. (a) Use the method of least squares to develop the estimated regression line.

(b) Plot this estimated regression line on the scatter diagram developed in problem 1.

(c) What grade would you predict in English for a student who sits 5 feet from the professor's lectern?

3. Give the assumptions of regression analysis that must hold true in order for the estimated regression line to be valid.

4. How significant is the relationship between x and y? (Use a t test with $\alpha = .10$.)

5. Find SSR, SSE, SST, MSR, and MSE. Give your answer in the form of an ANOVA table for the two-variable regression analysis.

6. Find and interpret the coefficient of determination, r^2.

7. Answer the question posed in problem 4, "How significant is the relationship between x and y?" by performing a test using an F statistic with $\alpha = .10$.
[Note: $F_{.10}$ with (numerator dof = 1, denominator dof = 2) = 8.53.]

8. Find and interpret r, the sample correlation coefficient.

9. Harry wishes to estimate, with a 95% confidence interval, the mean grade for a student in the English class who sits a distance of 7 feet from the professor's lectern. Can you help him?

10. Harry sits a distance of 3 feet from Professor Jover's lectern. Predict, with a 98% interval, Harry's grade in the English class.

Chapter 15

Multiple Choice Questions

1. The objective of linear regression analysis is to

   (a) determine the strength of the relationship between two variables
   (b) establish a cause-effect relationship between two variables
   (c) develop an equation showing how two variables are related
   (d) determine the correlation between two variables.

2. In the regression line for the population, $E(y) = \beta_0 + \beta_1 x$, the term β_1 is

   (a) the independent variable
   (b) the y-intercept of the regression line
   (c) the slope of the regression line
   (d) the estimated value of y at $x = \beta_0$.

3. The objective of the method of least squares is to

   (a) minimize $\Sigma (y_i - \hat{y}_i)^2$
   (b) minimize $\Sigma (\hat{y}_i - \bar{y})^2$
   (c) maximize $\Sigma (y_i - \bar{y})^2$
   (d) minimize SSR.

4. In the ideal case, when the least squares fitted line passes through every data point,

   (a) SSR = 0
   (b) SSE = 0
   (c) $r^2 = 0$
   (d) SST = SSE.

5. For a given set of 20 data points, SSR = 314.65 and SSE = 159.53. The sample correlation coefficient for these points is closest to

   (a) 1.97
   (b) 0.664
   (c) either 1.40 or -1.40
   (d) either 0.81 or -0.81.

6. For a given set of variables, n = 20, SSR = 314.65 and SSE = 159.53. The estimate of σ^2, the population variance of the y values about the regression line, is

   (a) 8.863
   (b) 7.977
   (c) 15.733
   (d) 26.343.

7. The purpose of drawing a scatter diagram of the data is that it

   (a) gives us an easy method of calculating MSE
   (b) allows us to visually determine the least squares line
   (c) provides an overview of the data and enables us to draw preliminary conclusions about a possible relationship between the variables
   (d) all of the above.

8. In order to test the hypothesis that β_1, the slope of the population regression line, equals 0, we use a test statistic based on the

   (a) t distribution
   (b) F distribution
   (c) neither of the above
   (d) either of the above.

9. For a sample of size n, the difference between the total degrees of freedom and the regression degrees of freedom in the ANOVA table for two-variable regression analysis is

   (a) n
   (b) n - 2
   (c) n - 1
   (d) 1.

10. Confidence intervals for predicting an individual value of y at a particular value of x

    (a) will always be narrower than those for predicting the mean value of y at that x
    (b) will always be wider than those for predicting the mean value of y at that x
    (c) will sometimes be wider and sometimes be narrower than those for predicting the mean value of y at that x
    (d) will determine whether or not the null hypothesis of a significant relationship between the variables is rejected or not.

Chapter 15

Answers to Problems

1. (a) Since the distance from the lectern is being used to predict the grade, the distance of the student's desk, x, is the independent variable. The grade the student makes in the course, y, is the dependent variable.

   (b) The scatter diagram is

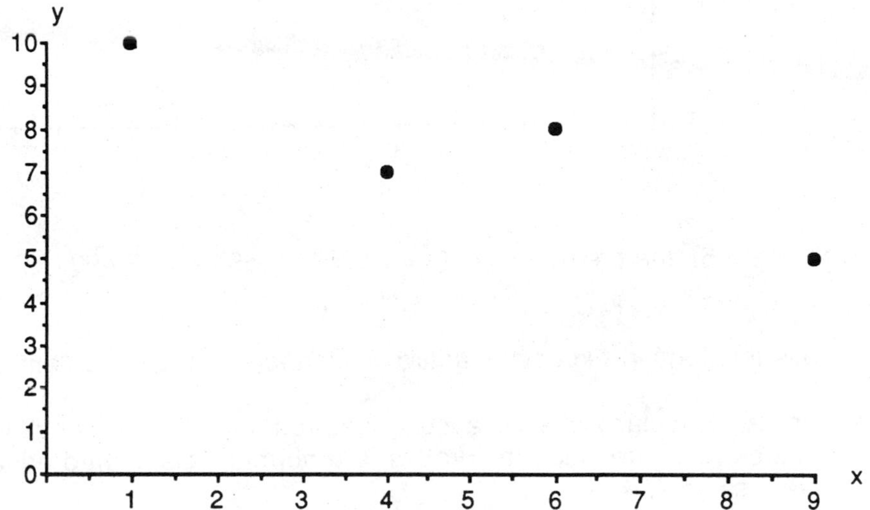

   (c) Visually, it appears that x and y are <u>linearly related in a negative sense</u>. Thus, as the distance from the professor's lectern increases, it appears that the student's grade decreases.

2. For this data, $n = 4$, $\Sigma x = 20$, $\Sigma y = 30$, $\Sigma xy = 131$, $(\Sigma x)(\Sigma y) = 600$, $\Sigma x^2 = 134$, $\Sigma y^2 = 238$, $\bar{x} = 5$, $\bar{y} = 7.5$.

   (a) Thus, $b_1 = -0.559$ and $b_o = 10.294$. The equation of the estimated regression line is therefore $\underline{\hat{y} = 10.294 - .559\,x}$.

   (b) Plotting the line on the scatter diagram, the line does appear to "fit" the data.

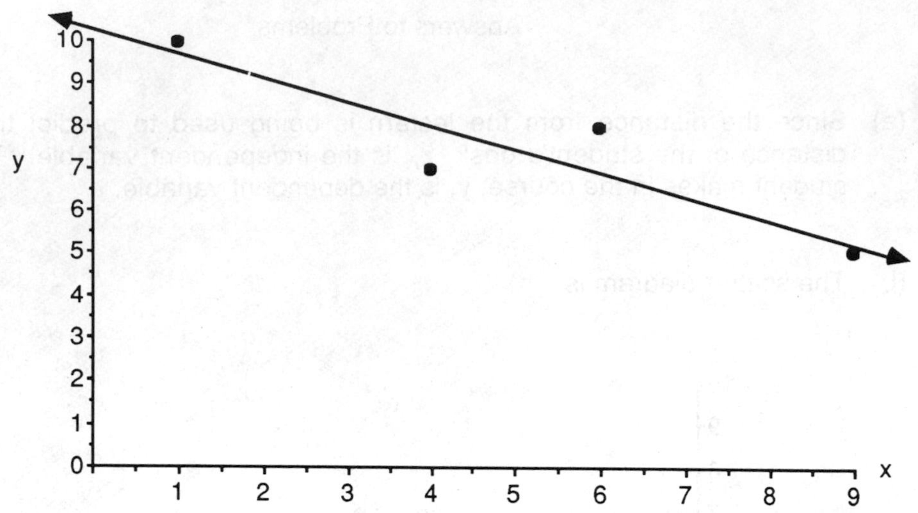

(c) For $x = 5$, the prediction is $\hat{y} = 10.294 - .559\,x = \underline{7.499}$.

3. The assumptions in regression analysis, as applied to this problem, are:

   (a) For a particular x, the distance in feet from the student's desk to the lectern, the values of y, the students' grades, are normally distributed about the population regression line.
   (b) The variance of the students' grades, σ^2, are the same for each value of x.
   (c) The values of the students' grades are independent.

4. Test the hypotheses: $H_0\colon \beta_1 = 0$

   $H_1\colon \beta_1 \neq 0$

   The test statistic is given in formula [13] with $n - 2 = 4 - 2 = 2$ degrees of freedom.

   The decision rule is Accept H_0 if $-2.92 \leq t \leq 2.92$

   Reject H_0 otherwise.

   From formula [13], the value of the test statistic is $t = -2.986$.

   Thus, reject H_0 and conclude that there is a significant linear relationship between the students' distance from the lectern and their grade in the English course.

5.

ANOVA Table for Two-Variable Regression Analysis

Source of Variation	Sum of Squares	Degrees of Freedom	Mean Square
Regression	10.618	1	10.618
Error	2.382	2	1.191
Total (about the mean)	13	3	

6. r^2 = .817

The estimated regression line has accounted for 81.7% of the total sum of squares.

7. F = 8.914 where the F statistic has 1 degree of freedom for the numerator and 2 degrees of freedom for the denominator.

Since the decision rule is "Accept H_o if $F \le 8.53$; Reject H_o if $F > 8.53$", the decision is that x and y are significantly related.

8. r = -.904

There is a negative linear association between x and y. Since this value is close to -1, the association is a strong one. One must be cautious, however, not to imply a cause-and-effect interpretation here. Certainly, a student's grade is not determined by where that student sits in the class.

9. At $x_p = 7$, $\hat{y}_p = 6.381$. Using $t_{.025} = 4.303$, formula [15] gives

$$6.381 \pm (4.303)(.662) = 6.381 \pm 2.847 = (3.534\ ,\ 9.228).$$

10. At $x_p = 3$, $\hat{y}_p = 8.617$. Using $t_{.01} = 6.965$, formula [16] gives

$$8.617 \pm (6.965)(1.276) = 8.617 \pm 8.889 = (-.272\ ,\ 17.506).$$

Chapter 15

Answers to Multiple Choice Questions

1. c
2. c
3. a
4. b
5. d
6. a
7. c
8. d
9. b
10. b

Chapter 16
MULTIPLE REGRESSION

WHAT AM I LEARNING?

Chapter Outline and Summary

In Chapter 15, we considered the techniques of regression and correlation analyses for models that contained exactly one independent and one dependent variable. Recall that the variable being predicted or explained by the equation (model) is called the *dependent variable* and the variable being used to predict or explain the value of the dependent variable is called the independent *variable.* In this chapter, we extend our discussion of linear regression to models that contain two or more independent variables.

In *multiple regression analysis,* two or more independent variables are used to construct a linear equation for the purpose of estimating the value of one dependent variable. The same basic concepts that were developed in Chapter 15 apply for multiple regression analysis. However, the mathematics involved in working with the multiple model is much more complex and time-consuming. For this reason, computers are used to do most of the routine calculations involved in multiple regression analysis.

The general form of the *multiple regression equation* for the population is

$$E(y) = \beta_o + \beta_1x_1 + \beta_2x_2 + \cdots + \beta_px_p$$

where the x_i values for $i = 1, 2, \cdots, p$ represent the p independent variables, E(y) represents the average of all possible values of y that could occur at a given value of each of the x_i's, and the $\beta_o, \beta_1, \cdots, \beta_p$ are the *population parameters* or *coefficients* for the equation. Note that if $\beta_i = 0$, then the corresponding x_i is not related to y.

Although a "best fit" is still defined in terms of the *least squares criterion*, the presence of two or more independent variables makes it difficult to graph the resulting scatter diagram. In the case of two independent variables, the best fitting line becomes the best fitting plane, and so forth.

The same assumptions that we made in Chapter 15 for the one independent variable case still hold true in multiple regression, although their statement becomes more involved. We state these *assumptions in multiple regression analysis* for the case of two independent variables:

(a) For a specified value of x_1 and x_2, the values of y are normally distributed about the regression equation $E(y) = \beta_o + \beta_1 x_1 + \beta_2 x_2$.

(b) The variance of y, denoted by σ^2, is the same for all values of x_1 and x_2.

(c) The values of y are independent.

The least squares method gives the values $b_o, b_1, \cdots, b_p$ which are the point estimates of the population parameters $\beta_0, \beta_1, \cdots, \beta_p$. Thus, the *estimated regression equation* is written as

$$\hat{y} = b_o + b_1 x_1 + b_2 x_2 + \cdots + b_p x_p .$$

In the general multiple regression case, matrix algebra and methods of linear programming are used to solve the equations that result from the least squares method for the values $b_o, b_1, \cdots, b_p$. For the special case of two independent variables,the least squares criterion is

$$\text{minimize } \Sigma (y_i - b_o - b_1 x_{1i} - b_2 x_{2i})^2$$

where $\hat{y}_i = b_o + b_1 x_{1i} + b_2 x_{2i}$. The equations that yield the estimates b_o, b_1, and b_2 to give the estimated regression line are called the *normal equations.* The interpretation of each regression coefficient is as follows:

> b_i represents the change in y corresponding to a one-unit change in the independent variable x_i when the other independent variable x_j is held constant.

The appropriate test for determining whether or not there is a significant relationship among x_1, x_2, and y is to test the hypotheses

H_0: $\beta_1 = \beta_2 = 0$ (there is not a significant relationship between x_1, x_2, and y)
H_1: At least one of the two coefficients is not zero
(there is a significant relationship among x_1, x_2, and y)

To test these hypotheses, we should use the summary provided in an ANOVA table and use the test statistic $F = MSR/MSE$ with numerator degrees of freedom equal to 2 and denominator degrees of freedom equal to $n - 3$. The two mean squares in the ANOVA table upon which this statistic is based are $MSR = SSR/2$ and $MSE = SSE/(n - 3)$. Using similar reasoning to that of Chapter 15, the decision rule is for a significance level of α is

Accept Ho if $F \leq F\alpha$
Reject Ho if $F > F\alpha$.

The appropriate hypotheses in the general case for p independent variables to test for a significant relationship are

H_0: $\beta_1 = \beta_2 = \cdots = \beta_p = 0$
H_1: At least one of the p coefficients is not equal to zero .

Again, if we reject H_0, we can conclude that there is a significant relationship. The F statistic used in this test is, as before, $F = MSR/MSE$ with the summary statistics and appropriate degrees of freedom available from the *ANOVA table for multiple regression analysis* involving p independent variables and a random sample size of n:

Source	Sum of Squares	Degrees of Freedom	Mean Square
Regression	SSR	p	$MSR = \dfrac{SSR}{p}$
Error	SSE	n - p - 1	$MSE = \dfrac{SSE}{n - p - 1}$
Total (about the mean)	SST	n - 1	

If, after using the F test, we conclude that the multiple regression relationship is significant (that is, we reject H_0), tests can be conducted to see which of the individual parameters, β_i, are significant. The t test used in Chapter 15 for the corresponding case of one independent variable may be used to test for the *significance* of the individual parameters in multiple regression analysis. That is, to perform the two-tailed test

$$H_0: \beta_i = 0 \qquad (\beta_i \text{ is not significant.})$$

$$H_1: \beta_i \neq 0 \qquad (\beta_i \text{ is significant.})$$

use the statistic t given in formula [4] of this Guide with n - p - 1 degrees of freedom. Of course, for the results of any of these tests to be valid, the assumptions in multiple regression analysis must be true.

A measure of the strength of the relationship, that is, the goodness of fit of the regression equation to the data, is given by the *multiple coefficient of determination,* R^2.

$$R^2 = SSR/SST$$

When multiplied by 100, the multiple coefficient of determination represents the percentage of variability in y that is explained by the estimated regression equation. In general, it is always true that R^2 will increase as more independent variables are added to the regression equation because adding variables to the equation causes the prediction errors to be smaller, thus reducing SSE. Since SST = SSR + SSE, this causes R^2 to increase. R^2 can be adjusted for the number of independent variables to avoid overestimating the impact of adding an independent variable on the amount of unexplained variability. The *adjusted multiple coefficient of determination* is

$$R_a^2 = 1 - (1 - R^2)[(n - 1)/(n - p - 1)].$$

Once a regression equation is developed, confidence intervals for the mean value of y and prediction intervals for a particular y at a specific set of values for the independent variables can be constructed by methods similar to those in Chapter 15. Computer packages often provide these confidence intervals once the user specifies the particular values of the independent variables.

Chapter 16

WHICH FORMULA SHOULD I USE?

Formulas

When:

defining the population multiple regression equation involving p independent variables

Use:

$$E(y) = \beta_o + \beta_1 x_1 + \beta_2 x_2 + \cdots + \beta_p x_p \quad [1]$$

When:

defining the estimated regression equation

Use:

$$\hat{y} = b_o + b_1 x_1 + b_2 x_2 + \cdots + b_p x_p \quad [2]$$

When:

testing for the significance of the relationship between the variables in multiple regression analysis for a sample size of n and p independent variables

Use:

$$F = \frac{MSR}{MSE} \quad [3]$$

where the F statistic has numerator degrees of freedom = p and denominator degrees of freedom = n - p - 1.

When:

testing the hypotheses H_0: $\beta_i = 0$ versus H_1: $\beta_i \neq 0$ to determine the significance of the individual parameter β_i in multiple regression analysis at the specified significance level α

Use:

$$t = \frac{(b_i - \beta_i)}{s_{b_i}} \qquad [4]$$

where s_{b_i} is the estimate of the standard deviation of the sampling distribution of b_i and the t statistic has n - p - 1 degrees of freedom with the decision rule: Accept H_o if $-t_{\alpha/2} \leq t \leq t_{\alpha/2}$; Reject otherwise.

When:

calculating the multiple coefficient of determination

Use:

$$R^2 = \frac{SSR}{SST} \qquad [5]$$

When:

computing the adjusted multiple coefficient of determination

Use:

$$R_a^2 = 1 - (1 - R^2)\left(\frac{n - 1}{n - p - 1}\right) \qquad [6]$$

HERE'S HOW IT'S DONE!

Examples

1. An experiment was done to study the relationship of the volume of the water in a fish tank, the temperature of the water in a fish tank, and the amount of food the fish are fed daily to the length of the fish at maturity if the fish were hatched and raised in the fish tank.

   (a) What are the independent variables and what is the dependent variable?

<u>Solution</u>:

(a) The length of the fish at maturity would be predicted by the other variables. Thus, the dependent variable is

y = the length of the fish at maturity.

The independent variables are:

x_1 = the volume of the water in the fish tank
x_2 = the temperature of the water in the fish tank
x_3 = the daily amount of food the fish are fed.

(b) A biologist developed the following estimated regression equation relating these variables for a particular species of fish. Interpret the coefficients in this estimated regression equation.

$$\hat{y} = 1.21 + .034x_1 + .21x_2 + .45x_3$$

<u>Solution</u>:

b_1 = .034 represents the change in the length of the fish corresponding to a one unit change in the volume of the water in the fish tank when the temperature of the water and the daily amount of food the fish are fed are held constant.

b_2 = .21 represents the change in the length of the fish corresponding to a one unit change in the temperature of the water in the fish tank when the volume of the water and the daily amount of food the fish are fed are held constant.

b_3 = .45 represents the change in the length of the fish corresponding to a one unit change in the daily amount of food the fish are fed when the volume and temperature of the water in the fish tank are held constant.

2. A random sample of 10 families in a particular area was studied in order to determine the factors which influence the purchasing of major home appliances. The study revealed

$$\hat{y} = 2.588 + .91x_1 + .529x_2 + .09x_3 + .249x_4$$

where y = purchasing index (which increases as purchase is more likely)
x_1 = wage rate of family
x_2 = house size index of family
x_3 = number of children in family
x_4 = mean age of currently owned major appliances (in years).

(a) Complete the following ANOVA table for this multiple regression problem.

Source	Sum of Squares	Degrees of Freedom	Mean Square
Regression	467.163		
Error	22.937		
Total (about the mean)			

Solution:

(a) For this example, the sample size is given as $n = 10$, and the number of independent variables is $p = 4$. Thus, the degrees of freedom for regression is $p = 4$; the degrees of freedom for error is $n - p - 1 = 5$, and the total degrees of freedom is $n - 1 = 9$.

$$SST = SSR + SSE = 467.163 + 22.937 = 490.1$$

$$MSR = SSR/p = 467.163/4 = 116.791$$

$$MSE = SSE/(n - p - 1) = 22.937/5 = 4.587.$$

Thus, the completed table is

Source	Sum of Squares	Degrees of Freedom	Mean Square
Regression	467.163	4	116.791
Error	22.937	5	4.587
Total (about the mean)	490.1	9	

(b) Is the multiple regression relationship statistically significant? Use $\alpha = .05$.

To answer this question, we test the following hypotheses:

H_0: $\beta_1 = \beta_2 = \beta_3 = \beta_4 = 0$
H_1: At least one of the four coefficients is not zero.

The statistic is $F = MSR/MSE$ with 4 numerator degrees of freedom and 5 denominator degrees of freedom.

The decision rule is Accept H_o if $F \leq 5.19$
Reject H_o if $F > 5.19$.

Computing the value of F from formula [3], we find

$$F = 116.791/4.587 = \underline{25.46}.$$

Thus, H_o is rejected and we conclude that there is a significant relationship among x_1, x_2, x_3, x_4, and y at the 5% level of significance.

3. Refer to example 2 above concerning the purchasing of major home appliances. A computer output reveals the following:

Regression Coefficient	Standard Error	t-value
b_1	.241	3.776
b_2	.224	2.362
b_3	.459	.196
b_4	.294	.847

Test for the significance of the individual parameters β_1, β_2, β_3, and β_4 at the .10 level of significance.

Solution:

For each of the parameters, we wish to test the hypotheses

$$H_0: \beta_i = 0$$
$$H_1: \beta_i \neq 0$$

The test statistic in each case is $t = b_i/s_{b_i}$ which has already been calculated in the computer output where the t statistic has $n - p - 1 = 5$ dof. (Recall that the "standard error" of the estimate is another name for the standard deviation of the sampling distribution of the statistic.)

For each test, the decision rule is Accept H_0 if $-2.015 \leq t \leq 2.015$
Reject H_0 otherwise.

Since $b_1/s_{b1} = 3.776 > 2.015$ and $b_2/s_{b2} = 2.362 > 2.015$, we reject the null hypotheses that $\beta_1 = 0$ and $\beta_2 = 0$, concluding that the parameters β_1 and β_2 are significant in the multiple regression analysis at the .10 level of significance.

Because $b_3/s_{b3} = .196$ and $b_4/s_{b4} = .847$ do not fall in the rejection region, we conclude that β_3 and β_4 cannot be considered different from zero and are therefore, not significant in the multiple regression analysis at the .10 level of significance.

4. Again referring to example 2 concerning the purchasing power of major home appliances,

(a) Calculate the multiple coefficient of determination.

Solution:

(a) Obtaining SSR = 467.163 and SST = 490.1 from the ANOVA table for this example, we calculate from formula [5]

$$R^2 = \frac{SSR}{SST} = \frac{467.163}{490.1} = \underline{.953}\,.$$

(b) Interpret this value of R^2.

Solution:

95.3% of the variability in the purchasing index is explained by the estimated regression equation.

(c) Calculate the adjusted multiple coefficient of determination.

Solution:

Using formula [6] we obtain

$$R_a^2 = 1 - (1 - R^2)\left(\frac{n-1}{n-p-1}\right) = 1 - (1 - .953)\left(\frac{9}{5}\right) = 1 - .085 = \underline{.915}.$$

5. Use the least squares equation given in example 1,

$$\hat{y} = 1.21 + .034x_1 + .21x_2 + .45x_3,$$

to estimate the length at maturity for the particular species of fish that are hatched and raised in a fish tank holding 10 gallons of water kept at a constant temperature of 70 degrees and are fed 5 grams of food daily.

Solution:

We are given the values $x_1 = 10$, $x_2 = 70$, $x_3 = 5$ and asked to predict y, the length of the species of fish at maturity. Substituting these values into the estimated regression equation, we have

$$\hat{y} = 1.21 + .034(10) + .21(70) + .45(5) = \underline{18.5} \text{ units of length.}$$

HAVE I LEARNED THE MATERIAL?

Problems

Data on eight elementary school teachers was collected for the following variables: the yearly salary of the teacher (in thousands of dollars), the number of years teaching experience for the teacher, and the age of the teacher (in years). The data is being collected as part of a study to determine salary scales for teachers applying for positions in elementary teaching.

1. What are the independent variables and what is the dependent variable?

2. A statistical consultant for the school board has developed the following estimated regression equation relating these variables. Interpret the coefficients in this estimated regression equation.

$$\hat{y} = 7.137 + .582x_1 + .336x_2$$

3. Complete the following ANOVA table for this problem:

Source	Sum of Squares	Degrees of Freedom	Mean Square
Regression	121.161		
Error	8.714		
Total (about the mean)			

4. At the .05 level of significance, test to determine if the fitted multiple regression equation given in this problem represents a significant relationship between the independent variables and the dependent variable.

5. For this data on the elementary teachers' salaries, a computer output reveals the following:

Regression Coefficient	Standard Error	t-value
b_1 = .582	.200	2.910
b_2 = .336	.115	2.922

Test for the significance of the individual parameters β_1 and β_2 at the .05 level of significance.

6. (a) Find and interpret the multiple coefficient of determination.

(b) Determine the adjusted R^2.

Chapter 16

Multiple Choice Questions

1. The regression coefficient may be interpreted as

   (a) the change in one independent variable corresponding to a change in the other independent variables
   (b) the change in an independent variable corresponding to a one-unit change in the dependent variable
   (c) the change in the dependent variable corresponding to a one-unit change in the independent variable when the other independent variables are held constant
   (d) none of these.

2. The adjusted coefficient of determination

   (a) will always be larger than the coefficient of determination
   (b) will sometimes equal the coefficient of determination
   (c) will always be smaller than the coefficient of determination
   (d) none of these.

3. The values of the regression coefficients in a multiple regression problem can be solved by using

   (a) a computer package
   (b) matrix algebra
   (c) simultaneous equation methods
   (d) all of the above.

4. For the multiple regression model, the term β_0 is interpreted as

   (a) the coefficient of correlation
   (b) a measure of the significance of the relation between y and the independent variables
   (c) the estimated value of the dependent variable when every independent variable equals zero
   (d) none of these.

5. A problem in multiple regression is characterized by

   (a) more than one independent variable and one dependent variable
   (b) more than one dependent variable and two independent variables
   (c) more than two independent variables and more than one dependent variable
   (d) all of the above.

6. In multiple regression analysis, a test of the null hypothesis that the p population regression coefficients are all zero versus the alternative hypothesis that at least one of the p coefficients is not equal to zero is based on the

(a) t distribution
(b) normal distribution
(c) F distribution
(d) none of these distributions.

7. The number of degrees of freedom for the statistic that is the answer to question 6 is

(a) n - p - 1
(b) p for the numerator and n - p - 1 for the denominator
(c) p for the numerator and n - 1 for the denominator
(d) none of these.

8. The population regression model for two independent variables is represented graphically as

(a) a straight line
(b) a plane
(c) a trapezoid
(d) a rectangle.

9. An assumption that is made in multiple regression analysis is

(a) for specified values of the independent variables, the values of the dependent variable are normally distributed about the population regression equation
(b) the values of the dependent variable are independent
(c) the variance of the dependent variable is the same for all values of the independent variable
(d) all of the above.

10. If the coefficient of determination for a problem in multiple regression analysis with 5 independent variables and a sample size of 10 is .680, the adjusted coefficient of determination is

(a) .28
(b) 1.53
(c) .32
(d) none of these.

Chapter 16

Answers to Problems

1. Evidently, the teacher's salary is to be predicted by the other variables. Thus, the dependent variable is

$$y = \text{the salary (in thousands of dollars) of the teacher}$$

The independent variables are:

x_1 = the number of years teaching experience of the person.
x_2 = the age in years of the teacher

2. $b_1 = .582$ indicates that as the number of years teaching experience is increased by one, the teacher's salary is expected to increase by .582 thousand dollars when the age of the teacher is held constant.

$b_2 = .386$ indicates that for each one year increase in the teacher's age, the yearly salary is expected to increase .386 thousand dollars when the number of years of experience of the teacher is held constant.

3.

Source	Sum of Squares	Degrees of Freedom	Mean Square
Regression	121.161	2	60.581
Error	8.714	5	1.743
Total (about the mean)	129.875	7	

4. To answer this question, we test the following hypotheses:

H_0: $\beta_1 = \beta_2 = 0$
H_1: At least one of the two coefficients is not zero.

The statistic is F = MSR/MSE with 2 numerator degrees of freedom and 5 denominator degrees of freedom.

The decision rule is Accept H_0 if $F \leq 5.79$
Reject H_0 if $F > 5.79$.

Computing the value of F from formula [3], we find

$$F = 60.581/1.743 = \underline{34.757}.$$

Thus, H_0 is rejected and we conclude that there is a significant relationship among x_1, x_2, and y at the 5% level of significance.

5. For each of the two parameters, we wish to test the hypotheses

$$H_0: \beta_i = 0$$
$$H_1: \beta_i \neq 0$$

The test statistic in each case is $t = b_i/s_{bi}$ which has already been calculated in the computer output where the t statistic has $n - p - 1 = 5$ dof.

For each test, the decision rule is Accept H_0 if $-2.571 \leq t \leq 2.571$
Reject H_0 otherwise.

Since $b_1/s_{b1} = 2.910 > 2.571$ and $b_2/s_{b2} = 2.922 > 2.571$, we reject the null hypotheses that $\beta_1 = 0$ and $\beta_2 = 0$, concluding that the parameters β_1 and β_2 are significant in the multiple regression analysis at the .10 level of significance.

6. (a) $R^2 = 121.161/129.875 = \underline{.933}$.

93.3% of the variability in the teachers' salaries in explained by the relationship of it to the teachers' experience and age.

(b)

$$R_a^2 = 1 - (1 - R^2)\left(\frac{n-1}{n-p-1}\right) = 1 - (1 - .933)\left(\frac{7}{5}\right) = \underline{.906}.$$

Chapter 16

Answers to Multiple Choice Questions

1. c
2. c
3. d
4. c
5. a
6. c
7. b
8. b
9. d
10. a

Chapter 17
NONPARAMETRIC METHODS

WHAT AM I LEARNING?

Chapter Outline and Summary

Most of the techniques of hypothesis testing that we have encountered so far are based on the assumption of normality of the population probability distribution. Fortunately, slight deviations from the assumption of a normal population still give reasonably reliable tests, particularly when the sample size is large. However, what do we do in a situation when the population from which we are sampling definitely does not meet this requirement? Another situation we may encounter is the case where we cannot assign specific numerical values to the observations. In this case, sample statistics such as mean and standard deviation are not able to be calculated and used.

The type of techniques we have studied so far have mainly been *parametric* techniques; that is, methods where the test is concerned with some particular parameter of a population with an assumed distribution. When one or more of the assumptions of a parametric technique are not met, *nonparametric techniques* can usually be used. Nonparametric tests, for the most part, compare the populations from which the samples were obtained rather than comparing specific parameters such as μ and σ^2. Nonparametric statistical procedures do not require knowledge of the form of the probability distribution of the population from which the sample is chosen. Thus, they are often referred to as *distribution-free methods.*

Nonparametric tests have many advantages. First of all, there are very few assumptions that need to be made about the samples and the populations being tested. Secondly, the error caused by assuming a population is normally distributed when it is not is avoided. Thirdly, the data may be easier to collect and the calculations involved in nonparametric tests are usually very simple.

Unfortunately, there are also some disadvantages associated with nonparametric methods. In the first place, the hypotheses are less clearly defined than in parametric methods; that is, nonparametric methods provide more general comparisons of populations. For instance, rejection of the null hypothesis in a nonparametric test may indicate that two populations are different, but we do not know if the difference or differences lie in the means, variances, or distributions of the populations. Also, if it is possible to use a parametric method for a particular test, the parametric method will normally give a smaller Type II error than a nonparametric test for a fixed Type I error. Thus, in that case, the nonparametric method would be less reliable.

Probably the main advantage of nonparametrical statistical inference is its general applicability. The methods of nonparametric statistics often provide useful alternatives to the parametric tests we have encountered in previous chapters.

Many nonparametric methods use the relative ranks of sample observations rather than their actual numerical values. One such test is the *Wilcoxon rank-sum test* which is used to determine if there are any differences between two populations. To use this test, two random samples should be independently chosen from each of the populations. Instead of testing for the differences between means of two populations (as did the independent sample t and z tests of Chapter 11) the Wilcoxon rank-sum procedure is used to test whether or not the two populations are the same.

A nonparametric test that is equivalent to the Wilcoxon rank-sum test is the *Mann-Whitney test.* The Mann-Whitney test uses a test statistic based on the test statistic used in the Wilcoxon rank-sum test. Either test can be used to determine whether or not two populations are identical under the assumptions of the tests.

Whenever the samples are paired or matched such that each observation from one sample has a corresponding matched observation from the other sample, the *Wilcoxon signed-rank test* can be used to test the hypothesis of identical populations. This test provides a useful alternative whenever questions exist concerning the appropriateness of the assumption of normally distributed differences in the paired difference t test discussed in Chapter 11. It is also used when it is possible only to rank-order the differences in two samples.

In some situations the matched-sample design is appropriate but it is not possible to obtain the quantitative measure for each population required by the Wilcoxon signed-rank test. If a preference for a particular item can be determined, a nonparametric method called the *sign test* can be used to determine if the preferences for two items are identical. In this test, preference for a particular item is denoted with a plus sign. The sign test compares the observed proportion of plus signs to the hypothesized proportion of $p = .5$ under the assumption of no preference for one of two items. Hence, the binomial distribution is the distribution of the number of plus signs when the null hypothesis is true. The sign test can also be used to conduct hypothesis tests about the value of a population median.

The exact form and procedures for these nonparametric tests are covered in the formula section of this Guide.

For measuring the degree of relationship between two variables, we may calculate the *Spearman rank correlation coefficient,* r_S. It is used to consider measures of association between two variables when only rank-order data are available. The Spearman rank correlation coefficient ranges from -1 to +1 and is interpreted similar to the sample correlation coefficient discussed in Chapters 4 and 15. Inferences about the population rank correlation, ρ_S, between two variables can be made using the Spearman rank correlation coefficient as was done with the population correlation, ρ, in Chapter 15. As expected, the nonparametric r_S does not require the assumption of normality as did the methods of Chapter 15.

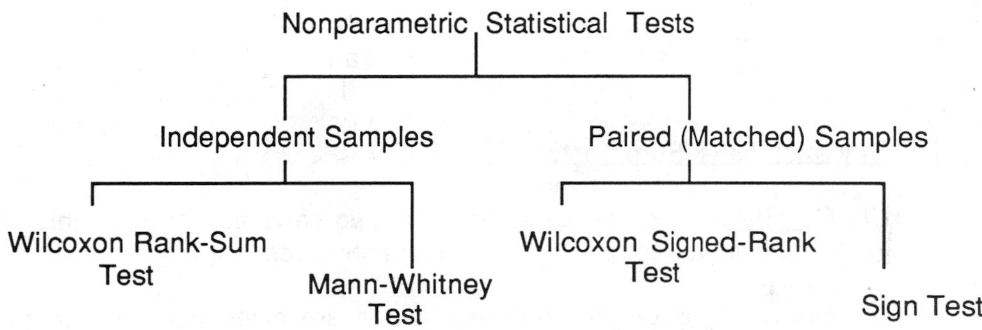

Chapter 17

WHICH FORMULA SHOULD I USE?

Formulas

When:

a) testing the hypotheses

H_0: Two populations are identical
H_1: Two populations are not identical

b) using the data obtained from two independent random samples of size n_1 and n_2, one sample from each population

c) $n_1 \geq 10$ and $n_2 \geq 10$

Use:

The Wilcoxon Rank-Sum Test:

Step 1: Combine the data values from the two samples and rank this combined data from lowest (rank of 1) to highest values.

Note: If ties occur, the tied values are given the average ranking of their positions in the combined data set.

Step 2: Compute W, the sum of the ranks for the first sample.

Step 3: Use the (approximately normal) test statistic

$$z = \frac{W - \frac{1}{2}n_1(n_1 + n_2 + 1)}{\sqrt{\frac{1}{12}n_1 n_2(n_1 + n_2 + 1)}} \qquad [1]$$

with decision rule

Accept H_0 if $-z_{\alpha/2} \leq z \leq z_{\alpha/2}$
Reject H_0 otherwise

to perform the two-tailed test of hypothesis.

When:

a) testing the hypotheses

H_0: Two populations are identical
H_1: Two populations are not identical

b) using the data obtained from two independent random samples of size n_1 and n_2, one sample from each population

c) $n_1 \geq 10$ and $n_2 \geq 10$

Use:

The Mann-Whitney Test:

Step 1: Obtain the Wilcoxon rank-sum for the first sample, W.

Step 2: Compute

$$U = \left[n_1 n_2 + \frac{n_1(n_1 + 1)}{2}\right] - W \qquad [2]$$

Step 3: Use the (approximately normal) test statistic

$$z = \frac{U - \frac{1}{2}n_1 n_2}{\sqrt{\frac{1}{12}\, n_1 n_2 (n_1 + n_2 + 1)}} \qquad [3]$$

with decision rule

Accept H_0 if $-z_{\alpha/2} \leq z \leq z_{\alpha/2}$
Reject H_0 otherwise

to perform the two-tailed test of hypothesis.

When:

a) testing the hypotheses

H_o: Two populations are identical
H_1: Two populations are not identical

b) using the data obtained from two paired (matched) samples of size n each

c) $n > 10$

Use:

The Wilcoxon Signed-Rank Test:

Step 1: Compute the differences of the n paired observations to obtain a data set of n differences

Step 2: Rank the absolute value of the differences by

a) discarding any differences of zero
b) rank the remaining absolute differences from lowest (rank 1) to highest
c) tied differences are assigned average rank values

Step 3: Determine the signed rank by assigning the ranked absolute differences the sign of the original differences in the data.

Step 4: Compute the sum of the signed rank values, T.

Step 5: Use the (approximately normal) test statistic

$$z = \frac{T}{\sqrt{\frac{n(n+1)(2n+1)}{6}}} \qquad [4]$$

with decision rule

Accept H_o if $-z_{\alpha/2} \leq z \leq z_{\alpha/2}$
Reject H_o otherwise

to perform the two-tailed test of hypothesis.

Chapter 17

When:

a) testing the hypotheses

H_0: No preference exists
H_1: A preference exists

b) using the qualitative data obtained two paired samples of size n

c) $n \geq 10$

Use:

The Sign Test:

Step 1: Assign a response indicating a preference for the category of interest a + sign; assign a nonpreference a – sign.

Note: If no preference exists, the response is removed and n reduced according.

Step 2: Compute the number of + signs in the sample.

Step 3: Use the test statistic

$$z = \frac{\text{number of plus signs} - .5n}{\sqrt{.5n}} \qquad [5]$$

with decision rule

Accept H_0 if $-z_{\alpha/2} \leq z \leq z_{\alpha/2}$
Reject H_0 otherwise

to perform the two-tailed test of hypothesis.

When:

testing the hypotheses

H_0: population median $= m_o$
H_1: population median $\neq m_o$

Use: the <u>sign test</u> described by formula [5] with

1) a + sign assigned to data values in the sample greater than m_o

2) a – sign assigned to values in the sample less than m_o

3) any data values equal to m_o being discarded.

When:

computing a measure of linear association between two variables when only rank-order data are available

Use:

The <u>Spearman Rank-Correlation Coefficient</u>

$$r_s = 1 - \frac{6 \Sigma d_i^2}{n(n^2 - 1)} \qquad [6]$$

where

n = number of items being ranked
x_i = the rank of item i with respect to one variable
y_i = the rank of item i with respect to a second variable
$d_i = x_i - y_i$.

When:

a) testing the hypotheses

H_o: $\rho_s = 0$ (there is no significant rank correlation)

H_1: $\rho_s \neq 0$ (there is significant rank correlation)

b) the rankings are independent

c) $n \geq 10$

Use:

$$z = r_s \sqrt{n-1} \qquad [7]$$

with decision rule

Accept H_o if $-z_{\alpha/2} \leq z \leq z_{\alpha/2}$

Reject H_o otherwise

to perform the two-tailed test of hypothesis.

HERE'S HOW IT'S DONE!

Examples

1. Two real estate appraisers, called A and B, were asked to each independently appraise ten properties. The results of the appraisals are shown below. (All appraisals are dollar values of assessed valuation.)

Property	Appraiser A	Appraiser B
1	46300	27700
2	26800	13000
3	8710	5220
4	7300	6100
5	47400	48200
6	4320	3400
7	5380	3190
8	30500	26660
9	1730	2050
10	5920	5400

Can it be said that the two appraisers differ in their assessed valuation of different properties? Use a level of significance of .05.

Solution

Using the Wilcoxon rank-sum test, we combine the data values from the two samples and rank this combined data from lowest (the value of 1730 with rank 1) to the highest (the value of 48200 with rank 20).

Property	Appraiser A	Rank	Appraiser B	Rank
1	46300	18	27700	16
2	26800	15	13000	13
3	8710	12	5220	6
4	7300	11	6100	10
5	47400	19	48200	20
6	4320	5	3400	4
7	5380	7	3190	3
8	30500	17	26660	14
9	1730	1	2050	2
10	5920	9	5400	8
	Total	114		

Next, we compute W, the sum of the ranks for the first sample as $W = \underline{114}$.

Substituting in formula [1], we obtain

$$z = \frac{W - \frac{1}{2}n_1(n_1 + n_2 + 1)}{\sqrt{\frac{1}{12}n_1 n_2(n_1 + n_2 + 1)}} = \frac{114 - (10)(21)/2}{\sqrt{(100)(21)/12}} = \underline{.68}$$

The decision rule is to accept H_0 if $-1.96 \le z \le 1.96$ and reject H_0 otherwise.

Since $z = .68$ does not fall in the rejection region, we conclude that the two appraisers do not differ in their assessed valuation of different properties.

2. Rework example 1 using the Mann-Whitney test.

<u>Solution</u>:
Using the Wilcoxon rank-sum $W = 114$, we compute

$$U = \left[n_1 n_2 + \frac{n_1(n_1 + 1)}{2}\right] - W = (100 + \frac{110}{2}) - 114 = \underline{41}.$$

We next compute the z statistic for the Mann-Whitney test:

$$z = \frac{U - \frac{1}{2}n_1 n_2}{\sqrt{\frac{1}{12}n_1 n_2(n_1 + n_2 + 1)}} = \frac{41 - 100/2}{13.23} = \underline{-.68}$$

With the same decision rule as in example 1, since $-.68$ does not fall in the rejection region, we reach the same conclusion as above.

3. A car rental agency is trying to decide whether the use of radial tires instead of regular belted tires improves fuel economy. Eleven cars are equipped with radial tires and driven over a predetermined test course. Using the same drivers, the cars are then driven over the same course with the regular belted tires. The number of gallons of gasoline used was recorded for each car as follows:

Car	Radial Tires	Belted Tires
1	2	1.7
2	1.9	2.1
3	3.2	2.8
4	2.7	2.7
5	3.3	3.5
6	1.7	1.9
7	2.2	2.5
8	2.6	2.9
9	3	2.9
10	2.8	3
11	1.9	2.3

Do the data indicate that the tires are significantly different in terms of automobile gasoline consumption? Use $\alpha = .05$.

Solution:

Since we have paired samples, let us use the Wilcoxon signed-rank test to test

H_0: The tires are identical in terms of gasoline usage

H_1: The tires are not identical in terms of gasoline usage.

We must compute the differences in the paired observations:

Car	Radial Tires	Belted Tires	Difference
1	2	1.5	.5
2	1.9	2.1	-.2
3	3.2	2.8	.4
4	2.7	2.7	0
5	3.3	4	-.7
6	1.7	1.9	-.2
7	2.1	2.9	-.8
8	2.6	2.9	-.3
9	3	2.9	.1
10	2.8	3.4	-.6
11	1.9	2.3	-.4

Next, we rank the absolute value of the differences, assigning average rank values to the tied differences. Notice that since car 4 had the same value for both types of tires, the difference is zero and therefore discarded.

We then assign the ranked absolute differences the sign of the original difference in the data.

Car	Difference	Absolute Value of Difference	Rank	Signed Rank
1	.5	.5	7	7
2	-.2	.2	2.5	-2.5
3	.4	.4	5.5	5.5
5	-.7	.7	9	-9
6	-.2	.2	2.5	-2.5
7	-.8	.8	10	-10
8	-.3	.3	4	-4
9	.1	.1	1	1
10	-.6	.6	8	-8
11	-.4	.4	5.5	-5.5
			Total	28

The last step is to compute the z statistic using formula [4] with T = 28 and n = 10 (since one value was discarded). Substituting these values in formula [4], we obtain

$$z = \frac{T}{\sqrt{\frac{n(n+1)(2n+1)}{6}}} = \frac{28}{\sqrt{385}} = \underline{1.43}$$

The decision rule is

Accept H_0 if $-1.96 \leq z \leq 1.96$

Reject H_0 otherwise.

Since 1.43 does not fall in the rejection region, we come to the conclusion that the two types of tires are identical in terms of gasoline usage.

4. Eighteen students were asked to each taste two different cheese spreads and give their preference as to taste. Eleven students preferred Brand A and five students preferred Brand B. Two students could not distinguish between the two brands. Perform a test of hypothesis to determine if a preference exists for one of the two brands of cheese spread at the .10 level of significance.

Solution:

Because we are only given the data in terms of preferences, a sign-test for paired comparisons is appropriate. (Recall that the data is paired because the same student is testing each of the cheese spreads.)

For this problem, $n = 16$ since the students who showed no preference are removed from the study. The number of + signs (preferences) is 11.

Thus, substituting in formula [5], we have

$$z = \frac{\text{number of plus signs} - .5n}{\sqrt{.5n}} = \frac{11 - .5(16)}{2.828} = \underline{1.06}.$$

The decision rule says to accept H_0 (no preference exists) whenever z is between -1.645 and 1.645. Since 1.06 is in this region of values, we conclude that no preference exists for the two brands of cheese spread.

5. Compute the Spearman rank-correlation coefficient to consider the association between variables x and y whose ranks are shown below:

Rank of x	Rank of y
1	2
3.5	1
5	4
2	3
3.5	5
6	6

Solution:

To compute r_S, we need to calculate the differences in the ranks and use formula [6] which calls for the squares of those differences.

Thus, we have

Rank of x	Rank of y	difference	square of difference
1	2	-1	1
3.5	1	2.5	6.25
5	4	1	1
2	3	-1	1
3.5	5	-1.5	2.25
6	6	0	0
		Total	11.5

Substituting in formula [6], we obtain

$$r_s = 1 - \frac{6 \Sigma d_i^2}{n(n^2 - 1)} = 1 - \frac{6(11.5)}{6(35)} = 1 - .33 = \underline{.67}$$

It appears that as the rank of x increases, the rank of y increases.

Chapter 17

HAVE I LEARNED THE MATERIAL?

Problems

1. The score on a certain psychological test is used as an index of status frustration. The scale ranges from 0 (low frustration) to 20 (high frustration). The scores are not expected to follow a normal distribution. The test was administered to independent random samples of 12 corporate executives and 10 federal government "top" administrators with the following results:

Corporate Executive Test Scores	Federal Government Administrators Test Scores
19	13
10	5
9	12
8	10
17	1
19	13
14	11
18	7
15	3
11	4
20	
6	

Use the Wilcoxon rank-sum test at the .10 level of significance to see if the two populations of test scores can be considered identical.

2. Answer the question posed in problem 1 using the Mann-Whitney test at the .10 level of significance.

3. Twelve paintings are ranked by each of two judges. Their rankings are as follows:

Painting	Judge 1	Judge 2
A	2	1
B	3	4
C	6	2
D	1	5
E	8	9
F	10	7
G	4	6
H	9	10
I	7	8
J	5	3

(a) Compute r_S.

(b) Test, at the .05 level of significance, whether or not there is significant correlation between the two judges' rankings.

4. Twelve groups of identical twins are given standardized IQ tests. The resulting scores are

Twin A Score	(Matching) Twin B Score
113	101
130	125
117	123
120	110
127	132
119	108
120	104
98	101
127	119
105	96
113	110
107	106

Do these data give evidence, at the .10 level of significance, that the associated populations of test scores are identical?

5. In a taste test for a new brand of cola, fourteen people were each asked to taste the most popular brand of cola and the new brand, not knowing which they were tasting. Each person gave a preference. The preferences are listed below with a "+" sign indicating a preference for the most popular brand of cola and a "-" sign indicating a preference for the new brand. Is there evidence, at the .01 level of significance, that one of these brands is preferred over the other?

+	-	+	+	+	-	+
+	+	-	-	+	+	-

Chapter 17

Multiple Choice Questions

1. Which of the following is not a nonparametric test?

   (a) Wilcoxon signed-rank test
   (b) Sign test for paired comparisons
   (c) Paired sample t test
   (d) Mann-Whitney test

2. A method of statistical inference which requires few, if any, assumptions about the distribution of the sampled population is called a

   (a) distribution-free method
   (b) parametric method
   (c) nonparametric method
   (d) both a) and c).

3. A nonparametric method for determining whether or not two populations are identical for paired samples is

   (a) the paired sample t test
   (b) Wilcoxon signed-rank test
   (c) Spearman rank test
   (d) Wilcoxon rank sum test.

4. A variable is found to have the values 20, 24, 15, 20, 15. The rank that would be assigned to the first 20 that occurs is

   (a) 3.5
   (b) 1
   (c) 3
   (d) 2.5.

5. A nonparametric test should be used when

   (a) testing the equality of two population means
   (b) an experimenter knows that the populations involved are normally distributed
   (c) only rank-order data is available
   (d) in all of the above situations.

6. Fifteen people were asked which of two brands of toothpaste they prefer. Five of these people had no particular preference. The sample size, n, that should be used in the sign test to determine if no preference exists for the brands is

   (a) 15
   (b) 30
   (c) 10
   (d) none of these.

7. A plant manager wishes to determine if there is an association between a preemployment test score and the employee's performance after being hired. Fifteen employees were chosen at random and both of these quantities measured on a numerical scale and recorded. Which of the following procedures is best to use to determine the relationship between the preemployment test score and the employee's performance after being hired?

   (a) Sign test
   (b) Wilcoxon rank-sum test
   (c) Mann-Whitney test
   (d) Spearman rank correlation coefficient.

8. Which of the following tests is useful to test for a specified value of a population median?

   (a) Wilcoxon rank-sum test
   (b) Sign test
   (c) Mann-Whitney test
   (d) none of these.

9. Under the assumption that the null hypothesis is true, which of the following tests is based on the binomial probability distribution?

   (a) Sign test
   (b) Mann-Whitney test
   (c) Wilcoxon rank-sum test
   (d) Wilcoxon signed-rank test.

10. Which of the following tests are equivalent?

   (a) Sign test and Spearman rank correlation test
   (b) Wilcoxon signed-rank test and the sign test
   (c) Mann-Whitney test and the Wilcoxon rank-sum test
   (d) Wilcoxon signed-rank test and the Wilcoxon rank-sum test.

Chapter 17

Answers to Problems

1. We wish to test H_0: the two populations are identical
   H_1: the two populations are not identical.

   The decision rule is Accept H_0 if $-1.645 \leq z \leq 1.645$
   Reject H_0 otherwise.

   Using the Wilcoxon rank-sum test, find W = <u>174</u> (if the ranks of the corporate executives are used)

   Thus, z = <u>-2.374</u> and we reject the null hypothesis. The conclusion is that the two populations are not identical.

   <u>Note</u>: There are 4 tied observations in the rankings, and if the ranks of the federal government employees are used, W = 79.

2. For the Mann-Whitney test, U = <u>24</u> resulting in z = <u>-2.374</u> and the same conclusion is reached as in problem 1.

3. (a) r_s = <u>.673</u> since $n = 10$ and $\Sigma d_i^2 = 54$.

   (b) We wish to test H_0: $\rho_s = 0$
   H_1: $\rho_s \neq 0$

   The decision rule is Accept H_0 if $-1.96 \leq z \leq 1.96$
   Reject H_0 otherwise.

   Since z = <u>2.018</u> falls in the rejection region, we reject the null hypothesis and conclude that there is significant rank correlation between the two judges' rankings.

4. We wish to test H_0: the two populations are identical
H_1: the two populations are not identical.

The decision rule is Accept H_0 if $-1.645 \leq z \leq 1.645$
Reject H_0 otherwise.

For the data, there are 3 "+" ranks and 9 "-" ranks with 2 tied groups.

T = -52 giving z = -2.04. Thus, we reject the null hypothesis and conclude that the two populations of IQ scores for the identical twins are not identical.

5. We wish to test H_0: no preference exists
H_1: a preference exists

The decision rule is Accept H_0 if $-2.56 \leq z \leq 2.56$
Reject H_0 otherwise.

The number of plus signs is 9 and n = 14, so z = (9 - 7)/2.65 = .76. Thus, we do not reject the null hypothesis and conclude that no preference exists between the brands.

Chapter 17

Answers to Multiple Choice Questions

1. c
2. d
3. b
4. a
5. c
6. c
7. d
8. b
9. a
10. c